The Magneti Marelli Workers Committee

The "Red Guard" Tells Its Story (Milan, 1975-78)

Emilio Mentasti

The Magneti Marelli Workers Committee – The "Red Guard" Tells Its Story (Milan, 1975-78)
Emilio Mentasti

ISBN 978-1-57027-363-6

Cover design by Haduhi Szukis
Interior design by Margaret Killjoy

Released by Minor Compositions 2021
Colchester / New York / Port Watson

Minor Compositions is a series of interventions & provocations drawing from autonomous politics, avant-garde aesthetics, and the revolutions of everyday life.

Minor Compositions is an imprint of Autonomedia
www.minorcompositions.info | minorcompositions@gmail.com

Distributed by Autonomedia
PO Box 568
Williamsburgh Station
Brooklyn, NY 11211

www.autonomedia.org info@autonomedia.org

To those who died at work

Contents

Introduction to the English edition 5

Preface to the French edition 11

Introduction 15

Magneti Marelli 21
   Between the World Wars *22*
   From World War II to the mid-eighties. *26*

Struggles in the factory, 1945-1972 33
   Employment and the evolution of worker composition. *36*
   Labour conflict at Magneti Marelli Crescenzago. *40*

The story of the Workers' Committee. 79
   Piece work *81*
   Egalitarianism *92*
   The workforce. *100*
   The Workers Committee and Senza tregua *104*
   Corporate restructuring. *108*
   "Drive the delegates out of the 'bosses' palace'!" *113*
   The "April Days" *118*
   The struggle spreads to other workplaces *126*
   Political layoffs. *129*
   The expulsion. *140*
   The verdict of 15 July *146*
   Repression and restructuring *157*
   Birth of the Autonomous Workers Coordination of Milan *163*
   "Against the union-government-Confindustria social pact" *168*
   The end of the movement *182*

Introduction to the English edition

EVER SINCE THE 1970S THERE HAS BEEN A STEADY TRICKLE OF INFORMATION into the English-speaking world about the working class movement in Italy during its most intense phase in the whole of the second half of the twentieth century (roughly from 1968 to 1977). The flow of texts started with material translated and distributed by political activists sympathetic to what was happening in Italy. The Red Notes pamphlets (1974 onwards) were the first indication that many non-Italian speakers in the UK had of what was going on. Other translated texts sometimes appeared – for example, the group around the Rising Free bookshop in north London published the pamphlet "Take Over the City" (largely a reprint of an article of the same name by Lotta Continua)[1] in 1974, or thereabouts. The political group Big Flame was to a large extent influenced by the Italian movement[2] (particularly by the organisa-

---

1   Available on the libcom site: https://libcom.org/tags/rising-free
2   Indeed, an Italian member of Lotta Continua moved to England and joined Big Flame whilst doing a BSc in Mathematics at Liverpool University. See the blog by ex-BF members: https://bigflameuk.wordpress.com/tag/italy/

tion Lotta Continua), and sometimes published texts produced by the movement[3], along with news about Italy.

In the US, the bi-monthly magazine *Radical America* (founded in 1967 by some members of Students for a Democratic Society) contained quite a few very informative articles about Italy, between 1971 and 1976.[4]

More recently, references to the 1970s Italian movement and the political ideas which informed it and were produced by it – broadly speaking, the Marxist theoretical and practical current known as "Operaismo"[5] – have become common, in fact fashionable, in academia, and even in novels.[6]

All this has made available much useful material about political theory and some of the more inspiring activities carried on outside workplaces – "proletarian shopping" etc. It has also brought a certain obsession with armed groups, often divorced from any context of who carried out acts of armed violence and what their relationship was to the wider class struggle.

Despite all this, though, very few accounts have been made available of what Italian workers in large workplaces actually *did*. How they organised themselves, what their concrete relationship was with initiatives taken outside workplaces (around housing, self-organised price reduction, the student movement, the women's movement...), what their real relationship was with the unions, the political parties, student activists, armed groups…

From the late 1970s onwards, information also started to become available about the vicious state repression that comrades in Italy were being subjected

---

3   For example, they produced a pamphlet containing English translations of material prepared for the January 1975 Congress of Lotta Continua.

4   See the online archive: https://library.brown.edu/cds/radicalamerica/shelf.html
     Relevant issues are: vol 5, #5 (Sept-Oct 1971); vol 6, #3 (May-June 1972); vol 7, #2 (March-April 1973); vol 10, #4 (July-Aug 1976); vol 10, #6 (Nov-Dec 1976); vol 11, #6 & vol 12, #1 (double issue, Nov 1977-Feb 1978); vol 12, #5 (Sept-Oct 1978); vol 14, #4 (July-Aug 1980) and vol 18, #5 (Sept-Oct 1984).

5   The literal translation of this word is "workerism," but it must not be confused in any way with the English concept of "workerism" (meaning the doctrine that the class struggle only happens in workplaces), often espoused by trade-unionist Trotskyists, or the French word "ouvrierisme" (the populist glorification of the "ordinary worker"), often espoused by Stalinists!

6   The novelist Rachel Kushner published a book (The Flamethrowers, 2013) about characters in the US art scene of the 1970s set against the backdrop of car factory strikes and Red Brigade assassinations in Italy. Likewise, the novels of Nanni Balestrini have become available in English. This includes the famous We want everything, first published in 1971, a fictionalised account of the class struggle written from the point of view of a proletarian everyman migrated from the South of Italy to work in the factories of the North.

to.[7] It was possible to read about the arbitrary mass arrests and imprisonment and the absurd trumped up terrorism charges that forced many people into exile. But much less has been written about the real policies of "repression" which brought an end to the movement – the restructuring of the economy, partly carried out precisely to break up big concentrations of militant workers and (as in other industrialised countries) to subject wage labourers in general to the discipline of mass unemployment. It was the process of relocation, decentralisation and automation of workplaces that proved so hard for workers to resist. Much harder to resist, in fact, than false accusations of being leaders of the Red Brigades, even if direct state repression certainly played a role in the suppression of particular workers' committees, including the one at Magneti Marelli, as is described in this book.

So, apart from a desire to set the historical record straight, why do we want to dig up the story of the Magneti Marelli workers? After all, both the technology of production and the organisation of labour processes have changed a lot in the last 40 years. Why do we think that the struggles at Magneti Marelli have anything to teach us today?

For a start, however much technology changes and lifestyles of workers outside the workplace may change, the tendency for capital to recreate the *factory* in new sectors of the economy does not go away. The despotic command of the assembly line, whether a classical one in a car factory or a modern electronics factory (Foxconn!), or a slightly modified one in an Amazon warehouse, or a more "virtual" one imposed by just-in-time production and global supply chains,[8] doesn't change that much. Likewise, the figure of the hated foreman (even though they might now be called a "team leader" and not be a man) is as real as ever. And it is in the factory (in the widest sense) that the class contradictions are at their most stark and where there is the greatest potential for collective resistance on the part of the wage-labouring class. Nor have the immediate things that the workers fought against changed: the inhuman pace of work, wages that don't keep pace with inflation, wage hierarchies that set workers against each other…

The struggle of workers against the despotism of the factory is nothing new, nor is it particularly unusual, even in a period of relative social peace like the one we experience today. But workers' struggle and *organisation* in Italy in the 1970s went much further than anything seen in recent years. In fact,

---

7   For example, see the Red Notes pamphlet "After Marx, jail! The attempted destruction of a communist movement." Available on: https://libcom.org/tags/red-notes

   There was also an "Italy '79 committee" active in London in the early 1980s, but hardly any information is available about it online.

8   What Brian Ashton calls the "factory without walls."

the Italian worker's experience was possibly the highest expression of the last *proletarian political cycle*, to use a term which developed from the movement in Italy.

The notion of "political cycle" was, and is, in very common use in *Operaist* circles. It is best described in terms of a historical period in which struggles reinforce each other across the globe creating the conditions for a qualitative break from the working class politics (trade unionism and social democracy) in existence during periods in between political cycles. The beginning and end of a cycle are marked by strong elements of discontinuity in relation to the preceding and later periods. The "social contract," that is, the collective formalised consent between classes, is a main cause of inertia and conservation of social relations.[9] It is the main obstacle that the working class must overcome in beginning to carry out the mission of radical transformation of society. One of the pillars of the social contract is, of course, the trade unions. The beginning of a radical organisational and political break from the unions on the part of the workers is one of the signs of the birth of a new political cycle.

The movement in Italy didn't simply go further on a quantitative level – number of strikes, number of days on strike, profits lost etc. It is not a matter of the extent or duration or level of violence of the struggle. It went further on a *qualitative* level. In particular, the workers were not simply creating disruption in order to bargain with the boss from a stronger position. They were using their collective strength to take what they needed and to directly improve their conditions of life. As the *operaisti* of the time said: "We don't demand, we take, and we organise ourselves accordingly."

The "Red Guard" of the title has nothing to do with Maoist students! It refers to an episode of struggle (continued over several months) provoked by the company sacking some workers (naturally they were some of the most militant and politicised). But they refused to be excluded from the factory. A "Red Guard" of their comrades escorted them into the factory every morning against the wishes of the management and the threats of their thuggish security guards, insisted on their right to be present in the factory (now as "agitators" rather than workers productive for capital), and escorted them out again in the evening. They understood clearly that the bosses' right to fire workers consists in more than just the right to stop paying them. It also consists in the right to exclude them from the workplace and thus prevent them associating with their comrades. This right had to be fought against, and still needs to be!

---

9   Obviously, we're not just talking about the historical "Social Contract" agreed between the Labour government and the trade unions in Britain in the 1970s (widely derided by workers as the "Social Con-Trick"). But this is a good example of how a social contract is manifested, and how it can be smashed by worker militancy.

A final postscript

The necessity for a "workers' history" like this one is underlined by the fact that the Magneti Marelli company still exists, and is still in the car parts business.[10] It employs 43,000 people worldwide, including around 10,000 in Italy. The company website has a "history" section, making no reference to the strikes of the 1970s whatsoever…

---

10   See: https://www.magnetimarelli.com/company

Preface to the French edition

EVERY REVOLUTIONARY ASSAULT BY THE PROLETARIAT CONFRONTS A NEW SITUation. But the weight of the past, the experience of previous defeat, obviously plays a crucial role in the course of events. Understanding the strengths and weaknesses of the attempts of yesterday is therefore vital for the movement of today. Amongst these attempts, the latest to date is constituted by the cycle of autonomous workers' struggles which shook Italy between 1968 and 1979. This cycle is remarkable for the following reasons:

- its duration: it began with the foundation of the Unitary Base Committee at Pirelli in Milan, in February 1968, and ended in Turin, on 14 October 1980, when the "demonstration of 40,000" managers and white-collar employees of FIAT went out to support their employer in the face of the strike against redundancies. That makes it more than twelve years;
- the forms of organisation that the workers created for themselves, which enabled them to push forward and lead strikes and, for a long time, to be as influential as the Italian Communist Party (PCI);
- its class composition. The movement affected all industries (first of all the big factories), from chemicals and electronics, to metalworking, engineering, and, most definitely, car manufacturing. It mobilised all categories of workers, from the least skilled to the most skilled, from technicians (in the case of Montedison in Porto Marghera or Sit Siemens in

Milan) to engineers (such as at IBM in Vimercate, close to Milan);
- its reaffirmation of the centrality of the factory. Starting from the concrete reality of exploitation, the movement opposed itself not only to the despotism of the factory but called into question the wage hierarchy and the differences in treatment between blue and white-collar workers. It imposed control over the pace of work and went as far as questioning wage labour itself;
- its political centralisation built up from the shop floor, founded on the refusal of delegation and the active participation of the greatest number;
- its propagation outside the factory. Very quickly it took on questions of housing, transport, energy and means of subsistence by organising the self-reduction of prices and the seizure of housing. The workers' groups coordinated themselves and centralised themselves by local area and then on a regional level, as happened for the last time in Milan in 1977.

The movement in Italy went through several stages. The first, in 1968-1969, began with the strikes at Pirelli and Borletti (Milan) and blossomed in the "Hot Autumn" of 1969. It was a time of great optimism as the appearance of an autonomous workers' initiative caused consternation on the part of the bosses, unions and parties. However, this period ended on 12 December 1969, the day of the bombing at the Bank of Agriculture on Piazza Fontana in Milan, which caused 12 deaths. This attack showed that the state, or at least a fraction of its apparatus, was ready to use all possible means to stop the movement.

The movement was also original at the time because the nuclei of workers were formed following the intervention of young external militants (at Montedison in Porto Marghera, for example) or/and from splits in traditional parties, the PCI, PSI and PSIUP (at Pirelli in Milan, for example).

Calling into question the traditional methods of struggle and organisation of the institutional parties and unions, the workers' groups gave themselves their own theoretical tools, helped by the "outsiders." On occasions of important days of struggle, which they had often driven forward themselves, groups in the factories would push for the creation of national political groups,[11] the first attempts at centralisation on the level of the country, organised around agitational newspapers.[12]

---

11 The three groups were: Avanguardia Operaia ("Workers' Vanguard"), founded in December 1968 around the experience of the CUB in Milan; Potere Operaio ("Workers' Power"), founded in August 1969, principally around the experience of the workers' assembly of Porto Marghera; Lotta Continua ("Continuous Struggle" or "The Struggle Continues"), founded in October 1969 around the worker-student assembly of FIAT in Turin.

12 All this is set out in detail in La Fiat aux mains des ouvriers. L'automne chaud de 1969

Preface to the French edition

The second period (1971-73) ended with the defeat of the occupation of the FIAT Mirafiori factory.

The third period (1975-77) was marked by the end of the political groups,[13] the revival of workers' committees and the entry into struggle of workers from small and medium-sized workplaces in the most important industrial areas of northern Italy. It is in this period that the activity of the Magneti Marelli Workers' Committee took place. But the context had changed. It had become distinctly less favourable to the workers. The bosses had regained the offensive, and, progressively, control of the factories. The crisis of 1973 helped them and allowed them to restructure by means of mass redundancies, factory closures, and a wage freeze.

The political groups became a break on workers' autonomy. Incapable of embodying and organising the political centralisation of the movement, they dissolved themselves or changed their nature. So, once again, starting from the terrain of base organisation, the worker left took up the red thread of its struggle. The centre of gravity of this was the Milan region, the industrial capital of Italy where there already existed the Autonomous Assembly of Alfa Romeo, the CUB (Unitary Base Committee) at Pirelli, the committee of SIT-Siemens, along with many other autonomous workers' organs. But it was the Workers' Committee of Magneti Marelli in the Crescenzago factory which would be the most advanced expression of the committees in the Milan region and thus in the whole country.

The vigour and duration of the Italian revolutionary movement went far beyond that of the French "May '68",[14] even if it is slandered today and largely ignored, even in Italy. Despite this, some rare researchers and historians are trying to rehabilitate the period and, beyond this, all the experiences of workers' autonomy. The work of Emilio Mentasti is within this framework. This work is made difficult by the subject itself and by the fact that the sources consist almost entirely of leaflets, pamphlets and posters from the period, in a style which is often repetitive and impenetrable, and which, despite our efforts, risks making the translated text equally dense.

    à Turin ("Fiat in the hands of the workers. The Hot Autumn of 1969 in Turin"), by D. Giachetti and M. Scavino, Les Nuits Rouges, n°22, Paris 2005.

13 Potere Operaio dissolved itself in summer 1973; Lotta Continua broke up in summer 1976 but its death was already pronounced at the Rome Congress in January 1975 when the workers' groups left; Avanguardia Operaia degenerated into trade unionism and electoralism.

14 So we can see the idiocy of the "concept" of "the creeping May" as a way to describe the movement in Italy.

Nevertheless, the great moments of the life of the Committee are (very) precisely described: the strikes for wages and against the pace of work, supported by marches through the factory; strikes aimed at supporting the canteen workers and the cleaners; the street battles during the hot days of April 1975; the determination to allow sacked members of the Committee to enter the factory every day, starting from 10 September 1975, and continuing for ten months; the confrontations around the court in Milan; the "workers' patrols" organised to support the workers in small workplaces; the self-reduction of prices in the shops; and finally, the demonstration on 18 March 1977 called by the Coordination of Workers' Committees which united 20,000 proletarians in Milan, as many as were on the official union demonstration on the same day.

The committee progressively dissolved itself in 1979 under the blows of repression. The factory where it was born, lived and fought, has been demolished. But the description of this experience seems to us to be useful and necessary to all those who understand the inevitability of the struggles to come. Perhaps soon...

Introduction

Workers' history has benefited from a considerable revival in interest following the extraordinary experience which culminated in the "Hot Autumn" of 1969. In the 1960s and 1970s, the working class appeared as a force which struggled consciously for itself, as a "class for itself" and not just as a "class in itself." According to one widely held opinion, it had to "make the state," that is to say it was credited with being able to lead Italy better than the political class of the era, by way of its moral rectitude and spirit of "sacrifice" given by the "value" which it attached to work. Or, it represented the irreplaceable kernel of the socialist revolution, capable of basing itself on the ideals of communism to create a freer and more just society, by way of its "autonomy" and "refusal of work."

Other currents which took very divergent positions as to the final objective also arrived at the conclusion that the real actor in any reformist or revolutionary transformation in Italy had to be the working class.

Yet, in the course of the 1980s, when the defeat of the workers was completed, the lights went out and all the attention which had been focused on these questions suddenly fell away again. In fact, research, articles, books and documents on workers' struggles from the end of the Second World War to the end of the 1970s have become rare. It is true that the 1980s and 1990s, a period of successive defeats in the factories, were hardly inspiring. The interest in revisiting the historic transitions cannot be appreciated without understanding that this period, with its thrilling struggles in the factories (which ran from the beginning of the 1960s to the end of the 1970s), was one of upheaval at all levels of Italian society.

What are the reasons for this lack of interest? I think that we have to see a desire to hide a movement of the "people at the bottom" which produces concrete results, but also the difficulty in recognising that the reformist and radical parties of today are not capable of repeating this experience or of learning from it. Today these parties who consider themselves to be parties of the (working) "class" only defend their own position. They arrogantly proclaim themselves its representatives, without wanting to recognise that, when the working class takes the lead, the first to be ejected from their position are, quite rightly, its "old representatives."

We have to take up the thread of workers' history again out of respect for its actors (the workers themselves) and also because it can help us better understand what we are and how we have arrived at the present situation. It is therefore essential to start from documents produced at the time and particularly those from the active participants in struggles. It is important to understand how they organised themselves, what the slogans and immediate objectives were, but also the longer term aims and the eventual political errors, and to appreciate the importance of various practices in this phase of upheaval which affected workplaces, unions and society.

One of the most fascinating experiences of this period was that of the Workers' Committee of Magneti Marelli, a factory situated in Crescenzago, a district of Milan close to Sesto San Giovanni, which, starting from 1975, was one of the sites of Italian "workers' extremism." It has an exemplary character because its protagonists confronted all the worker, union, political and organisational problems of the era.

— This experience is situated in a fundamental historical period, a few years after the "Hot Autumn." The economic crisis has become overt and it is obvious to the bosses that they have to restructure the industrial system and restore order in the factories. The strength of the workers is still important but their cohesion is weakening on the level of their demands. Torn between the "historic compromise" and the revolution, the workers very often choose not to be interested in the question. It is therefore the moment where Italy finds itself in the midst of full-blown industrial restructuring, in the course of a period of extremely difficult transition, that the Workers' Committee is formed. It clearly demands egalitarianism and the refusal of the delegation which had characterised the recent past, and considers that the working class can organise itself in an autonomous way.

- At this time there were many other experiences of autonomous organisation in the factories, but few among them had the strength of the Marelli Committee, which could cause the re-election of Baglioni (a founding and leading member of the Workers's Committee) to the Factory Council [the official representative body, usually dominated by the unions], even though he stood accused by the courts of being a partisan of armed struggle. In the Milan region, only the Autonomous Assembly of Alfa Romeo could claim to exercise a similar major influence on the events going on inside the workplace. To find a comparable example it would be necessary to go back to the days of the Unitary Base Committee (CUB) of Pirelli in 1968.
- In these years of the 1970s, the unions and the PCI [Italian Communist Party] wanted to regain absolute control of the factories. They wanted to impose the "historic compromise," without tolerating any organised presence other than the official structures. They violently attacked those who opposed the restoration of order in the factories, accusing them of lacking political experience and preventing them from exercising the slightest trade union activity (they could not participate in factory assemblies, in strikes, in publishing or distributing leaflets). They subjected them to measures of intimidation and physical aggression, denounced them to the judicial authorities and the management and expelled them from the union branch structures and the Factory Councils. These methods were used whenever worker "extremists" tried to develop a political and union activity. It is obvious that the relations between the two components of the social movement were most often translated into violent confrontations and total incompatibility, but the fact that the Marelli Committee succeeded in functioning despite the extremely hard clashes with the union structures, and sometimes had a more important influence than the unions amongst the workers, confirms the extent to which the members of the Committee were implanted inside the workplace.
- The Workers' Committee of Marelli also embodied "the complete workers' organisation." The workers gave themselves an instrument (the "Red Guard") that was in a position to respond in a general fashion to the needs of proletarians in the factory and in the surrounding area. It was a question of showing that the working class had no need of union or political superstructures which imposed choices or means of action which escaped the direct control of the workers.
- The involvement of workers in struggles also took on another exceptional character: their participation and the quality of their intervention illustrated the decisive role of women in the workers' struggles of this era.

- During this period, it seemed that workers' struggles had to leave the factories because the contradictions touched the whole of society: there's no point in obtaining a substantial wage rise, or an improvement in rights within the factory, if prices immediately rise exponentially, if the right to housing is put into question or if other workers are exploited in place of those who have won a victory. Strongly interested in this aspect of things, the Workers' Committee intervened in the neighbourhoods close to the factory, serving as an example to a whole series of workplaces (including small and medium-sized ones) heavily hit by the process of restructuration. These workplaces, which had to face massive lay-offs and site closures, were also concerned with other questions not linked directly to the factory, such as the rising cost of living. For this reason, right from the beginning, the Committee took many initiatives: patrols against overtime; pickets in front of small workplaces where the workers had a harder time confronting the boss; responses to fascist provocations and police repression. Strongly present in the housing occupations of Sesto San Giovanni, they organised the self-reduction of prices in the supermarkets in working class neighbourhoods, forcing the managers not to excessively increase their prices, and opened the factory canteen to workers who occupied their places of work.
- The Committee was conscious of its role as the locomotive of workers' struggles. It therefore participated in the launching of the Milan Workers' Autonomous Coordination which was created at the end of 1976 and openly opposed the official union organisations. The Coordination gathered together all the "extremist" workers' groups of the Milan region. In a position to launch general strikes and to organise demonstrations without the unions, it represented one of the most advanced experiences of the autonomous movement of that time.
- The Committee got involved in the debate on proletarian justice and the necessity of arming the workers. Some of its representatives were arrested after a clandestine military training session. In the courtroom they proclaimed the workers' right to respond to the bosses' attacks. They were certainly not the first to defend such positions, since the Red Brigades had already chosen armed struggle. What's more, large layers of the movement had already had recourse to violence, which they justified by reason of circumstances, or as the fruit of a precise strategic choice. It must however be stressed that inside Magneti no armed brigade was ever formed, even if some workers were prosecuted on the basis of this accusation.
- The Committee also had the honour of participating in the review *Senza Tregua* ("Without Compromise"), some of whose participants went on

to form the fighting communist organisation Prima Linea. The Marelli Committee, along with the other workers' committees which supported *Senza Tregua,* formed the best of the movement which got down to the job of constructing the "workers' poles" of a future revolutionary organisation.

The first part of this book is devoted to the history of Magneti Marelli. It illustrates the evolution of the restructuration undertaken during the 1970s, and stresses that the company was one of the first Italian factories to introduce "*scientific management.*" It also shows how Fiat (boss and main customer of the factory) had the decisive influence on decisions about production and also those concerned with the management of the workforce. This work is the result of a great deal of detailed research.

The second part sets out an overview of the struggles undertaken by the workers of Magneti Marelli de Crescenzago between the end of the Second World War and 1972.

Finally, the third part retraces the history of the Workers' Committee of the factory from its creation to its end.

To carry out this work I consulted the Gallinari collection of the Biblioteca Pannizzi de Reggio Emilia, which has archives of leaflets, bulletins and journals of the Workers' Committee, as well as numerous books on the history of the workers' movement, works cited in the notes.

chapter one

Magneti Marelli

Creation

LA FABBRICA ITALIANA MAGNETI MARELLI (FIMM) WAS CREATED ON 8 OCTOBER 1919 with a registered capital of 7,000,000 lire, underwritten equally by Fiat of Turin and Ercole Marelli of Milan. The aim of the company was "the construction and trade of magnetos and electrical appliances, especially for application to the automotive industry, aviation and navigation."[15] The company was established with a very high level of participation by Fiat, which was a constant factor in the history of Magneti Marelli, and in the wider Italian and global automotive supply chain.

From an international point of view, we can see two schools of car production: the American one, that gave priority to the organization of the production process, and the European one, that put the design of the final product first. In the United States, Frederick Winslow Taylor's "scientific management"

---

15   Constitution of the limited company Fabbrica Italiana Magneti Marelli, act of 8 Oct 1919, signed in front of notary Federico Giusti (Milan), cited in Renzo A. Cenciarini-Stefania Licini, *Magneti Marelli, la storia e la business transformation*, Giuffrè editore, Milano, 1996. Much of the information in this introduction is taken from this book, which was published especially for Magneti Marelli.

was applied by the industrialist Henry Ford, who in 1913 introduced innovative systems of production and assembly: "The first based on a sequence of many elementary processes handled by specialised disposable machines at an extremely fast pace, while the second was based on a chain of workstations where the parts to be assembled reached the assembly workers, and not *vice versa*, and the fragmentation of operations allowed for levels of performance previously unheard of. This revolutionary form of organisation, known as 'mass production,' seemed difficult to imitate, both because of the enormous technical requirements of implementation and for the sheer volume of cars that you had to make and sell for the investment to be cost-effective."[16]

Hence, while American car production in the first decades of the century was oriented towards simple, inexpensive and standardised products, the European one was oriented towards high-performance machines for an elite market.

In Italy, Fiat (Fabbrica Italiana automobili Torino) was founded in 1899 and represented a breakthrough in the nascent domestic auto industry, mainly thanks to the entrepreneurial skills of Giovanni Agnelli, ensuring the competitiveness of the company both from the technical/design and organisational point of view. From the beginning, the idea was to broaden the narrow internal market and to launch internationally. To do this it was necessary for Fiat to compete with other European and American manufacturers, using the latest technology and organising its presence in developing markets in the best way possible.

One of the most important components of the automotive industry appeared to be the magneto, "namely the electromechanical device which produces the electrical potential difference needed to ignite the spark between the electrodes of the spark plug." The quality of the magneto became essential to ensure electricity supply to the spark plugs even at high-speeds, so as to avoid starting problems, high fuel consumption and other irregularities. In the early years of the twentieth century, the German company Bosch, founded in Stuttgart in 1896, monopolised the European market.[17]

Between the World Wars

From the beginning, Magneti Marelli boasted some features that differentiated it in terms of innovation from other Italian companies of the period. One of these was the clear separation between ownership and control: on the

---

16   Giuseppe Volpato, *L'evoluzione dello scenario competitivo della filiera automobilistica*, in Renzo A. Cenciarini-Stefania Licini, *Magneti Marelli*, op. cit.

17   Ibid

one hand Fiat and Ercole Marelli, on the other capable managers such as the Quintavalla brothers. Like Fiat and Olivetti, Magneti Marelli stood out in the Italian industrial landscape between the wars as one of the manufacturers most inspired by Fordist and Taylorist methods, with its rationalisation of production and scientific organisation of labour, and with fundamental importance given to the "human factor."[18]

Magneti Marelli operated within an industry that, for Italy at the beginning of the twentieth century, was absolutely new. And so, it tried to break into the domestic and world markets (dominated by the German company Bosch) seeking a path of specialisation and standardisation of high quality production, helped by the mass production carried out by the parent company, Fiat, through a better rationalisation of production and the introduction of scientific management.

The organisational orientation of Magneti Marelli is clear from the description in a corporate brochure for "plant A" in Sesto San Giovanni, the company's first production department:

> the factory was divided into a number of workshops, each devoted to the production of one or more parts of the magneto… we have long since left behind the old idea that each workshop should contain a single type of machine. Each of our workshops contain all the machine tools necessary for the production of a certain piece, arranged in such a way that the raw materials and semi-finished products arrive at a certain point, then they move from machine to machine and work bench to work bench according to the needs of production so that, at the end of the line, a completely finished piece is ready to leave the workshop… in this way, any unnecessary movement of material is avoided and each worker can remain in his place, getting the piece from the previous worker, perform the action assigned (and nothing else) and pass the piece to the next worker.[19]

The results of this type of organisation were immediately evident as in the first eight years production tripled while the labour force increased by only 40%. Inspired by American workshops, a "Time" office, in charge of

---

18   For further study on the scientific management at Magneti Marelli in the period between the two world wars see the book P. R. Willson, *The Clockwork Factory. Women and work in Fascist Italy*, Oxford, 1993.

19   Brochure *Nei campi della gloria* ("On the fields of glory"), 1924, quoted in P. R. Willsson, *The Clockwork Factory*, cit., p. 47-48.

pre-calculating production times and overseeing workers' productivity, was introduced. The machines were constantly updated, introducing an increasing automation of production with greater efficiency for machine and worker.

The "human factor" enjoyed a great deal of attention within Magneti Marelli, not only regarding performance but also in the choice and selection of workers. It was the only Italian company of the time which had a department of industrial psychology, entrusted to the factory doctor and also involved in recruitment. In Italy in the twenties industrial psychology was still a completely theoretical discipline, its greatest exponent being Agostino Gemelli, from Milan's Università Cattolica where a specific laboratory was set up. Magneti Marelli was the only practical case where there was a psycho-technical laboratory based on the American model, which had to examine "individual faculties in relation to job requirements."

An example of the laboratory's duties applied to the predominantly female winding department:

1. Determine the individual production curve of workers already in the workshop
2. Establish the psychophysical characteristics of the good worker
3. Establish the minimum production for each category of workers
4. Remove, by process of elimination, the workers in the workshop who don't satisfy the desired requirements
5. Hire only workers who have good characteristics (to be assessed in accordance with section 3)
6. Create optimum working and production conditions, collaborating with the technical department for any modification of machines and working positions and with the specially created office of organisation that looks after welfare, support and health."[20]

Workers were employed only if they met the specific requirements and were sent to work in the various departments according to their personal abilities. The results of this policy

---

20 *Sprazzi e bagliori* ("Sparks and flashes"), no. 27, "The selection of personnel in an industrial enterprise of great importance." This is the corporate magazine published between 1924 and 1942, for employees, but also for spare parts vendors and authorized representatives (the so-called *targhisti*) and customers of Magneti Marelli.

Magneti Marelli also gave great importance to organising assistance in the form of nurseries, farm shops, holiday camps for employees' children, paediatric and gynaecological surgery, and committees against accidents and for protecting health outside the factory.

were immediately evident, as the winding workshop achieved a 30% reduction of production times with a 5% increase in production.

The recognition of the "human factor" was carried out through the continued training of workers. In 1926, the "Vedette" business school was founded, aimed at training young workers through six months of theory (applied mathematics, geometry, industrial design, principles of physics and electrical engineering, technology and industrial organization) and six months placements in all departments. Afterwards, a school was created for shorthand typists and one to prepare "foremen.[21]

Another area of innovation introduced at Magneti Marelli was that of Research and Development, specialising in design, with the creation as early as 1924 of a department for studying magnets. Only twenty years after its establishment, the company had 13 research and experimentation laboratories (raw materials, injection moulding, aptitude tests, radio, shortwave, television, sound, radio receiver design, radio transmitter design, chemistry, measurement, testing and military radio) and two test rooms (for technical and radio equipment).

Eventually "quality control" was introduced, carried out by special inspectors and discussed at weekly meetings at the highest level, in which defective pieces were examined.

In addition to high quality production and modern manufacturing systems, Magneti Marelli was efficiently organised. In 1924, both general and plant management were created and in 1929 both commercial and industrial management structures were set up. Therefore, within a few years, the company had a sufficiently complex structure to allow it to maintain a competitive market position. From a commercial point of view, the company signed a lucrative joint venture agreement with Bosch (Mabo) and launched original and creative forms of advertising such as sponsorship of the Grand Prix car races, air shows, regular participation at exhibitions, fairs and shows, classified and print ads unique in their graphics and style and the establishment of prize competitions for "targhisti."

Magneti Marelli couldn't restrict itself only to the Italian market and from the start it extended its sales network all over the world.

The 1927 replacement of magnetos with distributors caused an obvious crisis in the sector, due to the distributor requiring two thirds less work and its sale price being up to 30% less than that of magnetos. At Magneti the solution

---

21   Ibid

was found immediately and consisted in the conversion of production to automotive accessories: the Magluce (starting system and electric lighting for motorcycles), spark plugs for aviation, electric horns and wipers for cars, batteries etc. In 1929 the company began its activity in the field of radio, the following year Radiomarelli was set up with commercial and distribution functions. In 1932 Fivre was created for the production of radio valves.

In 1936 a new plant (Magneti) was built in Sesto San Giovanni and a second one (Fivre) in Florence. In 1939 the Truciolo plant in Carpi (near Modena) was acquired and part of the production of magnetos for the Air Force was transferred there (although no longer used in cars magnetos continued to be used in aircraft, as they still are today). The same year the company bought the land in Crescenzago where the plants N and D would be built.[22]

From World War II to the mid-eighties

Magneti Marelli took full advantage of the war, enjoying a monopoly in the provision of military components indispensable for the Italian war effort, such as starter and electrical equipment for aviation, and radio and broadcast systems for ships and land vehicles. Despite the difficulty in getting the necessary supplies and in recruiting enough people, an incredible production rate was achieved during the war, generating extraordinary profits.

With the first reversals of Italian fortune in the war, many plants were hit by Allied bombing such as Florence's Fivre plant in 1942, Apuania in 1943, Carpi in 1944 and Plant B in Sesto San Giovanni in 1945. After the conflict, plants and factories were quickly rebuilt, but the economic recovery was difficult because of the shortage of raw materials (steel, lead, aluminium, copper, antimony, Bakelite and plastics), the lack of liquid assets and the uncertain political and social situation.

On 16 August 1945 the National Liberation Committee of Upper Italy (CLNAI) proposed the appointment of Leonardo Brasco as special commissioner for Magneti Marelli to the Allied Command. The Allies accepted on

---

22 In 1939, Magneti had 13 plants, coordinating the activities of six subsidiaries, 7,000 employees (in 1919 it was 200) and produced a diverse range of products. The plants were: "A" Sesto San Giovanni (electrical and radio equipment), "B" Sesto San Giovanni (batteries and accumulators), "C" Sesto San Giovanni (workshops), Carpi (Milan) (aviation magnetos), Samas in Caravaggio (Bergamo region) (machine tools), Savam in Milan (glasses), Savep in Pavia (glasses), Star in Livorno (piezoelectric quartz crystals), Bregnano (Milan) (mobile radio and packaging), ICS in Canonica (Bergamo region) (Bakelite), Apuania (Macerata) (spark plugs), Fivre in Pavia (radio transmitter valves), Fivre in Florence (valves again). The group also included Radiomarelli and Mabo already described above.

condition that the company honoured its debts towards the state and Bosch, discipline in the factories was restored and surplus workers were made redundant. The Commissioner concerned himself with the immediate establishment of business relationships with US companies that required the situation in the factories to be back to normal. His main worry was the presence of workers' representative bodies like the "Consigli di gestione" (management councils), and at the same time an absence of representative bodies for property owners. The latter would be restored only on 23 July 1946, after several talks with the National Liberation Committee of Lombardy. It should be pointed out that the experience of the "management councils" was to end in 1948 due to the new Italian political situation.

Once normal management of the company was restored, owners and management had to face problems such as lack of liquidity and supplies, and above all, the collapse of the productivity rate in the last months of the war caused by constant mass sabotage by workers. To further aggravate the situation, the company was forced to hire more than 1,000 employees between the end of the war and January 1946 (the workers employed in all of Sesto San Giovanni thus increased from 2909 to 4091). This recruitment included the application of the provisions introduced by Decree Law no. 27 of 14 February 1946 requiring the reinstatement of employees "that, not being in their probationary period, had to leave the job to be interned or deported by the Germans or Fascists, or to participate in the liberation struggle or who, enlisted into the military, had been detained."

The situation tended to stabilise in subsequent years as far as reorganisation of the company, liquidity (by taking out loans) and surplus of workers (480 workers were allocated to initial training courses) were concerned, thus ensuring a sufficient level of economic equilibrium.

For Italy, the years between 1952 and 1963 were those of the so-called "economic boom," characterised by its final transformation into an industrialised nation, doubling the national income and with economic growth rates lower only than those of Japan and West Germany. Investments saw strong growth, unemployment was drastically reduced and the "consumer society" triumphed.

The symbolic goods of this "boom" were the automobile and the television, two areas in which Magneti Marelli was directly concerned.[23] The steady growth of Magneti Marelli is therefore unsurprising, given that it had chosen the path of intensification of investment and productivity, with consequences for the organisation of work and the composition of the workforce. There was a strong

---

23   The number of cars on the road went from 342,000 in 1950 to 1,675,000 in 1960. In the year 1950 79,862 new cars were registered, while there were 393,524 in 1960. In 1954 TV owners numbered no more than 100,000, in 1964 there were more than 5,000,000.

increase in the percentage of female workers, especially in plants A in Sesto San Giovanni and N Crescenzago where the process of mechanisation of production systems developed. Since the early fifties, the number of women employed on the assembly line ("on the carpet") doubled.[24] The significant improvement in production can be seen by an increase in production in 1962 by 9.6%, despite the loss of 1.2 million hours of work due to strikes by electro-mechanical workers. The company's workforce increased from 10,722 in 1959 to 12,022 in 1963.

In 1963, Magneti Marelli gave up on the telecommunications sector – international competition had become too strong to be able to afford product diversification and it was better to focus on processes related to automotive production.

In 1964 the Italian economic miracle can be seen to have ended. The next stage was affected by wage demands, a rapid increase in prices, loss of export competitiveness, a difficult balance of payments followed by a credit crunch which curbed inflation but also development, squeezing domestic demand. Magneti Marelli was strongly influenced by the new situation, being a company linked to the production of consumer durables (cars, radios, TVs etc.). Hundreds of workers were immediately suspended or put into the "Cassa integrazione" (see below), others were forced to work part-time.

The situation improved in 1966, and at the end of 1967, Magneti Marelli decided to proceed with a merger incorporating Fivre (receiver and transmitter valves, picture tubes, and other components for radio and TV), Mabo, Radiomarelli (both commercial only) Imcaradio (quality radio), Iniex (by now only Real Estate), Turin's F. Rabotti and Potenza's Rabotti South. This corporate concentration was in line with what was happening in other European industries, it being a necessary tool for greater market competitiveness through greater financial coordination, standardisation of purchases, reorganisation and expansion of the sales network. The merger also allowed the company to combine a number of sales offices, with obvious savings for Magneti Marelli. At the same time, electronics developed in the automotive industry, the company improved the workings of colour and closed-circuit TV, radio and sound reproduction (radios, cassette players and hi-fis), aiming at the introduction of new products. In 1971, a research centre was formed together with Fiat, which in 1973 set up its headquarters in Turin. All this was done in order to gradually convert production from electromechanical to electronic technology, supporting Fiat in its

---

24   In 1959 the construction of the "UQ" factory Romano di Lombardia (Bergamo) began. It was characterised by a high level of automation. They also expanded the plant "N" Crescenzago, and in the same area plant "D" was completed and the construction of the "S" plant was initiated. In 1955 Imcaradio of Alessandria (radio receivers) was acquired, later Rabotti was transferred to a new plant in Turin and the construction of a plant in Potenza (Rabotti South) began.

production initiatives. In the period between 1968 and 1972, the Rabotti plant in Potenza was expanded, Crescenzago's spark plug section was improved and new wire drawing and electrical equipment departments set up. In addition, a new battery production line was set up in Romano di Lombardia, a plant was built in Bursa (Turkey) along with another two large ones for the production of batteries and electrical equipment in San Salvo (near Chieti in Abruzzo).

Thanks to corporate decisions and the expansion of the automotive industry, Magneti Marelli maintained a positive economic trend until 1971. This was in spite of increasing labour costs and taxes with the simultaneous decline in hours worked and the progressive increase in worker absenteeism since 1967. In 1973, the situation got worse due to the "oil shock" that greatly increased the tendency within the Italian economy towards stagnation, accompanied by – for the first time in the country's history – inflation (a similar phenomenon had already been seen in the Weimar Republic of the 1920s, although the Italian case was nowhere near as extreme). The lowest point was reached in 1975, while the next three years appeared to guarantee some recovery. Yet in 1979 the Western economy (except for Japan) entered a new recession. This crisis in Italy would go on into the early eighties and was characterised by high inflation, trade and payments deficits, public debt, contraction of domestic demand, investment and production, and a sharp decline in industrial employment. The automotive sector was one of the hardest hit sectors in Italy, also due to government austerity measures that limited energy consumption.

In such a situation and with the strong labour unrest that characterised this period, Magneti Marelli attempted to deal with the crisis, maintaining an appropriate balance between costs (greater organisational efficiency and rigidly contained expenditure) and revenues (sources of alternative income to the automotive industry and new planning skills) while waiting for better times.[25]

---

25   Sales revenue and staff costs (In millions of current lire) – see table.

Years	Sales revenue	Labour costs
1973	9,34	3,38
1974	11,78	4,75
1975	13,16	5,96
1976	17,18	7,70
1977	23,09	8,73
1978	26,02	9,56
1979	30,84	11,82
1980	40,92	13,26

Source: Cenciarini-Licini, op. cit.

In autumn 1973, Magneti Marelli proceeded to restructure the company into different divisions, resulting in decentralisation of operations. Four production divisions (equipment, batteries, Fivre and Rabotti) and two commercial (Parts and Service exMabo and Radiomarelli) were formed.[26] Clearly all divisions complied with a central strategy that was responsible for general management with the support of the corresponding administrative staff such as the Central Board, the research and development headquarters, marketing head office, human resources, purchases, construction and plants, and licenses. In 1977 a new and major decentralisation was implemented, so the Equipment division was divided into Compressed Air, Spark Plug and Electrical equipment, while three new divisions were introduced: International activities, Systems and electronics, and Basic production.

Starting in 1975, corporate policy aimed at limiting costs through hiring freezes, postponing investments in development and abandoning production that brought little profit.[27] Even in the most critical years, such as 1975 and 1976, Magneti Marelli managed to make a profit and to raise turnover despite increasing labour costs (see table in footnote 10), thanks to ever increasing integration into international markets. In 1974 the company opened subsidiaries

---

26   The *Equipaggiamento* was responsible for the full range of electrical equipment for cars (alternators, dynamos, motors, ignition coils, washers and accessories), spark plugs and air braking systems for commercial vehicles (plants Crescenzago, San Salvo, Carpi and Alessandria). The division produced batteries for automotive starter batteries, traction batteries for electric truck transport and lifting, stationary batteries and lighting for trains (plants Romano di Lombardia, San Salvo and Crescenzago). Fivre made picture tubes in black and white (plants in Pavia and Florence). Rabotti was concerned with testing and made various products such as electric fans, inductors and traction motors (Turin and Potenza).

27   Employees of the Magneti Marelli 1968 to 1983 – see table.

Year	Staff	Year	Staff
1968	8.320	1976	11.689
1969	9.071	1977	10.917
1970	9.791	1978	10.812
1971	10.006	1979	10.441
1972	11.381	1980	9.044
1973	12.834	1981	8.480
1974	13.011	1982	7.730
1975	12.780	1983	7.350

Source: Cenciarini-Licini, op. cit.

in Barcelona and Paris. In 1977 Magneti Marelli Germany and France were born and by 1978 the company operated in Portugal, Great Britain, Argentina and Nigeria. In the same year Magneti Marelli Holding s.a. was born with headquarters in Lugano, Switzerland, where the company's foreign investments were brought together.[28]

In 1977 the company acquired 60% of Fabbrica Batterie York. In 1978, it established the *Compagnia generale accumulatori* (Cga), to whom four factories of *Fabbriche accumulatori riuniti* (Far) in Casalnuovo, Melzo, Monza and Bari were assigned. Far had previously absorbed Tudor, Titan and Hensemberger, so Magneti Marelli found itself in absolute control of the battery and accumulator sector in Italy.

In 1979 25 million shares were sold, increasing share capital from 36 billion to 51 billion lire[29]. In collaboration with Fiat and Weber, Magneti Marelli established Marelli Autronica. In 1980 the company sold its block of shares in Fivre and increased its stake in Fabbrica Batterie York, and in 1981 began construction of a spark plug factory in Iraq.

On 8 November 1982, the Minister of Labour declared that Magneti Marelli was in crisis, and in 1984 the company moved its headquarters from Sesto San Giovanni to Cinisello Balsamo (Milan) and signed a technical cooperation agreement with the Japanese company Nippodenso.

In 1985 and 1986 the company underwent several renovations, up until 1987 when its business areas went through a process of transformation. These business areas became: instrumentation, electromechanics, electronics, lighting, air conditioning and power systems.

Retelling the history of Magneti Marelli will stop here as its story goes beyond the remit of this work. It is enough just to remember that the Crescenzago plant no longer exists and the area has been converted into residential property.

---

28 The share of turnover derived from exports rose from 10% in the early seventies to 17% in 1977.

29 The "azione di risparmio" or savings share: shares that do not allow the holder the right to vote at ordinary and extraordinary meetings. To compensate for this restriction, the holders of such securities have preference in the distribution of profits and capital in the event of liquidation of the company.

chapter two
Struggles in the factory, 1945-1972

IN ITALY, AFTER THE CYCLE OF STRUGGLES OF 1960-1962, THAT REPRESENTED A real turning point for trade union initiative and organisation, there was a return of employer repression, together with a decline of unionisation in the factories, and the consequent weakening of workers' organisation. Only in 1968-69 was there a return to workers' combativeness, with the resumption of trade union initiatives often overridden by the will of the workers, the development of new forms of struggle and, for the first time, the acceptance by factory workers of interventions by external forces such as students. All of this could only weaken control over the working class by the unions, who could not maintain a clear and continuous line, with workers' autonomy often forcing union leaders to accept a *fait accompli* and "ride the tiger."[30]

---

30 For documentation of this part I used, or rather plundered, the beautiful monograph on Magneti Marelli Crescenzago (Milan) contained in the monumental research of *Istituto per la storia della società contemporanea*, edited by Alessandro Pizzorno, *Lotte operaie e sindacato in Italia: 1968-1972*, Il Mulino, Bologna, 1974. The monograph is the work of Luigi Dolci and Emilio Reyneri (dealing specifically with Magneti Marelli) and is part of

Starting in 1968 the first Unitary Base Committees (Comitati unitari di base) were created. Then it was the turn of the Autonomous Assemblies, which sometimes participated, sometimes not, in the elections to the official Factory Councils. Later on, there were Workers Committees, Workers Political Collectives etc., some more oriented to political issues and others more to the needs of workers. All, however, were equally characterised by a strong critique of the union line, which was considered too soft, if not actively pro-employer, and by the idea that workers were or could become revolutionary subjects.

The experience of Magneti Marelli fits into this context of class conflict, which since the sixties had taken on different characteristics from that of the previous period. This was for several reasons:

- the greater spread and intensity of workers' struggles;
- the use of new (or at least partially new) forms of struggle;
- the objectives, that often completely overturned those of the traditional trade unions, so as to create a new relationship between unions and workers.[31]

This "workers' power" found its highest expression in the figure of the workshop delegate, a real change in post-war Italy's industrial relations system. At the beginning, this representation was felt only on the factory level, and did not intervene in external issues. Later, in the early seventies, it also expressed itself outside the factory walls and workers' autonomy was felt in the areas where workers lived (through self-reduction of utility bills, the occupation of houses, the creation of self-organised schools). A sort of counter-power appeared that, for a while, made the partisans of workers' autonomy believe that they were more powerful than official institutions and were able to assert their own legality.

---

the third volume (of six) of the work cited.

31   According to the reconstruction carried out by Renzo Del Carria, the objectives for which the workers struggled in those years were:
- Same wage increases for everyone;
- Minimum wage;
- Second category for all; abolition of, or at least a decrease in the number of, categories;
- Significant reductions in the time and pace of work;
- Immediate and complete equalization between workers and salaried employees;
- Reduction of working hours with no loss of pay;
- Elimination of piecework and overtime;
- Elimination of the monetisation of harmful processes.

Renzo Del Carria, *Proletari senza rivoluzione*, Volume V, Savelli, 1977.

The Statute of Labourers (1970)[32] and the parallel rise of Factory Councils constituted without doubt the conquest of dignity and power by the working class. However, those workers closest to the extra-parliamentary organisations implanted in the factories believed that these two achievements could adversely affect the power of the delegates within the larger factories, and that this power would be absorbed by the unions.

The influence of outside groups (students or extra-parliamentary militants) suffered its first setback with the return of union control of struggles in the factory, due to an increase in membership and organisation. The strong disagreements on the manner and timing of struggles therefore now took place within the union, which managed most of the time to control or contain them, using its own organisational skills and a greater attention to requests from the rank and file than it had shown in the past.

In the factories, workers' dissent against the union line could not be measured only on the basis of the intervention of autonomous groups, since it was reasonably present within the union itself, which, however, was always dampening the influence of such dissent. The establishment of the Factory Councils allowed the unions to "territorialise" its interventions, preventing more general demands, while the electoral system in the factories was gradually changed to make it harder to elect delegates who were misaligned, or belonged to extra-parliamentary groups. The risk for "dissident" delegates was, obviously, that of falling into corporatism. To be able to stand out from the candidates aligned with the union, they had to mobilise the forces of the rank and file, which were sometimes marred by spontaneism.

Another root cause of the strengthening of trade unions after 1968 was, contrary to what had happened in the past, recognition by employers, who went so far as to seek dialogue with the unions, considering them the only intermediary able to control struggles and workers' demands. This happened at all levels, including workshops, where employer repression and control diminished in proportion to the "responsibility" shown by the unions.

---

32   The Statute of Labourers (*Statuto dei lavoratori*), established by Law 300 of 20 May 1970, was the state and the unions' reply to the struggles of the Hot Autumn of 1969. It provided certain benefits for workers but not as many as for the unions. It consisted of no less than 41 articles, grouped under six headings (Freedom and Dignity of the Employee, Trade Union Rights, Trade Union Activity, Diverse and General Measures, Hiring Norms, Scope and Punitive Measures) and hundreds of sub-articles. This law was brought in by Carlo Donat-Cattin (1919-1991), the Christian Democrat minister of labour of the time, a former leader of the CISL union.

Employment and the evolution of worker composition

The professional structure of Magneti Marelli remained constant over time, even if employment was cyclical, with obvious consequences for job security and the age range of the workforce.

Between 1952 and 1956 the number of employees varied between 2,300 and 2,400, while in the following three years it dropped by 400, before increasing by 50% during the "economic boom" (1960-62), reaching 3,000. Immediately after there were new job losses and massive use of redundancy pay: in the period 1964-66 there were 400 less workers and 500 were suspended at zero hours for a period of a year and a half. These drops in employment were accompanied by attacks by the bosses on union organisation and a decline in class conflict.

In 1968 the company started to recruit at a high rate, fishing in the labour market of southern Italy until 1973, when the production department of Crescenzago had an extra 1,000 factory workers and 200 office employees, a small part of which was transferred to Sesto San Giovanni, coinciding with a period of recession in 1971-72.

From 1968 the data on workers' composition[33] saw a sharp increase in male workers, young and southern, while the employment of women was characterised by a high "natural" turnover. This new reality had a direct consequence for class conflict due to the different attitudes of the new employees towards work. An alliance between the young workers from vocational schools, with frustrated expectations, and southern immigrants, instinctively rebellious given their harsh social conditions, came into being. Only a few smaller departments (tooling, maintenance, the foundry) were not affected by this new composition and were therefore disconnected from the attitude of the remaining departments at the Crescenzago plant.

Worker composition at Magneti Marelli Crescenzago in 1972 could be described as follows: internal organisation of the factory saw some auxiliary departments (tooling, maintenance, inspection) employing 700 workers, while those related to production numbered 3,200, employed in fragmented and repetitive tasks of automatic and semiautomatic machine tools, transfer

---

33 This concept was developed by the journal *Quaderni Rossi* to analyse modifications in the structure of the working class in its various job roles and qualifications, not from the static point of view of sociology but from the dynamic point of view of struggles. To put it another way, the analysis of class composition has for its aim the understanding of what does or does not favour workers' struggles and their modes of organisation in relation to the position in the productive process of this or that group of workers.

or conveyor belts for assembly.[34] This resulted in very low skilled workers and a high proportion of women (40% of the total, 50% in production), considered suitable for handling small parts in a way which is mentally rather than physically stressful.

At the end of 1970 the first category workers (the highest) represented 10.5% of the total (they were all men, especially in auxiliary departments and maintenance staff), those of the second category made up 28.5% (all men), those of the third were 39% (half of which were women), the fourth were 22% (all women). Already in 1973, the qualification structure changed considerably: the fourth category disappeared, half of the workers then fell into the third category, the second numbered little less than 38%, and first 13% (most of them in "first super," a category which did not exist in 1970). The movement from one category to another was obtained through company agreements, commissions for qualifications or unilaterally granted by management.[35]

In 1970, office workers represented 10% of employees (about 400), in 1973 this reached 13% (about 600). The administrative offices were located in Sesto San Giovanni where white collar workers amounted to more than 70% of the staff (in 1970 it was 40% out of 1400 employees, but some operative departments were dismantled immediately after). In summary, we see an elite of professional workers alongside a vast majority of ordinary workers who performed unskilled work with very short cycles, sometimes of few seconds, subject to rigid time control through a piece rate system and with no prospect of a professional career. Women were used where there was less muscular effort (assembly, small machine tools, transfer lines[36]), while the men took care of

---

34   Centro di ricerche sui modi di produzione, *L'organizzazione del lavoro della Magneti Marelli di Crescenzago*, Milan, 1970, typescript.
35   Dolci-Reyneri, *op. cit.*
36   The transfer machines are part of the third phase of mechanization in factories:

The first phase is that of multi-purpose machines or generic tools first operated directly by man, such as drills and universal lathes. The worker keeps a wide field of initiative, for each machine carries out a large number of different operations, the precision of the work is high, though depending in large part on the ability of the worker. This is the first phase of production in small batches.

The second phase is that of machines which are specialised or single-purpose or single-focused, designed and built for only one or a few operations. This phase corresponds to the development of large scale production, for which the work must be divided into operations fragmented, assigning to a machine one or a few operations, simplifying the machine itself, making it very precise and at the same time avoiding or substantially reducing the work of adjustment. If in the first phase, the worker saw the work as a whole, now only those who oversee the line of simple machines see the work as a whole, this view

the larger machine tools. The workers were not tied collectively to the pace imposed by the plants, there were no assembly lines like those in automotive or home appliance companies. The work of female workers was often carried out at an "imposed" rhythm[37], like at electromechanical light factories such as Borletti and Sit-Siemens, but with the difference that Magneti Marelli women did not represent the majority of the workforce and were isolated in women-only departments. The production flow was not organised by the type of work but by product. Therefore, men working on machine tools that processed parts could work in the same department as the women who assembled them. The strong presence of women, well integrated into the life of the factory,

---

leaves the worker rather fragmented.

The third stage is one in which partial operations are recomposed and entrusted to individual special machines and then comes the so-called automatic machine, mainly suitable for large scale production. A single machine or a complex of machines performs a series of operations and thus it exceeds the phase of decomposition of work of its second phase of mechanization. Machine transference is one of the features of this third phase, the planning and organization have a dominant weight to which they fit the individual elements of production. The single operating department is designed as a function of the complex machine that unites it. In the previous step, the one of chains of production, each piece was transported by the chain in front of the individual machine, leaving the conveyor belt, it was worked on by the machine and then it was put back on the conveyor belt to proceed to the next machining process. Now it is rather the operating unit (the machine) that moves to perform the operation of a piece that remains fixed to the conveyor, until the end of all the operations.

In the fourth phase these transformations result in automation, that is the replacement of man in different loading functions, monitoring and control of machines and then with the liberation of man from the same performance more simple and repetitive. Maurizio Lichtner (Eds.), *L'organizzazione del lavoro in Italia*, Editori Riuniti, 1975

37 "In factories, the worker often works with one or more machines that may or may not operate automatically, using a predetermined period of time to perform a given operation. During the period in which they work, and then during the total cycle time of work, the worker cannot accelerate the pace of work, and therefore the total cycle time. The worker can save time only when the machine is stationary, since when the machine is working the rhythm is predetermined. If the worker has to monitor the machine for a fraction of the total machine-time, the company will tend to assign them to the control of other machines, so that they are always busy even during the period in which they could just be waiting." Marino Regini-Emilio Reyneri, *Lotte operaie e organizzazione del lavoro*, Marsilio editori, 1971

influenced the strong trade union militancy of women and the structure of workers' representation.[38]

The factory was divided into various buildings, themselves divided into roughly twenty departments. Almost everybody worked on two shifts, with a presence ranging from 30 to 250 workers at a time.

The 1968-72 cycle of struggles would mostly affect those departments where there was a greater presence of machine operators not tied to the pace imposed by the plant. Only later would the relationship with the corporate hierarchy break even in the smaller or predominantly female departments.

In each female team there were the so-called "teachers": older workers of a higher category than that of their workmates who accelerated the pace of work by means of group piece work which existed in all areas of production. In fact, group piece work, adopted also for jobs that were not interdependent, resulted in the spread of a strict mutual control amongst workers to ensure certain earnings, as could be seen by the frequent quarrels between the "lazy" and those who wanted to "do the piece."[39] This happened especially in situations with poor working-class solidarity and weak unions.

The workers employed in auxiliary departments or with auxiliary tasks in production, around 600 "economisti" (workers not directly employed in production, e.g. maintenance, tool-making) and piece workers, were almost all of the first or second category, and amongst them consistent and differentiated merit increases were the normal practice.

---

38   Leaflets by comrades, and even by the unions, often addressed workers in an impeccably non-sexist way as: "*Lavoratrici, lavoratori*" – "Female workers, male workers," or perhaps as "*Compagni, compagne*" – "Male comrades, female comrades." This has been rendered in the English translation as "workers(f/m)" or "comrades(f/m)" just to remind readers that, although the radical groups in the factories were mostly composed of men, they did make a real effort to address women workers, even in the phrasing of their leaflets.

39   Comitato di coordinamento del Gruppo Magneti Fim-FIOM-UILM, "Documentation about the Group and labour problems," Sesto San Giovanni, July 1971. The "piece" is a wage system aimed at achieving a higher return by the worker through a monetary incentive, that is, to pay the worker depending on the amount of work delivered in a unit of time. Among the workers' more "subversive" demands by this time is the breaking of the link between wage increases and productivity gains. Wages must become a "independent variable," not determined by the profits of the company or the economic situation. It is obvious that the system of piecework proceeds in the opposite direction. You can understand why its abolition was the constant object of worker platforms. Paul Ginsborg, *Storia d'Italia dal dopoguerra a oggi* ("History of Italy from the post-war period to today") – 2 volumes, Einaudi, 1989.

Up until 1970 technological innovation was gradual, resulting in increased levels of mechanisation and automation of machines that made the work even more repetitive, and at a rhythm imposed by the machine.[40]

Labour conflict at Magneti Marelli Crescenzago

a) From the end of World War II to 1968

Italian industry emerged almost untouched by the armed conflict, as is reflected in the 1946 guidelines for industrial imports, where it was estimated that "for the northern regions production capacity has been reduced by 5-7% due to serious destruction."[41] In contrast, the average index of national industrial production, set at 100 in 1938, was only 29 in 1945, while the national income, again assuming 100 in 1938, dropped to 51.9 in 1945. This was not due to damage to the industrial apparatus during the war, but to the lack of energy and raw materials, the destruction caused to the transport and communication systems as well as the disastrous condition of agriculture.

This quantitative reality goes along with a qualitative one that saw an industrial apparatus living in a condition of self-sufficient "perfect isolation" from 1935. A number of barriers and customs protectionism had allowed the survival and development of industries significantly more backward than in the rest of Europe. Therefore, after the war, Italy resurfaced in the international competitive arena with the need for strong industrial restructuring in order to enter markets.

Bosses pushed for a productivity increase and a reduction in employment, estimating a surplus of industrial labour of 38% in September 1945. This was certainly an overestimation, but there is no doubt that, immediately after the Liberation, problems arose concerning how to use a large part of the workforce.

Already in 1946, industrial productivity picked up thanks to better transport and supply of raw materials (coal, cotton, wool) and a significant increase in exports. The war damage had been largely repaired, industry was returning to pre-war efficiency, the process of conversion from war production to peace production did not present any technical problems since in most cases

---

40 *Dibattito unitario* ("Unitary Debate"), 1970.

41 *Piano di massima per le importazioni industriali dell'anno 1946*, paper by the Ministry of Industry and Commerce in collaboration with the Central Economic Commission of the National Liberation of Italy and the Technical Commission of the Committee of National Liberation of Naples, October 1945, from p. 46.

factories went back to their old production without modernising their plants or ways of working.[42]

In Lombardy the company CLNs (Committees of National Liberation), and then the Consigli di gestione ("Board of Management" with representatives of bosses and workers), raised the question of the restoration of damaged plants and machinery, the recovery of production and conversion of military production, the use of labour and the search for raw materials necessary for production. At Magneti Marelli war damages were completely irrelevant, production continued as it had during the war, while the workforce increased from 2,909 workers in April 1945 to 4,091 in January 1946.

Amongst the new recruits there were 330 veterans, 68 who'd refused to be drafted to work in Germany, 148 ex-Partisans and others in the Resistance, 131 recalled to their previous employment positions and 105 women and men in particularly difficult economic conditions. In 1947, in Crescenzago Plant N, important innovations were made that introduced the assembly line, making the plant suitable for the production cycle of the car. Between 1948 and 1954, Magneti Marelli tripled production without increasing employment, thanks to a policy of radical plant modernisation.[43]

---

42   Istituto per gli studi di economia, *Annuario della congiuntura economica italiana*, 1938-47, Florence, 1949, pp. 313 et seq.

43   *Un minuto più del padrone, i metalmeccanici milanesi dal dopoguerra agli anni settanta*, Vangelista, 1977. Of great importance was the struggle of the workers for the achievement of equal pay between women and men, already enshrined in the Constitution in 1948 but not applied in practice. The female labour force was historically more malleable, subject to greater mobility and lower skilled, and trapped by various moralistic conventions. Women were included in the labour market when there were production requirements, for example during a time of war, but were driven out when the economy was slow. This is what happened at the end of World War II, when veterans and supporters from the front and from prisons demanded jobs, so that companies thought about "getting rid" of women or exploiting the huge disparities in pay between men and women to keep the female workforce where high performance was guaranteed at low cost. At the end of the war, in the industrial area of Milan there was a significant use of female labour in the field of radio (Safar, Geloso, Magneti Marelli, Philips, Autelco, Siemens and Face). Already in 1945, the issue of equal pay was identified by the workers, who made it a reason to create the *Gruppi di difesa della donna* (groups for the defence of women) of Alfa Romeo and Magneti Marelli, but it would have to wait until 16 July 1960 before an agreement was signed by union and bosses' organizations that provided equal pay for equal work between men and women. In the category of metalworkers this equal pay for equal work and qualifications was achieved with the contract signed in 1963 which abolished so-called "female categories" and gave increases of 35 lire per hour for female

After an initial phase of collaboration between established political parties and business people, a new phase began in 1948 in which workers' parties and trade unions used the Boards of Management as an official oppositional political force. The electoral victory of the conservative coalition changed the balance of forces in the political and trade union arena, increasing the demand for redundancies in Italian factories. Hence, the weekly newspaper *Il Rondò* (the name of a square in Sesto San Giovanni, a suburb of Milan, which became known as the "the Stalingrad of Italy"), proclaimed the need to transform "every factory into a fortress."[44]

It was in this climate that the attack on Togliatti occurred (he was shot and seriously wounded on 14 July 1948, leading to a brief period of strikes and insurrectionary upheaval, damped down by Togliatti himself). From that moment, trade union unity came to an end. In all of Milan's factories an air of Liberation took hold, with each of the union tendencies undermining workers' unity in favour of entrenching their ideological positions. Meanwhile, "as it is not possible anymore that union membership fees are paid through the bosses' institutions… the rapid creation of a vast network of collectors is required," in the ratio of one for every 15 workers. The network was created in August at Magneti Marelli, Ercole Marelli and Breda.[45]

In October 1948 management made a serious attack on employment, suggesting sending away 1,119 workers to be retrained and the dismissal of 250 employees. Redundancies hit all the major factories in Milan, and there were lockouts followed by factory occupations. These occupations demonstrated that workers were able to work and produce without the bosses. Battles were fought at Falck, Breda and Magneti Marelli, but were disconnected because the Confindustria (Italian employers' association) forbade the entry of trade unionists in to the factories. On 13 December, Marelli and Breda management left the premises of their companies that continued production under workers' occupation. On 11 January, a general strike took place, but reached massive numbers only in Sesto San Giovanni. On 21 January, there was a big demonstration in Milan's Piazza del Duomo, which was joined by workers from Sesto. A few days later, agreements were signed at Breda and Marelli that envisaged a number of resignations equal to the number of redundancies requested.[46]

---

    workers and 9,900 lire a month for the female employees. Of course, these agreements were not enough to eliminate inequalities between male and female workers regarding working conditions, qualifications and career. *Ibid.*

44 *Il Rondò*, a Sesto San Giovanni weekly, Year III, n. 14, 4 May 1948

45 *Il Rondò*, Year III, n. 33, 30 Aug 1948

46 Istituto milanese per la storia della Resistenza e del movimento operaio, *Verbali CE*, 30

In 1953, the legislature came to the end of its term and the conservative coalition tried to permanently settle its accounts with the working class and its political organisations, proposing the so-called "legge truffa" (fraud law), with strong opposition from the CGIL union confederation, while the other union confederations, CISL and UIL, defended the law as democratic.[47] The "fraud law" did not pass. Centrism was in crisis, but the absence of real political alternatives gave new breath to employer repression, launching its latest anti-worker attack. This time the target was the internal committees of the major factories (elected bodies representing all workers, union and non-union), which saw their rights taken away. For instance, the posting of announcements and newspapers on company notice boards, the presence of party and union headquarters within the factory premises, the possibility for trade union committee members to move around the factory, the right to hold meetings during working hours, workers' control over welfare institutions – CRAL (Company Workers Social Club), insurance etc. Workers' resistance was hard, despite CISL and UIL supporting the undermining of FIOM (the metalworkers' branch of CGIL) and organisations representing workers. This attitude, and the abundant availability of labour, encouraged employers to carry on with this policy of repression. It consisting of: cutting production times, decreasing piece rates, extending working hours, wage discrimination against women, so that high profits and restructuring were unimpeded.

The majority of Italian industrialists, spearheaded by Fiat, used a production method called "poor man's Taylorism." This involved the following procedure: the employers "estimate a certain time, without any research, without any effort to improve the work itself. The incentive encourages the worker to reach the time set, but the worker is left to himself, that is to more physical and mental effort to meet this time. The company management doesn't do

---

Nov 1948, 12 Dec 1948 and 17 Dec 1948, quoted in *Un minuto più del padrone*, op. cit.

47   In Italy, in the period of history we are concerned with, the existing union confederations were:
- CGIL: *Confederazione Generale Italiana del Lavoro* (Italian General Confederation of Labour), close to the Stalinists of the PCI but also containing numerous Socialists and numerically the most important union with around 3 million members in 1969.
- CISL: *Confederazione Italiana Sindacati Lavoratori* (Italian Confederation of Workers' Unions) very close to Christian Democracy, with around 2 million members in 1969.
- UIL: *Unione Italiana del Lavoro* (Italian Union of Labour), close to the Socialists and Republicans, with around 1.5 million members in 1969.

There was also the CISNAL, *Confederazione Italiana dei Sindacati Nazionali del Lavoro* (Italian Confederation of National Labour Unions), a fascist union with around 400,000 members.

anything or very little. Hence, it abdicates its responsibility for the improvement of the organisation and methods of work... Once the set time is reached, with any excuse or even without any, you cut the time and assign another. The worker, again driven by need and incentive, puts his physical and mental strength to work again to meet the second time. And so on until a time is reached that cannot be further reduced because it borders the limits of physical and mental possibilities."[48] The workers of Magneti Marelli, a company linked to Fiat where the method was strongly applied, reported in a document that "conservative calculations suggest that from the beginning of 1953 production at Plant N increased by about 40%. Only 20% is due to technical innovations, while the remaining 20% was obtained with the increase in the pace of work, and therefore with greater physical effort by the workers...For coils, flywheel magnets, coil ignitions, dynamos, compressors in particular, but also in general for all other materials one can calculate that in just eight months, from June 1953 to February 1954, there was an average increase of over 20%. In response to this increased production, the average percentage of piecework during the same period decreased by 13%. It is therefore evident that increased production is not followed, as it should be, by an increase in workers' income."[49]

Magneti Marelli boasted a strong fighting spirit and a significant CP presence in the workplace. It is easily understandable that management, from the mid-fifties, tried to regain control by destroying the trade union and political organisation of the workers. The first wave of layoffs took place in 1953 (office workers), the second in 1956 (factory workers). In the first case the reaction of the workers was extremely strong, with about 40 days occupation of the factory. The second was much weaker. However, the result was the same: the objective was not achieved. Job insecurity and a lack of tangible results, despite the high level of conflicts with the boss, frustrated the expectations of workers, and caused a disconnect between the union leadership and the rank and file. The employer repression could thus continue. This resulted in a factory "cleansed" of old CP political and union frameworks (FIOM and PCI members).

---

48   S. Leonardi, *La vera produttività del lavoro* ("The true productivity of labour"), in *Rinascita*, nn. 11-12, 1954.

49   Document *Memoriale dei lavoratori della Magneti Marelli* N, 1954. "On the moving belts for assembly of our products, where you cannot sit down without being replaced so as not to stop the line, the team that work there should have a reserve worker to replace those who have to sit down. The lack of such a person represents considerable practical difficulties resulting in further sacrifices by the workers of the team and by the technicians, as the latter are often forced to compensate for this deficiency themselves. On some assembly lines replacements exist but their cost is entirely met by the team thus contravening the most basic rules of the contract." *Ibid*

The company sought to restrict the freedom of action of union representatives, an effort that ran parallel with the national agreement on the *Commissioni interne* (Internal Commissions) already disempowered and with limited functions and effectiveness. This agreement, which saw the eradication of "relocated" members (that is, removed from the factory) and drastically reduced the possibility for the Internal Commissions to meet together and with workers, would remain in force until 1969.

But, despite all this, FIOM still achieved successive electoral victories.[50]

The company's policy moved along two lines. On the one hand, the company practiced a "paternalism" which developed a wage policy through productivity bonuses – linked to piecework and to specific increases in the cost

---

50   In 1952 there were 1,152 enrolled in FIOM, in 1958 only 340, in 1961, 627, peaking in 1963 with 948 members of FIOM and 594 of Fim (metalworkers' union in the CISL), then there is a considerable drop in union membership until 1970.

Unionisation of the workforce

Years	FIOM	Fim	UILM	Unitarians
1952	1185			
1958	340			
1959	387			
1960	450			
1961	627			
1962	862			
1963	948	594		
1964	742	558		
1965	512	423		
1966	413	321		
1967	492	423		
1968	586	528		
1969	592	503		
1970	1015	688		
1971	1024	636		
1972	1091	636	205	519
1973	1188	672	199	670

Voting percentages in elections to the Internal Commissions:

Years	FIOM	Fim	UILM	Cisnal

of living – and "merit" increases granted by supervisors. On the other hand, it promoted the development of the business union Fim (a "democratic and modern" union), which drew up separate agreements from FIOM without using the threat of strike action. In particular, it should be pointed out that the 1954 agreement, clearly anti-FIOM, granted wage increases only to workers who had already accepted the national agreement about "conglobamento" (aggregation) signed only by CISL and UIL.[51]

1952	67,9%	32,1%		
1953	73,3	26,7		
1954	67,0	33,0		
1955	69,5	30,5		
1956	68,7	25,4		5,9
1957	56,9	37,5		5,6
1959	59,9	35,8		4,3
1960	62,7	32,5		4,8
1961	61,4	30,9	7,7	
1962	59,2	33,5	7,3	
1963	57,2	34,6	8,2	
1964	58,2	33,5	8,3	
1966	54,8	30,6	14,6	
1968	55,4	31,3	13,4	

Delegates elected to the Internal Commission:

Years	FIOM	Fim	UILM	Cisnal
1957	4	4		1
1959	5	4		
1963	6	4	1	
1964	6	4	1	
1966	5	4	2	
1968	6	4	1	

Figures come from the provincial federation of the FIOM of Milan and are quoted in Dolci-Reyneri, *op. cit.*

51 "Tempi moderni," *Potere sindacale e contrattazione aziendale alla Falck ed alla Magneti Marelli* ("Trade union power and company bargaining at Falck and Magneti Marelli"), n. 14, April 1959.

The structure of wages inherited from the post-war period provided a very fragmented and precarious composition. Everywhere the base pay was only a small part of total compensation, the rest was made up of various components (piece rates and other incentives,

The second half of the fifties, therefore, is marked by a strong split between the unions. CISL was used by management as a "union of convenience," inserting itself in the already hard ideological and political confrontation between Catholics and Communists that was going on in Italy in this period.

In 1958, the management of Magneti Marelli was one of the most reluctant to accept the application of the "conglobamento" agreements in Milan. In spite of CISL having a majority in the Internal Commission from the previous year, the unions were united enough to face down the bosses' ferocity. The summer of 1958 was marked by a wave of layoffs that hit large groups of workers in Sesto San Giovanni, starting from Breda and Magneti Marelli, to which unions responded with a joint demonstration that took place in Sesto on 11 July.

There was an episode in February 1959 where Magneti Marelli played a key role. In that month elections were scheduled for the Internal Commission of the company, in which FIM in the preceding years had had a majority. The management, as usual, sent a letter to employees' homes encouraging them to vote for FIM. This time the divisive manoeuvre failed, with FIM itself reporting "external interference" and withdrawing its representatives from the electoral commissions, and once the election had taken place, it made its elected representatives resign from their lists. This gesture had such a strong unifying power that the rest of the Internal Commission would continue to consult the FIM-CISL before taking positions.[52]

The situation changed in 1960, the year of the struggle against the "clerical-fascist" Tambroni government. In Milan, the unions launched a united policy, coinciding with the return of worker militancy, spearheaded by the electromechanical sector and Magneti Marelli. The dispute was prepared collectively, but the strike against the Tambroni government and the congress of the MSI (the fascist party) in Genoa, was called by CGIL and rejected by CISL and UIL, breaking the recently discovered unity and creating strong tensions between workers, who came to blows at Falck Unione.

---

allowances, contingency, category's minimum and superminimum, particular elements of the various companies). The fight for aggregation promised to combine multiple elements into a single wage, but the CGIL's positions on this issue differed from those of the CISL and UIL, which, together with the CISNAL (the fascist union), on 12 June 1954 signed a separate agreement with the Assolombarda that was described by the CGIL as a "scam agreement." *Il metallurgico*, year II, no. 3 June 1954.

In March 1956, two years after the agreement on aggregation, it had not been applied to Magneti Marelli. FIOM in the company was forced to sign this agreement so as not to lose support in their working-class base.

52   *Il magnete*, s. no., February 1960.

The workers' strength expressed itself above all in the bitter struggle over the contracts of electromechanical workers, for whom the national capital was Milan. The workers had to face an alliance of bosses who did not care about any "modern system of industrial relations." Apart from Sit-Siemens and Breda Electromechanics, the electromechanical industry in Milan was in private hands. On one side, Edison, a monopoly within the power industry that led the resistance to the nationalisation plans drawn up by the centre-left. On the other, there was Fiat (which controlled Magneti Marelli), certain of its triumph over its workers and therefore extremely aggressive towards their demands.

It's easy to imagine how Assolombarda (Association of Industrial and Service Companies of the Milan region – part of Confindustria) embraced the intransigent line that forced the obstinacy of workers in their struggles and it is not by chance that the last company to sign the company agreement was Magneti Marelli.[53]

This new wave of struggles at Magneti Marelli was facilitated by the renewed hiring of workers, job security, the unitary policies of FIM and FIOM and also by the more moderate and "realistic" demands of workers. The forms of struggle were extremely strong with half-hour strikes organised by workers that, due to their job, could move freely within the factory, sneaking away from checks that the company had imposed on members of the Internal Commission. Participation was also almost total, even amongst women. The result of the struggles was better than that obtained in the other Milanese factories owned by the same group, Ercole Marelli, where in the company agreement there was a clause to absorb wage increases in subsequent contracts. At Magneti workers followed the directives of the provincial FIOM office that opposed the more conciliatory position of other members of the Internal Commission, who were closer to management.

The revival of the workers' movement gave new strength to trade union negotiation that, in the period between 1960 and 1962, obtained the institution of a third wage element equal to 14% of the minimum wage, an increase in piece rates, paid breaks and a reduction of working hours. Unionisation of

---

53 *Un minuto più del padrone*, op. cit. After a very long struggle, the electromechanical contract was signed in February 1963 and provided a platform on which the unions built a strong bargaining position: wage increases were substantial, they obtained bargaining rights for piecework, bonuses and the pace of work, obtained the reduction of working hours, achieved equal pay for women and young people, the three first days absence due to illness were paid, union dues were taken out of wages every three months, the recognition of the union in the factory.

the factory increased considerably (FIOM membership doubled), massively exceeding the average for Milan.[54]

From 1964 to 1967, the economic situation reversed and therefore the workers' situation changed again: there were hiring freezes, redundancy requests and hundreds of suspensions from work. Trade union organisation was destroyed while corporate control was fully restored: the fighting spirit that had been expressed in the period immediately preceding could not resist the attack of the crisis. Indeed, the repressive policy at Magneti Marelli had already been felt after the contract fight in 1963, which saw poor participation on the part of workers, such that it was the only major company in Milan to deduct holidays following strikes, and was among those that violated the provisions of the contract.[55]

The company's reaction was particularly hard on FIOM, which suffered verbal intimidation, suspensions, transfers and threats. In this way, dozens of workers were driven out of the factory, and others directly fired. Among the tactics used to achieve this objective, Magneti Marelli abruptly transferred union activists to other plants, especially to the Romano Lombardo plant in Bergamo, considered as "company confinement." Another tool to remove activists was to put them in *cassa integrazione* on zero hours (in 1965-66), thereby preventing contact with the rest of the workers.[56] The members of the Internal Commission were not affected by such violent internal repression thanks to the new contractual protection, although they repeatedly received suspensions from work on charges of spreading information that was false or harmful to the interests of company, introducing union material into the factory, or staying at the factory after working hours. The company also tried to limit the involvement of Internal Commission members by way of censoring

---

54 Bianca Beccalli, *Scioperi e organizzazione sindacale: Milano 1950-1970*, in "Rassegna italiana di sociologia," January-March 1971. In Magneti Marelli Crescenzago, FIOM has a unionisation rate of 32% (average of 20.3% in Milan) and Fim 20% (average 9.3% in Milan). The establishment of this 14% incentives' increase had great importance in the struggles of 1968, as the management interpreted the agreement excluding those who passed qualification and new recruits. In 1968, at the Magneti Marelli there were about one thousand workers who were therefore discriminated against on pay incentives to piece rates, especially young recruits. Massimo Cavallini (ed.), *Il terrorismo in fabbrica* ("Terrorism in the factory"), Editori Riuniti, 1978.

55 FIOM, *Libro bianco sulle violazioni contrattuali* (White Paper on breach of contract), Milan, 1964

56 *La voce sindacale*, in May 1965 and August 1966

communication or preventing them from working in the workshops and even stalking them outside the factory or during trade union duties.[57]

Company intervention became unmistakable during the union elections of 1966, when it identified – in no uncertain terms – UILM as the "union of convenience," an organisation through which the factory would hire workers throughout the sixties.[58] The company repeatedly used the "lockout" in union conflicts, such as in 1965 in Crescenzago in response to a strike against a breach of contract and the suspension of some workers or in the Romano Lombardo plant for a strike against the on-the-spot dismissal of two members of the Internal Commission.[59]

Repression also directly hit workers with heavy and frequent fines for every little infraction, dismissal for poor performance, the continued intensification of the pace of work, demotions, and the reduction of wages by blocking collective bargaining and not respecting agreements.

The management were able to shatter workers' unity due to the high turnover of the female workforce, and mass suspensions on zero hours at the same time as asking overtime from other workshops. The small size of the workshops themselves allowed for strict authoritarian or paternalistic control by employers.

In this context, it is quite understandable that company-level agreements from 1963-1968 were virtually non-existent. In 1964 the company nullified the 1957 agreement concerning the variable production bonus because, due to the high inflation of the time and the related cost-of-living increases, it was deemed too costly. The company then decided to freeze the "reward value" of the previous year if a certain piece average was reached.[60] In the absence of working class resistance, Magneti managed to significantly reduce labour costs by increasing the price of the canteen by 3,000 lire (1965), not recognising "Item 3" for new employees (although it was included in the electromechanical contract agreement), and finally by increasing the wage increments based on productivity. Management agreed to meet the Internal Commission only upon written request, sometimes

---

57   *La voce sindacale*, in May 1965 and July 1965
58   In this regard, we can read the account of a Catholic weekly in Sesto San Giovanni: "The management from then on decided to pamper the UILM but ended up interfering in the work of the Election Committee. While the FIOM won its last seat from the UILM by just a few votes, the director of personnel hastened to convene the Election Committee. Against its advice, he personally recounted the votes in open and flagrant violation of the rules." *Luce sestese*, "Ambiguity and company managements favour the UIL," July 1966
59   *L'Avanti!*, 4 Oct 1965; *L'Unità*, 4 Oct 1965; *La voce sindacale*, November 1966
60   *La voce sindacale*, December 1965 and November 1966

even denying a meeting, and even refused bargaining on changes in pay grade based on qualifications.

The complexities of the payslip in Italy

The direct wage, paid monthly, is made up of:
- Fixed elements:
  - the contractual minimum or basic pay,
  - the cost of living increase (or "escalator"),
  - the third element, a part of the wage coming from the boss-union accords on the regional and provincial level (therefore variable according to location),
  - periodic increases due to seniority every two or three years following existing conventions (linked therefore to presence in the same workplace),
  - various other bonuses given on an individual basis for a fixed period which can end up integrated into the wage;
- Variable elements:
  - overtime,
  - increases for shift work, night work, unpleasant work, being moved,
  - family allowances,
  - bonuses for the thirteenth and fourteenth months (if they are set out in the collective agreement),
  - work on public holidays,
  - paid sick leave,
  - various reimbursements (including PAYE),
  - various bonuses (study, regular attendance, car allowance, professional expenses etc.).

For the trade unions, the corporate attitude was incomprehensible because between 1964 and 1967 production performance was excellent, thanks to the decline in employment and working hours and the concomitant increase in production. However, workers' frustration was higher for those in less successful engineering companies.[61]

The strike of all Milanese private sector metal workers over production bonuses was called on 23 May 1964 by Fim and FIOM to reinvigorate the

---

61   *La voce sindacale*, March 1966 and June 1966

fight against Assolombarda. The latter held out, defining the recently signed company agreements as "experimental."

This opened a season of redundancies (500 at Magneti Marelli), resulting in all the factories in Sesto San Giovanni being brought to a halt in July 1964. At Magneti a struggle broke out that lasted more than a year, with company and general strikes that intertwined with the struggles for the enforcement of the contract. The Assolombarda front proved once again to be the most stubborn against the workers' struggles opposing redundancies, disciplinary letters and unilateral reductions of working hours. The fiercest battle was that imposed on Magneti Marelli by Fiat, where 900 workers were suspended, including 500 for 15 months.

On the other hand, the militancy at Magneti was definitely lower than the average in Milan at the time. It can be argued that the only strikers against the measures taken by management were sections of the Internal Commission and few other workers. Some even did overtime during this period of mass suspension. Hence, the union practiced forms of struggle that were often symbolic, such as a "picket tent" that was put up in front of the factory for 70 days (following the example of workers at Geloso and Borletti) and the sending of several delegations to Rome. Even the participation in the 1966 contract struggles was poor.[62]

In those years, unionisation at Marelli plummeted back to the levels of the mid-1950s, but remained higher than the average in Milan. The network of worker activists was destroyed, causing the non-renewal of trade union leaders who, due to protection for being members of the Internal Commission, held all union activity in their hands. Some delegates were listed only to collect votes, while the trend was towards one of strong centralisation of decision-making and participation in the union. Indeed, the same two FIOM and Fim delegates dealing with management had been re-elected without interruption from 1958 to 1968.

Trade unionists inside the factory had to link themselves closely to the organisation outside the factory, very large and active in Sesto San Giovanni, with the result that the internal FIOM was strongly influenced by the local union.

---

62 *La tenda*, bollettino straordinario della FIOM-CGIL per il presidio operaio della Magneti Marelli, undated but certainly distributed in November 1965; bulletin no. 2, 27 Nov 1965; FIOM, *Libro nero sulle condizioni di lavoro alla Magneti Marelli* ("Black Book on working conditions at Magneti Marelli"), October 1965; *La voce sindacale*, March 1966 and June 1966. The strike proclaimed in 1965 against the suspension of 500 workers totally failed and only the intervention of the external union allowed a partial success of the initiative.

The union split between FIOM and Fim was clear from the ideological and practical point of view until 1968, even though the internal management of the Commission was quite united. The clash with UILM, an organisation "welcomed" by management, was not heavy and sometimes the same Fim (which was strongly Catholic and anti-Communist) sided with the UILM against FIOM.

b) The period between 1968 and 1972

Until the early months of 1968, militancy at Magneti Marelli remained low, as in most other large engineering companies in Milan. This is shown by the fact that in some workshops, starting in May 1967, changes were made in the method of calculating piece rates and different wage elements were combined, disregarding old agreements and widening the space for discriminatory performance increases. Management and Assolombarda did not even respond to a request for a meeting from the Internal Commission and even tried to prevent the Commission from posting relevant information on the factory noticeboard. Meetings between the Commission and management took place but only seven months after the initial request. The company agreement on the renewal of productivity bonuses expired after the deadline set by the national contract had passed, forcing the provincial unions to open a dispute with Assolombarda. Among the reasons for the workers' passivity were the different positions taken by internal trade unions: on the one hand, FIOM organised only a few spontaneous stoppages while Fim was reluctant to mobilise workers at all.[63]

Only after the successful strike for pensions of 7 March 1968,[64] organised by the CGIL, did the unions at Magneti begin to timidly organise, with

---

63 *La voce sindacale*, June 1967, July 1967, October 1967, February 1968 and April 1968

64 The story of pensions is a real watershed in the Italian workers' struggles, as it represented the first victory of the season that would be called the "hot autumn." The dispute began in 1967 when the unions raised the demand for an improved pension, and then announced a general strike on 15 December, cancelled at the last moment. Many workers, however, were absent from work on the grounds that the revocation of the strike came too late, but this was a sign of renewed will to fight. On the night of 26-27 February 1968 the unions reached agreement in principle with the government. This provided big improvements but also contained some compromises: existing pensions were only very weakly increased, the retirement age for women was pushed back to 60, and those who wanted to carry on working, even though they had reached retirement age, did not have the right to draw a pension and a wage. From across Italy, thousands of retirees flooded the union offices with telegrams of protest, so that the CGIL withdrew its agreement and called a general strike on 7 March that attracted wide support. It was now clear that the trade unions

strikes lasting a few hours. In the spring of 1968 a series of company struggles broke out throughout Italy. The objective was a wage increase (the same for everyone) to make up for the "skinny" contract of 1966. Among the first companies to see mobilisations was Fiat, whose workers carried out the first large scale company dispute in more than 14 years, and in Milan struggles started at Borletti, Ercole Marelli, Magneti Marelli, Philips, Sit-Siemens, Innocenti, Autelco, Triplex, Brollo, Raimondi, Mezzera, Rhodex, SIAE Microelettronica, SECI, Ferrotubi, Elettroconduttture, Autobianchi, AMF, Fachini, Tagliaferri, Termokimik, Minerva, Amsco and twenty other small businesses.[65]

The union's platform at Magneti Marelli was based above all on demanding increases to recover wages lost and the defence of the existing pay system, strongly undermined by the unilateral changes made by management. At the beginning, the struggle was managed by old activists and external unionists, therefore in a rather authoritarian way. However, after a month some young factory workers began to put themselves forward and vigorously criticised "trade unionists and members of the Internal Commission on the methods and stages of struggle," changing qualitatively the forms of mobilisation, through strong pickets and internal factory marches to force employees to go on strike. On one occasion these workers spontaneously extended a strike by a couple of hours, forcing the unions to support them. This injection of new blood led to a massive participation in the struggle, increasing the duration of the strike. Demonstrations took place through the streets of Sesto San Giovanni, breaking through the gate of the company management building. The strikes continued, despite Assolombarda requesting they be called off for the start of negotiations. Factory workers' participation was total, though almost nothing happened, however, amongst office workers.[66]

---

faced a serious crisis of representation. After the elections of 18 June 1968, the meetings between the parties continued without any hiring decisions, so on 14 November there was a call for a unitary general strike, the first since the splits. The strike was repeated, and finally, on 5 February 1969, the law of pension reform was approved by the Council of Ministers, which introduced several enhancements: the relationship between the pension and the final salary rose 65-74%, with a commitment to reach 80% by 1975; a mechanism would be set up of a "sliding scale" appropriate to reassess pensions as the purchasing power of the lira decreased; restores the ability to draw a pension and a wage together for seniors who wish to continue to work; entitlement to the old-age pension for those who have at least 35 years of contributions but are not yet 60 years old; establishment of a social pension (12,000 lire a month for thirteen months) for the elderly without a pension due to lack of contributions; abandonment of raising the retirement age for women.

65   *Il metallurgico*, year XVII, nn. 1-8, January-August 1968
66   In the spring of 1967, Magneti Marelli took on a hundred young people from the

From mid-May the militancy reached its peak thanks to significant instances of spontaneity and solidarity expressed by a group of students from Sesto. These events culminated, after a rally in front of the factory, in students pushing for a demonstration marching to Milan, something which had not happened since 1949. The trade unions accepted and the march was a success in terms of participation and organisation. Once in Milan the union was dragged by young workers and students to demonstrate outside the Assolombarda headquarters, while other protesters went to a meeting at the University of Milan. The same evening a magistrate summoned the parties and in the night an agreement was signed, which the unions presented to the workers as a victory. However, the assembly that took place immediately after was full of conflict: amongst the accusations was that the unions had not called an assembly before signing the agreement. The most dissatisfied were young workers who had led the struggle, many of whom had been hired in the previous two years and had good professional training but were assigned to simple and frustrating tasks. Some of them knew each other because they had attended the same vocational institute close to the factory. Not having lived through the union repression of the previous years, they remained enthusiastic, though, while not under the union influence, they were not yet able to promote their own initiatives.[67]

ANAP-CISO vocational school which accepts orphans or youth recruited by means of a ministerial competition. After submitting their application to the Ministry, the kids did a brief medical examination and psychological aptitude and were sent to this school in Milan to learn the trade. At that time the school was run by a priest who would later be involved in several scandals, including the charge of organising for profit a true "marketplace of manpower" with Belgian and German companies, in addition to embezzlement of ministerial funds intended to finance the school. According to eyewitness accounts, at school "they filled your head with the bright future that you were preparing. They said that you would become a leader in the factory, that you would be doing a very satisfying job," however, having finished the course, the young men were routed to foreign companies or large factories in Milan, including Magneti Marelli where they ended up all doing piece work. About this group of young people, another testimony: "Strikes started and new recruits in the fight led a charge that caught by surprise even the old trade union framework. It was an irrepressible force, difficult to control, which railed against everything that, in some way, represented the company. It smashed tables and glass and they went inside the offices to sweep out the scabs without looking too closely. Their anger was enormous, and it was not always kept within the limits of good behaviour. I think that this anger, with the destructive charge that it carried, was one of the means of unifying the levels of struggle inside the factory to win over the remaining moderates in the union." *Il terrorismo in fabbrica*, op. cit.

67   *La voce sindacale*, July and September 1968.

This new period of worker ferment was therefore characterised by the intervention outside the factories of groups of students who were looking to connect with workers, often their peers. After the season of university occupations, out of some areas of student militancy came the need to encourage workers' struggles, identifying the factory as the centre of the overall restructuring of capital, which was also affecting the university.

At the same time as the student intervention, new organisations for the coordination and management of struggles in workshops and companies were created, often spontaneously, in which there was a very strong participation of young militants, who were not yet union members. There was a growing use of assemblies for decision-making, and the *Comitati Unitari di Base* ("Unitary Base Committees") were born.[68]

This negotiation started on 22 March and ended on 15 May after around 40 hours on strike. The platform of demands includes: a) connecting the Production Premium (blocked by 1963) to the work performance, b) aggregation of payroll agreed with the union, c) 3rd element: minimum guaranteed rate for all, d) apply also to new hires of agreements of the electromechanical (1962), e) piece work: full implementation of the system reported in 1963.

The agreement gives: a) increase in the production premium of 9,100 lire per year, b) definition of the criteria for payroll aggregation, c) 3rd element: hourly increase of 15.50 lire, d) application to those hired after 10 May 1962 (about 1,200 workers) of the old agreements with an increase in average hours of 20 lire, e) piece rates: recalculation on new minimum wage and the abolition of differences in age, f) commitment to a joint assessment with the Internal Commission of requests for transfer of category. Dolci-Reyneri, *op. cit.*

68 At the national level they conducted the struggle for the overthrow of the "wage cages." The Italian system was based on some sort of list of geographical areas, each of which would have a different contractual minimum. Italian provinces were staggered in seven steps, according to the levels of the cost of living, so if a worker in the zone 0 (including Milan, Turin, Genoa and Rome) earned 100, a worker with similar qualifications in the area 6 (two-thirds of Southern Italy and islands) was receiving a salary of 80. The strikes against the "cages" began in the autumn of 1968, meeting the tenacious resistance of private businesses, but also public companies, who showed themselves hostile to an agreement because contract renewals were on the way. After a long series of strikes a compromise is reached on 21 Dec. 1968 between the trade unions and the partly state-owned industries (the state being represented by Intersind and Asap): the gap had to filled by June 1971. Confindustria took a hard line all winter, despite gusts of strikes across Italy, but in March it was divided so that on 18 March 1969 the Minister of Labour Brodolini, trade unions and Confindustria reached an agreement levelling wages phased in over three and a half years.

From the signing of the agreement in May 1968 to the beginning of the contract dispute in September 1969, union activity at Magneti Marelli went through a period of transition. There were only a few workshop strikes and a resumption of negotiations between management and unions, with the recognition of the trade union presence at the factory. Some of the young workers, protagonists of spontaneous struggles, joined the trade union, reinvigorating it, while others were to form an autonomous group outside the factory.

The disputed outcome of the 1968 negotiations did not result in an increase in union members in Crescenzago. Its delayed implementation, then, did nothing but increase complaints from its working class base. Within FIOM the new recruits made their voices heard, with the result that in the following election four of these young activists were elected to the Internal Commission. In Fim, a similar conflict took place, where young people took positions so extreme as to go beyond those of the FIOM.

Among the various unions relationships began to change: Fim and FIOM broke sharply with UILM, while arguing among themselves on how to oppose management's policy of procrastination in the implementation of the 1968 agreement, aiming at winning hegemony amongst the new activists. In September 1968, FIOM proposed the establishment of trade union committees based in individual workshops, but this never came to fruition. At the electoral level, the composition of the Commission did not undergo any change.[69]

The autonomous group that had formed outside the union was born above all thanks to the students who had been so devoted during the recent company struggle. They were the ones who organised meetings attended by many young workers disappointed by the conclusion of the dispute and students belonging to groups of the extra-parliamentary left. After about two months in the autumn of 1968, a dozen workers formed first the *Comitato Operaio* (Workers Committee) and then the *Comitato di lotta* (Struggle Committee). Their level of education and training was quite high, while their union experience was almost absent, apart from one of them who had been a member of the Internal Commission for the CGIL in another factory. These two characteristics explain the lack of trauma in breaking with the union and the good relationship with the extra-parliamentary students. Leafleting in front of the factory was delegated to the latter, which caused frequent arguments with union activists who accused the workers of the Struggle Committee of not wishing to expose themselves publicly. The activists in autonomous groups rejected the logic of bargaining and blamed the unions for not being able to or not wanting to defend the interests of workers, preferring to compromise with the bosses. The

---

69   *La voce sindacale*, in July 1968 and September 1968, and the company bulletin of Sas-Fim, FIOM October 1968, and the FIOM leaflet, 13 Sept 1968.

relative immovability of workers' demands with regard to the contract renewal encouraged criticism of the internal union, which was often accused of being too passive, so that the young workers of the Struggle Committee announced an autonomous strike over wage demands. The strike failed because the picket line was not respected and workers were able to enter the factory. Among the reasons for the failure was the fact that the strike was announced exclusively by leaflets distributed outside the factory by the students close to the autonomous group. This was perceived as "the vanguard[70] escaping from the masses."[71]

In the early days of May, an agreement regarding the Magneti Marelli plants in Crescenzago and Sesto San Giovanni was signed, approved by workers' assemblies with a large majority and without strikes. The same happened in other engineering factories in Milan, perhaps because companies did not want to reignite tensions before the autumn contract negotiations that promised to be hot. The content of the agreement established wage increases with a marked egalitarian tendency, easing of norms for those on assembly lines, and wide recognition of trade union rights.

In this fight, there were no episodes of worker spontaneity and afterwards FIOM would double its membership, and FIM's increased by 35%.

Shortly after, the "capi-bolla" ("bubble-heads" – controllers) role was challenged for the first time. They were accused of being in league with the team leaders to modify the data on piecework. The young workers got one "capo-bolla" guilty of serious irregularities dismissed and managed to get the establishment of an administrative office to redo the calculations. In this way, the "mafia" of "capi-bolla," one of the traditional tools used by Magneti Marelli to control the workforce both socially and productively, was challenged.[72]

---

70 The word "vanguard" (*avanguardia*) was very commonly used in leaflets by the radical left in Italy at this time. It may sound rather stilted in English, but that is the word they used!

71 The picket regained importance starting from 1969. It contributed to breaking from and then completely eliminating a climate of weakness and worker passivity which had reigned for quite a while. Then it would be replaced by internal processions to departments and offices, which involved not only activists, but the bulk of the strikers, to search for scabs and sometimes temporarily seize the managers (the so-called "spazzolate" – "brush"). Ida Regalia-Marino Regini-Emilio Reyneri, *Conflitti di lavoro e relazioni industriali in Italia, 1968-75*, in Colin Crouch-Alessandro Pizzorno (eds.), *Conflitti in Europa*, 1977, Etas libri.

72 The Agreement of 6 May 1969 (discussed in only two hours of assembly for each of the three shifts) was approved at a meeting that saw only 60 votes against it. The platform of demands included: reduction in the cost of a meal from 200 to 150 lira; wage increase equal for all of 20 lira per hour; a short week for the day labourers, increase in holiday pay; three members of the Internal Commission to join the Committee on accident prevention; increase in the percentage of the "compartecipazionisti" ("participation") bonus;

The failure of the strike called independently from the unions led, within the Struggle Committee, to a strong self-criticism that caused the autonomous worker-student group to fall apart and to the adherence of a large number of young people to FIOM. This was, among other things, because of to its greater internal democracy, the opening up of the contract struggle and the spread of the myth of trade union unity. The intention was to refresh FIOM's policies and leadership from the inside. The effect was that the union was able to take full control of the working class base with a rejuvenation of their age demographic and organisational structure. In the new contract platform, a consultative referendum was held, approving, by a large majority, a proposal for an equal increase for all workers (despite opposition from the FIOM leaders). During the struggle to renew the contract, following the national union directives, the *Comitati sindacali unitari* (Unitary trade union committees) were set up at Magneti Marelli. Their members were not true delegates because they were elected and were not present in all factory workshops, but instead were contacted and appointed by the trade union.

Workers' spontaneity, which manifested itself regularly in the workshops, was felt in the period following the approval of the contract and was based on a hard-core of about 200-300 young male workers always ready to fight (especially those of the second and third sections where new unskilled recruits were concentrated). A few days after the signing, management decided to cut the end of year bonus (called the "tredicesima" – thirteenth month), deducting pay

---

the unification of the price of labour by piece and by qualification; commitment to study the question of eliminating piecework; commitment to improve conditions on the lines (breaks and replacement workers); commitment to elaborate a new union rule with the Internal Commission; limitation of disciplinary procedures; commitment to speed up exams required to obtain qualifications.

On 26 May 1969, an agreement was signed between the Assolombarda and provincial unions which only affected the employees. The platform of demands included: increased incentives, a forty hour week and improvements in the calculation of holidays, job description and corporate joint body control, revision of qualifications, internal mobility and communication of judgments. The agreement reached was: increase of 3,500 lire per month, gradual reduction of working hours from 42 to 40 hours, a commitment to review the requests for revision of qualifications submitted by the Internal Commission and to communicate the availability of places. Dolci-Reyneri, *op. cit.*

"The existence of a team piece rate also for workers employed in individual processes had raised the figure of the "capo-bolla," a worker elected by the team with the task of collecting processing bills and evaluating the number of pieces produced; this practice, however, often gave rise to collusion between team leaders and "capi-bolla," which favoured the division among the workers." Dolci-Reyneri, *op. cit.*

for strikes that had taken place during the year. This led to a real uprising by young workers who went against the advice of external union officials. A workers' demonstration invaded the head office of Sesto San Giovanni, where general management was based, and after hours of negotiations with the managers besieged in their offices, the inviolability of the end of year bonus was won.

Workers' militancy also manifested itself around the issue of working hours. The company had encouraged overtime, trying to take advantage of the workers' need to make up for wages lost during struggle. The union proposal, accepted in the assemblies, was that of self-determination of working hours with an overtime ban, anti-scab pickets and some spontaneous stoppages. The struggle began on 29 January and ended on 26 March with the overtime ban lasting the entire time. Support was total from piece-rate workers, while participation from *economisti*, those not directly involved in production, was almost completely absent. After a few months of frequent meetings, management and the Internal Commission reached an agreement.

This struggle was led by young assembly line workers and their delegates, followed by the women, who traditionally favoured reductions in working hours. They organised pickets against colleagues who wanted to work overtime, especially against the *economisti*, who were attracted by the strong economic incentives. The struggle brought the largest building of the Crescenzago factory to a complete halt, after a spontaneous initiative began in the workshop with the highest proportion of young workers, which spread throughout the whole factory using internal demonstrations.

It was in this department and another similar one that spontaneous stoppages and acts of rebellion against the workshop hierarchy and the pace of work started. These young workers saw the working conditions as unbearable, were aware of their collective strength and were unwilling to accept the reduction of production times proposed by the company, while trying to recover the wage increases granted by the contract:

in the wave of the great movement, for any wrong suffered by a worker, the whole team or department stopped immediately, with delegates at the head. Taking away the authoritarianism of the bosses, making them smaller: in this task we succeeded perfectly, with every tactic, even tough ones. These people had to come down from the pedestals on which the workers had put them. For instance, you could not go to wash five minutes early. Well, with delegates at the head, we went there 10 minutes early. When piece work was functioning very well, we made a big mess until everything was put right. We got to the point of having the strength to say, 'we're not paid enough for this piece, we're working too much,' and no one was able to force us to do it. We had gained the upper hand over all the institutions of company organisation.

These two testimonies of FIM and FIOM activists show that union delegates led the spontaneous mobilisations, with widespread action and without any centralisation.[73]

In May 1970, the first Factory Council was elected by secret ballot, and with the possibility of casting a blank vote. The candidates were elected (one for every 75 workers for assembly lines with at least 25 employees) without a formal candidature and without the need for a majority of votes, by the highest number of votes obtained by each candidate. In that way, politicised minorities were favoured and even workers not representative of the reality of the department or line. The Factory Council was made up of 63 elected members plus eleven more from the Internal Commission and three representatives appointed by each union branch and the RSA (Company Union Representatives).

The procedure for appointing RSA raised major differences within the trade unions. The internal statute conformed to the compromise reached during the National Conference of FIOM-FIM-UILM held in March 1970 in Genoa, which left it up to the freedom of choice of each trade union, encouraging them to choose from within the elected delegates. The advice was followed by FIOM (except for a new employee who was a Communist Party member), but not by FIM and UILM, the latter even discriminating against delegates elected because they were considered too "unitary," a fact that would have such strong internal repercussions that a split within UILM took place at the election of the second Factory Council.

---

[73] Leaflets by FIOM-Fim-UILM from 20 Jan 70 and 29 Jan 70 and *La voce sindacale*, April 1970, and interviews with a member of the Executive, FIM (1972) and a member of the Executive, FIOM and an extra-parliamentary (1972), cited in Dolci-Reyneri, *op. cit.* The workers' platform provides for the regulation of working time for shift workers with a short week and alternate weeks. The agreement incorporates in full the workers' demands. Some witnesses compare the previous climate in the factory to that in the prisons, "especially during night shifts, once every three weeks. It was not night work itself that bothered you: what were you doing in the habit. It was the fact that you seemed to be a lifer. During the day there was the foreman to watch you. Not that it was a big party, but at least there is a little flexibility. It was enough for you to do your job and they were not looking if you spoke a few words with the attendant standing at the machine next to you. At night, however there were guards, and they had orders to act as guards. It was enough for you to get up and look at the car and they fined you. I believe that they had a habit of hiding to catch you lying. And each time was a 800 lire fine, if not more. Then our salary, when we didn't stuff our neck with overtime, reached 70,000 lire a month. With 800 lire one day, 800 lire another day, it ended up that you lacked the money to eat. *Terrorismo in fabbrica*, op. cit.

In this first Factory Council a secretariat was elected made up of six members, two belonging to the Internal Commission as well. In reality, this secretariat did not serve any purpose because everything was in the hands of the Commission that dealt with both workers' demands and technical problems. It is important to underline the presence, amongst the three members of FIOM, of a representative of an extra-parliamentary group, demonstrating that at this moment FIOM was not aligned with the positions of the Communist Party.[74]

From the first meeting, the Factory Council decided to run a company dispute which led to a big internal debate: the clash focused on wage demands and the organisation of work and saw the union on one side and young activists on the other. The young workers' demand to get the "fourteenth month" was not approved, but the proposed wage increase through the renewed productivity bonus was approved. The proposal to include all workers in the second category was also rejected while the abolition of the fourth and fifth categories was taken into consideration, which would enshrine the equality between men and women inside the factory. Then there was the initial demand for a minimum guaranteed wage for those on piece work (equal to the average of the plant), which would result in the *de facto* abolition of piece work. Many of these demands lost prominence later on, when the platform came, in effect, to identify itself with that which had been proposed by FIOM a month earlier.

The only substantial difference was about trade union rights that had to be extended to the Factory Council, while the FIOM platform favoured only the Internal Commission. Only at the end of June (the proposal had been submitted on 3 June) were there general assemblies to decide on the forms of struggle. It began with a strike over overtime. An assembly approved the proposal to start go-slows from 1 July. This decision was kept in the background by the three unions and presented only as a hypothesis. In reality, among the workers, the discussion on piece work had been going on for some time, so on the first day of July, the go-slow happened without the approval of the unions – the first time ever at Marelli. The initiative started in two workshops where young workers were in the majority and had now been at the forefront of factory struggles since 1968. The strike spread rapidly, so that by the end of the day it already involved half the factory.[75]

---

74 FIOM-FIM-UILM, *Elezioni dei delegati*, April 1970

75 "Well, the day unfolded with a set of things never seen before. At nine o'clock two lines came out on strike, around noon 30% were on strike and with a gradual climb it reached 70% of all Magneti. All this, it must be said, with a certain euphoria, with people laughing and joking as they worked. For the first time the prestige of the chief was also challenged by women who, for obvious reasons, were always the most influenced by various leaders."

The Factory Council could not do anything but ratify the action, and in the evening it officially extended the go-slow to all departments where there was piece work.[76] Up to that moment it had seemed that FIOM and Fim controlled the evolution of the strike, but afterwards the situation was taken out of their hands as many assembly lines went well beyond the union recommendation of slowing production from 133% to 100%. Many workers slowed down to 50% and even to 30% in individual tasks, where it was not easy to control the real reduction in pace and where the most militant workers worked.

The strike went on for twenty days (1-21 July) and success was guaranteed by the fact that delegates could go around the various workshops safely. The Statute of Labourers established the absence of guards in the workshops, for example, allowing women to overcome their traditional deference to the corporate hierarchy.

The final result was the collapse of production and of company authority in the factory.[77] The participation in the struggle was total and saw women return to active participation.

- "Vento dell'Est," *Analisi della lotta aziendale del 1970 alla Magneti Marelli* ("Analysis of the company struggle of 1970 at Magneti Marelli"), nn. 19/20, December 1970

[76] "Trade unions in the meantime had not been stopped. FIOM had always been favourable and therefore its activists were among the promoters of the strike. The FIM, after a hesitant start by its members of the Internal Commission, who every morning went around telling people to wait, took a position for the strike under the pressure of its delegates and members. UILM in contrast, "consistent" as always, sent around its few henchmen to say not to do anything crazy, wait for the response of the Head office. However they were quite "marginal" to the workers. And now we come to the evening: in the Factory Council there was nothing to do but to sign off the announcement of the strike. But despite all this, UILM began to quibble about famous leaflets and meetings that, according to them, had not decided to strike. But they could not with this last attempt have any influence on the judgment that the Factory Council now had to take by force of circumstances, that the strike would have three signatures." *Ibid*

[77] "One thing stands out immediately in the eyes of the workers, for the first time after decades of misinformation: piece work is a weapon in the hands of the boss. By this strike we will really kill three birds with one stone. One, it is possible to show the workers the deception of piece work on the financial level. In fact, if the workers work at half speed they will lose less money than in a conventional strike (this being the first time in Italy that this type of strike was practiced it wasn't clear what the exact loss was going to be). Thus it was proved that the piece rate is not the main element in the wage of a worker. Secondly, the strike significantly reduced the level of production (for example, if Marelli had a turnover of 6 billion per month, all of a sudden it will be cut in two) and it is not a strike that exhausts the workers, quite the opposite. Thirdly, the workers will finally take

After the first week of the strike negotiations began between Assolombarda, Internal Commission, RSA, and, for the first time, factory delegates. The company's resistance continued for about a month, then, suddenly, at the end of July an agreement was reached. The workers, however, considered the agreement unsatisfactory: the only positive point was the sharp increase in the production bonus. Rather than achieving the elimination of piece work on the assembly lines where the machine imposed the rhythm, a new "special" piece rate was established that guaranteed the same wages only in the case of an interruption of production for technical or organisational reasons. The night shift was not abolished but an increase in pay was granted. The fourth and fifth categories were not immediately abolished, but there were staggered category changes for groups of workers. The unions presented the outcome without the usual exaggeration, because they were aware that the objectives set had not been achieved.

The workers' assemblies saw an absolutely contradictory trend. During the first shift, in the morning, a strong dissent towards the agreement showed itself, it was even rejected by 60% of the vote and called a "scam agreement." In the second and third assemblies, the attitude of the union changed and became much stronger than that of the morning assembly. Trade union officials presented the workers with the prospect, in the case of rejecting the agreement, of having to start fighting from the beginning again in September. Older activists intimidated those who wanted to declare themselves against

> account of the pace of work and their first reaction is to refuse to return to the rhythms of the past, to ask for a more "human" rhythm. This element will be, if it is used well, a demand which the company can no longer ignore: the workers will progressively understand that time is used against them.
>
> Another point is the loss of power within the factory by the team leaders, who truly live in a situation of a difficult balance between management and workers. In this time they cannot take any initiative before they see the reaction of the workers. In fact, if they had to make some decisions, to punish someone or put pressure in one way or another on some workers (as occurred in some rare cases) they immediately have to "talk" to a hundred people. In this climate, it is clear that the regulation as it is understood by the owner no longer exists.
>
> Finally, the principal department of the company doesn't work more than five hours a week because other employees, whether technical or the wage workers in the office, must leave earlier because of the overtime strike, despite the two hours a week that are used recover the losses caused by the workers' strikes. In this situation worker groups form that, during working hours, go on patrol to check out all employees and they are around even on half-hours counted as strikes, because there is no more control that can be established." *Ibid*

the agreement. The result is that in these two meetings the agreement was approved unanimously.

Once again it was the young unskilled workers who were at the forefront of the struggle, followed by the women's assembly lines that for the first time were able to create the unity necessary to oppose the company hierarchy and authoritarian organisation of production.[78]

The next phase was characterised by the attempt by the union to reabsorb the internal dissent that had been clearly expressed after the approval of the agreement, and above all by the desire to centralise decision-making and control spontaneity. This attitude of the union, however, caused the spread of an even greater dissent that would later lead to the establishment of independent workers' organisations.

In the last week of August, after the summer holidays, management notified the Internal Commission that they would be deducting the production quota that had not been reached from the July pay slip, something which affected all workers given the massive participation in the strikes. The intention of management was to redefine, to their own advantage, the balance of power inside the factory, showing how the go-slow, and more importantly the

---

78   Factory Council of Magneti Marelli, *Piattaforma rivendicativa*, in June 1970 and *Analisi della lotta aziendale del 1970*, op. cit. and leaflets FIM-FIOM-UILM, 26 June 70 and 27 July 70. It should be noted that a leaflet from FIOM in mid-June explains in detail how to calculate the piece rate and shows how you can slow down production without losing too much money.

The output strike was new in the techniques of struggle inside the factory (strikes in fits and starts, checkerboard pattern, sudden strikes, non-cooperation etc.) and back in vogue after the early fifties when bosses' repression aided by the judiciary drove strike action and union organisation out of the factory.

Agreement was reached on the following bases: a) Production Premium: an increase of 21,600 to 130,000 lire per year; b) overcoming the fifth and the fourth worker category and the fourth employee category; 250 workers to be immediately promoted to the higher category on the basis of their jobs; on the conveyor belts and assembly lines they introduced an output bonus, which went from a fixed value base to a given output, independently of technico-productive inconveniences; increasing the percentages for those who received a participation and monthly bonus; the night working bonus was increased; the management agreed to communicate to the Internal Commission the results of enquiries by the ENPI ("National board for the prevention of accidents"); agreement to make known jobs available for employees. Dolci-Reyneri, *op. cit.*

The women found it hard to engage in struggles due to the impossibility of physically moving from their jobs on the conveyor belts and deference towards the male supervisors that prevented women expressing themselves and communicating with each other. *Ibid*

delegates and Factory Council that had promoted and directed it, were not valid organisational tools. The attitude of the Internal Commission was clear in this regard: it consulted the provincial unions but avoided informing the Factory Council and the workers, so that after three days of negotiations with management a compromise was reached that the Factory Council could only ratify. Immediately afterwards a controversy broke out between the Internal Commission ("If it hadn't been for our responsible intervention, who knows what would have happened, and it wouldn't have been for the benefit of the union") and the most militant delegates who criticised the habit "of deciding things among two or three people," and observed the "fear of the Internal Commission of losing its power." The clash highlighted the weakness of the Factory Council, in that in the earlier struggle it had not played a real leadership role, as well as not proposing a monitoring body over the strike procedures it had itself established. Before during and after the struggle the union attempted to form a single union leadership centre in the factory which would eliminate the dualism between the Internal Commission and the *Esecutivo* (the Executive which often acted against the delegates) and take away autonomy from delegates, binding them to the decisions made by the Factory Council even over issues at workshop level.[79]

The July dispute represented the highest point of conflict reached at Magneti Marelli in those years. The union was repeatedly bypassed, but the enthusiasm of the youth did not come into conflict with the union leadership, in fact it seemed that the union had "ridden the tiger" of spontaneity to channel it into more negotiable demands for the company. The end of the struggle, characterised by conflicts – sometimes very strong – over the agreements reached, caused a clear change in the behaviour of the unions. This phenomenon took place at the same time in many other factories where young workers

---

79   Leaflet from FIM-FIOM-UILM, 28 August 70 and *Analisi della lotta aziendale del 1970*, op. cit. and Magneti Marelli Factory Council, *Bozza di documento per una discussione in C.d.F.* ("Draft document for discussion in Factory Council"), 31 August 70. In the comments of a group of workers close to marxist-leninist groups: "All this should make us reflect on vanguards, because we can see clearly when it suits the Internal Commission to sit on top of everything (workers, delegates, etc..) to decide on its own, and this is really a step back that we took in the recent past, we saw the fear of the Internal Commission of losing its power in a way that sees it fall in front of some delegate and try in one way or another to rise against them, weighed by their own experience and the privilege enjoyed by its members in the factory, but this clearly could not last long and reactions increased against this abuse of power by the Internal Commission (when that worked, because, in other cases, it tried to involve the others in the responsibilities which it assumed)." *Analisi della lotta aziendale del 1970*, op. cit.

upset the balance of the trade unions, with slogans such as "direct democracy," "egalitarianism," "question the boss/worker relationship." After the union had achieved a great deal of power within the company, it had to decide whether to risk losing the balance achieved, by supporting a permanent and radical mobilisation, or to consolidate its power by being recognised by their counterpart as a responsible and credible entity. The union was not a revolutionary political group so, therefore, taking note of its deficiencies in the last dispute, it decided to control more strictly the initiatives from the autonomous working class base and to centralise decisions.

This policy, characterised by the greater uniformity of its actions and the stiffening of its structures after having opened up to workers' spontaneity in 1969-70, produced strong criticism within the union itself and within the PCI, resulting in the haemorrhaging from its ranks of a good number of activists whose dissent had radicalised.

In the autumn of 1970 some union activists, who had been in contact for some time with left-wing extra-parliamentary groups, got together outside the union structures. Some of them had been members of the old autonomous group that had fallen apart before the contract struggles. The debate was of interest also to members of the PCI and FIOM at Magneti Marelli critical of the conduct of the union in the company. By the end of the year, all the members of the new "Circolo operaio" ("Workers' Circle") were sympathisers of the extra-parliamentary left, and as such they began intervening with leaflets and taking a stance on the Factory Council. In fact, at the beginning their opposition to the FIOM union guidelines was rather bland, particularly considering that three of the seven Magneti delegates that went to the July 1970 FIOM provincial congress were supporters of the new autonomous *Circolo*, and within the Factory Council ten delegates took part in the *Circolo*. The differences became more bitter when the members of the *Circolo* did not respect the discipline of the trade union or Factory Council, criticising their conduct.[80]

---

80 According to one testimony: "The *Circolo operaio* was basically a large group of young people who recognised themselves in a series of experiences and feelings in common: the vocational school, immigration from the South, the disappointment of piecework, anger against the employer, the desire to change everything and trust that all this could change very quickly. These were the common traits. Also, there were different codes borrowed from the world of the student protests. Inside the Circle was a bit of the whole '68 rainbow: *Lotta Continua, Servire il popolo* (Serve the people), marxist-leninist groups. Some, like me, had joined the FGCI [the PCI youth]. At that time there was also a group with a local implantation which referred to the *Circolo Lenin* of Sesto San Giovanni." *Il terrorismo in fabbrica*, op. cit.

The struggle of summer 1970 changed the climate reigning in Magneti between workers and the company hierarchy, as well as between the union and management. It is important to point out the euphoria that characterised the workshops where female workers were concentrated, "for the first time the boss's prestige was questioned by women." In male workshops, performance did not go back to the level before the summer struggles, and when the union talked to management to introduce the new piecework system, some assembly lines restarted spontaneous stoppages and "self-reduction" of performance to impose a pace of work the union itself deemed excessively low. This worker spontaneity was supported by the activity of some workers connected to the extra-parliamentary groups who managed to make it last for several months, despite the hard work of unionists in the assemblies to convince the workers to agree to a "normal" pace of work. Management was forced to give in.[81]

During autumn-winter 1970-71, two of the usually less militant departments stood out for frequent stoppages and strikes. One was the foundry, where there was a boss reputed to be "repressive and paternalistic." The dispute, viewed negatively by the union, lasted for two months and called for an increase in compensation for poisoning from noxious materials (doubled after the agreement).[82]

The company changed its attitude, becoming more approachable, and sought to establish a dialogue with the trade unions, after replacing the old leadership with younger staff. The July company agreement, among other things, was quickly applied, but there were delays on the part of the workers reluctant to return to the production levels from before the dispute.[83]

---

[81] *Analisi della lotta aziendale del 1970*, op. cit. About the slowdown of the pace of work: "This is an efficient fight for two reasons: a) It can significantly damage the boss not only in the sense that – thanks to the close interdependence of the various production flows – a few workers can block the workplace but also in the sense that it can devastate the entire organization of the company (which in a traditional strike is left intact and in its hierarchical authority and its functions, it can continue to "adjust" to anticipate, prevent, order) and all without much loss by the workers; b) It is a kind of struggle in which is emphasised the to the utmost the spontaneous initiative of each worker, and all workers, regardless of the party or trade union label to which they normally relate, and they have in common the need to acknowledge, manage and defend the autonomy that is created at the time of the fight. The fight against the pace of work is a particular battle: you no longer ask to enter into the employment relation but you attack immediately and to some extent you change it. You present the boss (and his organisation) with a *fait accompli*." *Lotte operaie e organizzazione del lavoro*, op. cit.

[82] *Dibattito unitario*, November 1970 and April 1971

[83] *Dibattito unitario*, December 1970 and April 1971

Also during this period, the Factory Council and the unions approved a restructuring that hit the most militant workshop in the factory, where there was a large concentration of young workers. Many assembly lines were transferred to a Magneti factory in the south of Italy, while the workers themselves were moved to other workshops. The union approval depended on the fact that this restructuring would guarantee greater employment in the south as well as offer security of wages, production norms and overtime authorisation.[84]

1971 was characterised by the first contract dispute that involved all the Magneti Marelli factories (apart from one non-unionised factory in southern Italy) with as many as 10,000 workers taking part. This union strategy, calling for structured bargaining at an industry level, came from a national directive. The first step was a meeting of all the Factory Councils at Magneti Marelli in March 1971, during which it resolved to establish a Coordinating Committee and to open a discussion on a common platform of demands.

In the Crescenzago plant, discussion on the platform started to heat up and led to a partial crisis of union control. The argument was about different ways of applying for a guaranteed minimum increase of merit and on whether or not to claim an automatic transfer from third to second category.

In almost all Italian companies, and so also at Magneti, significant and differentiated merit increases were only awarded to technicians (toolmakers, maintenance staff etc.) who fell into the two highest categories (second and first), while the others (piece workers involved in production, in the third and fourth categories) were left with crumbs. The union proposal, therefore, was to demand a more significant guaranteed minimum for the higher categories and technicians, so as to control wages by reducing discriminatory merit increases and pushing a demand that would benefit all workers. The delegates connected to extra-parliamentary groups were of a different opinion and several FIM and FIOM delegates intended to demand a guaranteed minimum equal for all, which would only benefit the lower categories, and the possibility to transform the third category (accounting for more than 60% of workers) into a transitional one. Both positions justified themselves on the basis of seeking workers' unity: the union position tended to unify the immediate economic interests of various strata of workers, the egalitarian position of the "groups" and union "dissidents" was based on the interests of the lower categories (the majority of the workers), aiming to reduce differences in wages and norms between the workers.[85]

---

84 *Dibattito unitario*, in December 1970, and leaflet by Magneti Marelli Factory Council, 25 Oct 1970

85 The entire relation can be found in the Dolci-Reyneri work that illustrates which of the two positions is best. According to one FIOM activist "requiring an equal minimum

In the Coordinating Committee and Factory Council at Crescenzago the position of the unions prevailed, but the situation was reversed in the assemblies, so that the union was forced to yield to the pressure of the pieceworkers, under the influence of the "groups," over the guaranteed minimum of the merit increase. Assemblies at other plants instead approved the union proposal, but both the Milan provincial trade union and the Coordinating Committee committed themselves to support the demand of pieceworkers at Crescenzago, the most militant workers at Magneti Marelli.

The union position was far more rigid regarding the proposal for automatic transfer from the third to the second category, considered an unacceptable demand as it was incompatible with the importance given by them to "professionalism." The proposal was approved at the assembly, but the workers' decision was blocked by an external union organiser who threatened to call into question the entire platform, so that in a second vote the proposal was rejected.

A conference of Factory Councils approved the platform that aimed at making all the plants the same as that of Crescenzago. Unlike the platforms presented in the large engineering companies in Milan in autumn 1970, the one at Magneti did not include the total abolition of piecework and automatic category transfer, two of the most important demands related to work organisation. This regression in the Magneti platform also stemmed from the changed union attitude that in the spring of 1971 was no longer willing to support these demands, given the different political climate in the country and the company's previous resistance to such requests.

If in the other plants of the Magneti Group the agreement was approved almost unanimously, in Crescenzago it can be considered as weak and certainly inferior, from a wage point of view, to those obtained in the other workplaces of Sesto San Giovanni. The production bonus increased by 50%, the guaranteed wage for piece work also increased, but only the piece workers and women benefited from the guaranteed minimum merit increases.

---

wage for all, the *economisti* did not gain anything and it therefore doesn't create unity of struggle among the workers. For the [extra-parliamentary] groups it was not fair that those who gained the most should get an increase; this idea could be acceptable, but it did not take account of the need for unity."

On the other hand, a member of the *Circolo operaio*: "Our speech was motivated by a need for class unity. We never defended the idea of a single category. We said that certain differences are justified by the organisation of work and others are not. We were aware of leaving out the higher categories. The union discourse was that instead you gave money to more people and then you united the factory. Which could also work, but with this difference in merit increases you legalise a weapon of the bosses."

The fight was carried on traditionally, first with an overtime ban, and the week after that with a 6-hour strike, after two weeks there was an additional go-slow, without falling below 100% productivity to avoid the curtailment of wages. "Groups'" activists proposed stronger forms of struggle but did not get to put them into practice – the union and most of the Factory Council accused them of dividing the workers. FIOM threatened to expel the "groups" but ended up doing nothing. All workers participated in the fight and it lasted six weeks, from 8 June to 21 July, with a 35-hour strike during which union control was never questioned, except once when a group of base union activists violently occupied the Directorate Generale of Sesto San Giovanni expelling the managers.[86]

In November 1971 the second election of the Factory Council happened, this time with only delegates elected by the workers, so the council became the only factory union body, as the Internal Commission had since resigned following the directions of the national unions. The rotation of delegates was extremely high, the re-elected were less than a third compared to the first Factory Council. The voting procedure was much more formal than in the first election. After a general preparation meeting, the departments were called one at a time in to the canteen where, before voting, the factory's top union leaders

---

[86] Leaflet of the Coordinating Committee, 31 May 71; leaflet of FIM-FIOM-UILM, 24 June 71; leaflet of the Coordinating Committee, 25 June 71; *Circolo operaio*, July 1971.

The platform of demands included: a) Production Premium: increased from 75,000 to 130,000 lire per year, b) unification of the third element, eliminating the differences between shift workers and monthly paid, men and women, by age, between plants, c) fourth element: definition of a guaranteed minimum wage equal for all workers, d) piece work: new calculation of the contractual minimums, unification of payment to the minute, increase in the output bonus, guarantee of a minimum of output pay, based on the output chart, e) increase in participation bonus (up to 75-100%), f) abolition of the night shift; g) full payment of half an hour to shift workers, h) improvements in holiday and severance pay, i) abolishing the fourth category for employees.

The agreement achieved can be summarized as: a) Production Premium: Increase to 115,000 lire per year, b) unification of the third element and defining a unique value for each category (directly proportional, with a sharp jump between second and first category), c) fourth element: a guaranteed minimum of 20 lire per hour for all, d) piece work: new calculation and unification of the rates of the calculation, gradual extension of the output bonus, increase in the guarantee of output pay, significant reduction in the output rating beyond the maximum levels reached, e) increase in participation bonus (up to 50-80%), f) increase in allowance for night work; g) full payment of half an hour to shift workers, h) improvement of holiday and end-of-job allowance, i) steps from fourth to third category for 50% of the employees. Dolci-Reyneri, *op. cit.*

again set out the tasks and responsibilities of delegates. Lists were created and, to reduce the weight of political minorities, a particular system of ballots was introduced. The only ones eligible were those with more than 50% of the vote: if nobody achieved this, then there had to be a runoff vote.

Another substantial change was the division of the electoral constituencies. In the most important plant (more than 40% of the workers) election was by section (three to five lines, i.e. from 250 to 500 workers, about seven delegates) and not more for lines. The homogeneous group was thus abandoned, a choice that the union justified by the impossibility of finding female line workers willing to be candidates. According to the extra-parliamentary groups however, this decision hid the uncertainty of electing members of the old Internal Commission, which did not carry out trade union activities in the workplace and could not be elected.

There were less women elected than in the previous Factory Council (from 12 to 8, out of 50 delegates in total), and a reduced number of representatives of the most combative departments, non-union members and UILM members. The weight of delegates linked to extra-parliamentary groups remained unchanged, nine, one of whom became a member of the Executive of the Factory Council. The position of the "groups," however, changed in substance. In the first Factory Council there was a group that carried out its action only as political propaganda, in the second the elected *Circolo operaio* delegates wanted to be representatives of direct and daily workers' interests, as well as in open dispute with the unions.[87]

In the autumn of 1971, the companies of the Magneti Marelli group introduced significant reductions in working hours, and around a thousand workers were put on technical unemployment, 10% of the total. The most affected plant was that of Sesto San Giovanni, in which nearly all the workers, employed in radio-TV in a crisis situation, were suspended. By contrast, in the Crescenzago plant technical unemployment was not applied, even though

---

87   According to a FIOM activist of the period: "The first group is on its own: in the last elections, two of its delegates were not re-elected, including one who was in the Executive. His policy was very different from that of the *Circolo operaio*: when a worker addressed them about the problems of the department, they didn't take it seriously, because they weren't ideologically for those things, they wanted to solve the problem radically by knocking down the boss, while the others are people that are doing things to solve the problems of the workers, even the smallest ones. If there is anything to do at the level of militancy, they are the first. And workers notice it beyond the politics. Among those who do not do anything and spread their politics and those who work, although there are differences, the worker prefers those who work." Interview with FIOM activist, cited in Dolci-Reyneri, *op. cit.*

some departments often lacked work. Crescenzago was one of the rare factories in Milan which, at the end of October, went on strike against rising prices – indicating indirectly that jobs were not considered threatened in this workplace, at least not by the workers. When the first suspensions began, the workers' reaction was immediate: meetings in all plants, indefinite overtime ban and a go-slow.[88] The problem with this new workers' mobilization was the fact that, with lack of work in the workshops, striking or decreasing performance helped the boss. On the other hand, however, the demonstration of labour strength allowed Crescenzago workers to remove the suspensions.

The company feared a severe reaction, so it was necessary to strike to prove that the workers' strength was effective. They rejected the idea of the performance strike and adopted articulated strikes – assembly at the factory and department level in order to keep the tension high among the workers. When some of them were transferred, the reaction was immediate and hard: the Management office was occupied and internal demonstrations "sweep up" employees and unskilled workers caught doing overtime, while foremen and the higher grades are thrown out of the departments.[89]

At the beginning of 1972 the suspensions continued and the fight went on without results. There were two possibilities: the first one, put forward by the extra-parliamentary groups, was to broaden the struggle, aiming to make non-negotiable demands on the Italian economy; the second one aimed at classic wage bargaining, always welcome for the workers. The union strongly approved of the latter and thus opened up a group dispute that called for the withdrawal of the suspensions and put forward economic demands.

Immediately, "complaining" broke out from the *economisti* who, on the margins of the last collective agreements, asked to restore their state of privilege. There were spontaneous initiatives by warehousemen and forklift drivers and they strike for three days. To avoid harder forms of struggle, such as blockading the stores, the union negotiates with the management for an increase in the percentage of "participation in piece work" and a guaranteed minimum of "merit increases" only for the *economisti*. The management accepts. First the assemblies reject, then they also accept.[90]

Meanwhile, thirty workers stopped work spontaneously, demanding immediate promotion to the first category without having to sit the examination. The strike became very determined and went on for 4 months. The strikers' delegate was part of an extra-parliamentary group that was able to kick off the struggle without resorting to an all-out strike. This was initially what the

---

88 Leaflets by the Magneti Marelli Factory Council, 29 Sept 1971 and 6 Oct 1971.
89 *Dibattito unitario*, March 1972
90 *Dibattito unitario*, "Un economista," March 1972 and *Dibattito unitario*, April 1972

workers wanted, but it would have petered out in a short time, so the group proposed instead to strike for a few hours a day to prolong the fight until it achieved its goal.

After a month of one or two hours a day stoppages, the workers began "non-cooperation," refusing to carry out machine maintenance, bringing the department to a standstill.

The fight showed a certain amount of creativity, with singing demonstrations around the factory and satirical drawings being stuck up. The union did not hinder the fight even if it always drew on the discourse of "professionalism," an argument considered acceptable by the management which, on one side, threatened a crackdown and, on the other, promised to examine all the demands for promotion to higher categories. The Factory Council's Executive urged the workers to accept the offers made by the Management at a meeting that ended this struggle. The workers only got a few rises in category on condition of being subjected to discriminatory tests, showing how strong union control of the worker base was. The same extra-parliamentary groups' activists were forced into contradictory behaviour: on the one hand providing an interpretation of the political period that leads them to bypass the union to generalise the struggle for employment, on the other they do not intend to stop worker spontaneity and so promote more particularist agitation.

The union is now recognized by the company as the only valid interlocutor and, to demonstrate this, an agreement provides for the recognition of the Factory Council and other labour representative structures.[91]

Finally, on 25 May the struggle for Crescenzago's new platform of demands began. However, in contrast to the national demands, this was only concerned with an increase in the performance bonus. The intensity of the struggle was lower than that of any strikes since 1968: participation in the strikes was total, but in the assemblies not very much. The only noteworthy event was on the last day when a worker demonstration in Sesto San Giovanni went to occupy

---

91   *Dibattito unitario*, July 1972. Negotiations began on 10 March 1972 and the agreement was signed on 24 March, without strikes or other forms of pressure on management. It recognised the Factory Council, its Executive and the Coordinating Committee of the Factory Councils group. Delegates could move within departments without limitations, the hours were calculated on the total number of hours allowed under this agreement only if used outside the company, so theoretically there was no limit of time for union activities performed in the factory. Delegates who did piece work were paid for the piecework missed, production by *economisti* was no longer checked. Just a couple of the 9 members of the Executive worked a few hours per month, the others were in fact exempt from work. Dolci-Reyneri, *op. cit.*

the management office. The agreement was reached on 21 June, was judged partially satisfactory by the union and was accepted without disagreement.[92]

c) After 1972

The six conflicts between 1968 and 1972 varied in terms of worker participation. The first phase was devoted to the demands of the majority sector of the workforce, that is to say the piece workers, unskilled young people and women, 85% of the workers of Crescenzago, to the detriment of professional workers. In the second phase, on the contrary, the area of bargaining widens and the platform becomes especially appealing for workers in all the companies in the Magneti Marelli group, rather than just Crescenzago, that had long since achieved many of its goals. In addition, from 1972, demands around working conditions disappeared, giving way to the demands of professional workers who wanted to restore the pay gap between themselves and the unskilled workers.

In 1973, the situation in the company saw a union now fully recognized by a counterpart that granted it maximum freedom of action within the workers' representative structures. It is important to remember that in the period between 1968 and 1972, the staff leadership had changed twice. There were no longer managers from the Fiat school, but young people who did not share the paternalistic and repressive aspects still present in factories related to Fiat. Precisely for this reason, it was hard to restore the corporate hierarchy in the departments. The prestige of the foremen was not maintained in the female departments and, to make the factory function, from now on the foremen sought the collaboration of the union delegates.

The company tried to bring back a more disciplined production process, began to send letters of complaint to those abandoning their jobs and checked

---

92   The proposals were made to the Management in mid-April, but the negotiations only started from 15 May. After two meetings with negative results, the strikes began and continued till the end. The platform of demands was as follows: a) increase in the production premium, b) full payment of wages in the case of illness, c) definition of the fourth element, d) further equalization for certain establishments in the group, e) end of layoffs through "technical unemployment" and guarantee of jobs.

  The agreement was as follows: a) Production Premium: Increase from 115,000 to 152,000 lire b) partial advance by the company of indemnity from INAM (health insurance), c) confirmation of the company and departmental agreements for the fourth element (20 lire to piece workers and 50 lire to *economisti*) and the participation bonus, d) equalization of certain conditions in the non-Milanese factories, e) letter from the Management in which it communicates the gradual return to full-time in all the plants and that it does not envisage future hour and job reductions. Dolci-Reyneri, *op. cit.*

the presence of workers at home during illness. It also restricted the right to put up union notices. Nevertheless, clashes were then resolved around the negotiating table with compromises on both sides.

The negotiations no longer involved the direct intervention from the shop floor. The delegate was fully recognised without support from worker initiative. The era of mass delegations to the management offices seemed to be really over. But this only really applied where the delegates were in line with the union, not where there were delegates belonging to extra-parliamentary groups. Delegates close to the union were given management functions in the departments that were previously assigned to "capetti" (low-level foremen). For a time, workshop delegates and managers made partial deals directly with each other, bypassing management and union, which did not disturb the company but it did annoy the union, that ran around reducing the autonomy of delegates. When there was a problem in their area, the relevant delegate had to explain it to the Executive of the Factory Council, requesting assistance. The decision to reduce the autonomy of union delegates had as a theoretical assumption that "the autonomy of the delegate ends when their action may give rise to a struggle in the department and therefore involve the entire factory. In practice, the distinction is very difficult to make, so the most important thing is the line taken by the union that pushes the delegates to see to a much larger extent the Executive or the committees (piecework, qualifications, working environment), where there is always a member of the Executive."[93] The centralization of negotiations was favoured by the fact that the entire Executive was exempt from production, so it had a lot of time for union activities, and that many delegates did not have the skills to do it themselves. But this was not the case for delegates from the "groups," who did not accept limits on their autonomy and took important decisions without involving the Executive.

This second position seemed to be more in line with the workers' struggles that had characterised the Italian factories in the years 1968-69, founded on the end of delegation, on the sovereign power of the assembly ("the General Assembly is the highest decision-making body" according to Art. 5 of the Statute of the Factory Council of Magneti Marelli Crescenzago), throwing into question the full-time union official being exempt from production and therefore disconnected from the workers.

This centralisation of decision-making in the hands of the Executive meant that its members were almost every day involved in negotiations, which facilitated the task of the management in that it faced a responsible counterpart that did not constantly change. There was daily negotiation concerning piecework, the working environment, overtime, promotion by qualifications (only

---

93   Dolci-Reyneri, *op. cit.*

those up to the second category, other promotions were decided unilaterally by management). Finally, the management "normally informed the trade unions about restructuring plans in an quite obvious effort to involve them in the technical and production choices in exchange for the extension of trade union power in all the factories of the Group and the political requirements for the satisfaction of employment development in the South" (of Italy).[94]

In 1972-73 the rate of unionisation of the plant in Crescenzago consolidated at more than 60%. If we add to this the full recognition by management, good control over the working-class base and a decent level of union activism, we can say that, despite the presence of the "groups," the trade union structures of the factory were at the height of their success. The union aim was the extension of their power in the other companies of the Group, which were poorly unionised. The method used was once again the centralisation of decision-making through the creation of the Secretariat of the Coordinating Committee, a body which served to concentrate bargaining to a maximum level. This Secretariat was in fact made up of 5 members of the Executive of Crescenzago and Sesto San Giovanni that "helped" the other factories, directly intervening with the Head Office of the company. This union intervention, especially in the southern factories, caused an increase in enrolment and stimulated the growth of new Factory Councils.

Also in these two years, the institutionalisation of trade union democracy was perfected. The active participation of the union was regulated and the protagonists became stable figures recognised by workers and management. The union leadership in fact coincided with the Executive of the Factory Council and consisted of a dozen workers belonging to Fim, FIOM and UILM. The elections for the Executive the previous year confirmed entirely the same people, except for one who had retired. Among these, those who had greatest prestige were the 2-3 members of the former Internal Commission, considered the most important trade union leaders of Magneti in Crescenzago since the early sixties. They were trusted unconditionally even outside of the union, so that no officer intervened regularly at the factory. The other members of the Executive were young people emerging from the union battles of '68-'69, more combative than the older ones, and which sometimes made alliances with the delegates of the "groups."

The level of the other delegates was quite varied. There were only about twenty workers (one third of the total of 54) that were definitely able to solve the problems of their departments, organising meetings and pickets of small factories near Crescenzago. Female labour activism remained low, with only 10 delegates and no real autonomy. While some concerned themselves with

---

94   Ibid

"women's issues," such as child care and maternity, none belonged to the union leadership or took part in the decisions that really mattered. The relationship with the male delegates amounted to paternalism on the part of the latter.

The proof of the institutionalisation of union democracy can be seen in the procedure for defining Group platforms of demands in 1973:

1) the *Comitato di collegamento* (Liaison Committee), composed of 28 members appointed by the Factory Councils, is convened by the Secretariat and suggests a proposal, and

2) the Factory Councils discuss it and propose a new document which is discussed in the department assemblies, and

3) there's a further meeting of the Factory Council that prepares another document including proposals that emerged in the assemblies,

4) a meeting of the Coordination of all Factory Councils of the Group (i.e. 100 delegates) that prepares the final platform;

5) ratification in the factory general assemblies.

Unlike in the disputes of 1971 and 1972, we are dealing with a much more involved procedure. Furthermore department assemblies were preferred over general assemblies because in the latter it is easier for dissidents to set out their positions (at general assemblies there are always the same people and "at the end when most people have left, those from the 'groups' then present their motion and it gets passed by the few who are still there").

Proof of the strained relations between the trade unions and the "groups" after the 1972-73 contract can be seen in an attempt to reduce the presence of "groups" in the Factory Council, which did not succeed. Signatures were collected to revoke two of their delegates, but they were subsequently re-elected. Another example was when the Magneti section of the PCI distributed a leaflet attacking, by name, the only Executive member belonging to the "groups."[95]

The assemblies became a site of conflict between the Executive and the extra-parliamentary groups, such as during the 1972-73 contract struggle when the delegates of the "groups" were trying to override the decisions of the Executive but they were defeated first in the Factory Council and then in the assembly. Or, in April 1973, when the Factory Council blocked the doors of the offices of the security guards, and the "groups" proposed blocking the gates as well.

The attitude of the delegates of the "groups" was regarded as unfair by the other members of the Factory Council, because even when their positions were defeated in the Factory Council they re-proposed them again in the assemblies, creating, according to the other delegates, confusion among the workers.

---

95   Ibid

chapter three
The story of the Workers' Committee

THE *COMITATO OPERAIO* (WORKERS' COMMITTEE) OF MAGNETI MARELLI WAS situated in the historical period characterised by the most serious international economic crisis since 1929. The end of the "boom" was announced by the devaluation of the US dollar, the explosion of wage rates in Europe, an excess supply in the labour market and a rapid decline in profits, but the final blow came when the OPEC countries decided, in the fall of 1973, to increase the price of crude oil by 70%, by decreasing the amount produced.

In 1974 the West went into a recession, marking the beginning of a decade of stagnation and unemployment, while the increase in oil prices increased the cost of production and finished products, resulting in a fall in profits and overall demand for goods and services.

Italy and Britain were the Western economies most vulnerable because of their excessive dependence on imported oil, to which in Italy we can add weak governments and business owners who chose to respond to the loss of power in the factories by blocking investments and taking their capital abroad. Italy faced four factors: the highest rate of inflation in the western world, the enormous growth of "black market" work and tax evasion, the partial decrease in production and the rapid increase in public debt.

The response of the Bank of Italy to the crisis was a strict deflationary policy accompanied by a credit squeeze which resulted in a large shift of production activities with a consequent increase in the "black economy," home working and work by young people, which provided low-cost production and high profits.[96]

The restructuring of production, even before the recovery of profit margins, was directed by the bosses towards the reconquest of the time and space that the struggles of workers had stolen from them. For industry, it was necessary to restore the basic functions of capitalist reproduction, productivity and discipline. That's why they tended to drastically reduce the workforce in production by increasing the role of technology and decreasing that of workers. It also explains very well the massive introduction of factory automation, mass layoffs, plant closures and decentralisation of production. If we analyse the restructuring, aimed at restoring flexibility and control over the workforce, the importance of the role of inflation is clear, as is that of employer-worker *inquadramento unico* and *Cassa integrazione*. The pressure of an increasing cost of living makes it easier to reintroduce overtime and wage incentives in the factories.

The "CASSA INTEGRAZIONE" (CIG)

This measure, put in place after the Second World War, allows industrial enterprises with more than 15 staff and other commercial businesses with more than 50 staff to temporarily suspend the payment of wages to workers put in "technical unemployment" (that is, their jobs have become technically unnecessary). The state makes up the loss of pay for the workers. There were two sub-measures: the *Cassa integrazione ordinaria* (ordinary CIG) in case of temporary economic difficulties, and the *Cassa integrazione straordinaria* (CIGS) reserved for structural crises during the process of restructuring and reconversion.

The ordinary CIG has a maximum duration of 13 weeks (eventually renewable). The (extraordinary) CIGS can be invoked for 12 months in a crisis situation, and for 24 months in the case of restructuring and reconversion. The CIGS is called "zero hours" when the employment contract is completely

---

96   *Storia d'Italia...*, op. cit., pp. 473 et seq.

suspended. The compensation corresponds to 80% of the salary normally received for the hours not worked.

The ordinary CIG is financed by contributions from companies, fixed at 1% of salaries (0.75% in companies with less than 50 staff), as well as by the state. During a period of recourse to the ordinary CIG, employers pay out an additional 8% of the salaries received in compensation by their staff (3% for small companies). Employers and employees finance the CIGS, at 0.6% of salaries for the former and 0.3% for the latter.

The *inquadramento unico* ("single framework"),[97] born in the name of a compromise between unions and employers, was only partially aligned with the grassroots egalitarian thrust that had helped to get it accepted. For the most part it was used to reintroduce the notion of individual "professionalism," defined according to "objective" rules that struggles were deleted from.

By imposing mobility bonuses, the boss undermined the cohesion of the working class. *Cassa integrazione* was used to reduce business costs, to dampen the conflict during periods of intense restructuring and intensification of the decentralisation of production, but also as an instrument of division of workers and an anti-strike deterrent. Another aspect was the emergence of a clear commitment by the bosses to strengthen the authority of their institutional counterpart, the union, based on the working class.[98]

Piece work

The Magneti Marelli Workers' Committee, taking stock of workers' struggles in 1969, stated that "the struggle aims to claim objectives that correspond to

---

[97] The agreement known as the "single framework," signed by the unions and the Italian bosses in 1973, consisted in establishing a single classification of employees, whether they were blue or white collar, founded on professional levels (based on technical capacity and position in production) and no longer by qualification groups inside professional categories. The application of the framework lead to a change in the relation of qualifications to pay packets, except for the least skilled workers who remained at the bottom. Beyond the reduction in differences between blue and white collar workers, the single framework had the aim of restoring "professionality" (see note below).

[98] Andrea Graziosi, *La ristrutturazione nelle grandi fabbriche 1973-1976*, Feltrinelli, 1979 and Primo Moroni-Nanni Balestrini, *L'orda d'oro* ("The Golden Horde"), 1988, SugarCo.

the immediate needs of the workers, to the practical criticism of the capitalist organisation of production. You arrive at the imposition by force of political freedom in every department, of every link, of every form of political agitation, of worker debate, up until the goods blockade organised independently by the comrades in '73."[99]

When, on 17 May 1973, Enrico Baglioni, future leader of the Committee, was taken on at Magneti Marelli, the extra-parliamentary presence in the factory was very strong, at up to 20% of the delegates. Inside the Crescenzago factory there were Lotta Continua and Circolo Lenin of Sesto San Giovanni, a small local group with a strong union orientation that shortly afterwards went into Lotta Continua. The internal section of Lotta Continua could call strikes on its own; the membership of the factory cell was 35; the newspaper sold 30 copies a day and was distributed in every department of the factory. Baglioni was immediately elected delegate for the department. He became a member of the provincial committee of Lotta continua, and was part of the National worker commission and of the National Committee of the organization. The section of Lotta Continua in Sesto San Giovanni was the strongest in the province of Milan.[100]

In September 1973, the workers of Magneti in Crescenzago took part in the strike to protest against the *coup d'*état of Chilean General Pinochet against the reformist president Salvador Allende. For the occasion the Circolo Lenin distributed a leaflet in which the Allende government was referred to as the result of the process of strengthening the political autonomy of the Chilean working class. The Allende government, however, had enormous contradictions, so "when the margins of economic development that enabled a temporary truce were lacking, class conflicts exploded ... Back in December 1972, the contrasts between the Chilean bourgeoisie and the proletariat were irreconcilable, but Allende rejected the path of class struggle, choosing reconciliation with the DC [Christian Democrats] and the army and politically disarming the working class with the theory of 'peaceful transition to socialism.' The Chilean

---

[99] In 1977, shortly after the arrest of seven Magneti Marelli and Falck workers in Valgrande, the Magneti Marelli Workers' Committee published a document entitled *Operai e Stato* ("Workers and State") about the history of struggles in the factory: "just when the attack against the revolutionaries in factories is most explicit and violent and a qualitative leap in workers' organisation shows itself to be most necessary." The basic fact was "the inability of the boss, the PCI and the union to block" the continuing process of growth of the organisation and workers' consciousness within Magneti Marelli at via Adriano 81 at Crescenzago.

[100] *L'orda d'oro*, op. cit., p. 326

workers are from now on armed with class consciousness and the *coup d'*état carries out a brutal repression to defeat them."[101]

In Italy, meanwhile, the government decided to increase the price of petrol and diesel, which resulted in "a new general payroll robbery of the workers" by an immediate increase in the price of private and public transport and rent increases due to the higher costs of heating. This "victory of the oil bosses" motivated other Italian capitalists to attack the workers, while the government proved once again that it had no intention "to look for money where it is," but intended to attack the workers' wage with indirect (price increases) and direct taxation (a new tax reform). This attack on wages was accompanied by restructuring in the factories, with the consequences of unemployment, underemployment, increased exploitation and work at home, maximising the output of the plants, increasing productivity. The government's plan had the support of the Communist Party and the Socialist Party, who shared responsibility for this attack on workers. The Communist Party agreed to block struggles and wage increases in exchange for a fake blocking of price increases, making it an accomplice in the impoverishment of the proletariat, rising unemployment and exploitation in the factory. Precisely for this reason the contemporary workers' struggles in Carlo Erba, Magneti Marelli, Alfa Romeo, in Marghera, Fiat and the small factories of Paderno Dugnano (a suburb close to Milan) should be understood as struggles against the boss, "but also against the will of the revisionists for their continued attempt to mediate and mystify."[102]

The *Circolo operaio Karl Marx* pointed out in a leaflet that almost all the women in the factory were in the third category: "but does this category make sense? We say no, we say that it is an unjustified division that the bosses put on us – on the basis of a different wage – to set us against each other, to break what they most fear: our unity of struggle." The Circle attacked the Qualifications Commission that supported the proposals for "rotation" and "professionality,"[103] which in reality served to push through bosses' decisions such as the reintroduction of shifts in the fifth section: "the Boss has good

---

101 *Dibattito unitario, Noi e il Cile* ("We and Chile"), no. 12, September 1973 and leaflet: "Against the coup in Chile, the working class arms itself with its political autonomy!" by Circolo Lenin, Sesto San Giovanni, 12 Sept 1973.

102 Leaflet "A new tax on wages! Another theft from the pay packet!" by Circolo operaio Karl Marx, 1 Oct 73 and the leaflet *"Against the division of categories, for better wages, let's get the fight started on the shop floor!"* by Circolo operaio Karl Marx, 8 Oct 1973.

103 We have chosen to translate "professionalità" by "professionality," a term which might appear a bit too sociological in the context of the struggles of the '60s and '70s. Nevertheless, in Italian, this word means two things: professional qualification, but also the attachment of the worker to doing a good job, their professional consciousness.

reason, from his point of view, to create shifts, so the machines run 16 hours continuously. For us, the shift system means: deep physical discomfort, it's impossible to organise our lives, discomfort with the children and the home, with nursery and normal living time. The shifts mean an attack on employment." In the third section the workers succeeded in pushing back the introduction of shifts by "blocking the carpets" (the Italian term for conveyor belt is "tapetto" – "carpet"), demonstrating that only struggle pays.[104]

On 10 September 1973, the Coordinating Committee of the Factory Councils of the Magneti Marelli group presented its platform of demands to the Marelli Head Office. Its main points were:

1. the application of the "single framework,"
2. wage equalisation within the same level,
3. an increase in productivity bonus,
4. an increase in the meal break time for shift workers and the reintroduction of breaks for assembly lines and work on harmful/toxic processes.

Demands for wage increases, made even more compelling by the high inflation affecting workers' income, had to be made in the framework of a single wage within the same classification level. The platform emphasised the importance of professionality, a mechanism identified by the unions to differentiate job positions, without prejudice to the automatic transition from the second to the third level as professionality certainly could not be achieved on the "lines." As for professionality, the Coordinating Committee wrote that "above the third level, we reiterate the concept of professionality as our objective cannot be to disqualify the job (as the boss does) but to enrich it. Certainly those who support automatic category promotion are proposing a simplistic objective, because they start only from the discrimination that the boss has introduced."[105]

---

104 Ibid.
105 Leaflet: "Present demands to the Management" of the Secretariat of the Coordinating Committee, Milan, 17 Sept 73, and *Dibattito unitario*, "The beginning of negotiations with the management and our demands," September 1973. The national agreement of 1973, signed in March, with Intersind and Asap and in April with Federmeccanica, achieved a single framework, and 150 payed hours for study, with increases the same for everyone. Within the single framework worker-employees formed 8 levels (seven, plus a super fifth) that unified the previous categories and subcategories that resulted in 20 different wages. For the Marelli Coordinating Committee the new wage structure of the employees of the Group was supposed to be as follows: basic wage equivalent to the minimum wage, a corporate component (called the third monthly element) equal

For the Circolo operaio Karl Marx, after the workers' assemblies, it was time to start the fight. The trade union platform was too vague: "Our conditions are worsening, and if we are not firm they will get even worse." For the circle, "there is no contradiction between the struggle of the department and the factory and the general struggle for pensions, family allowances and unemployment pay. The workers know that the fight nourishes itself in the workshops, in the factory to be stronger on the general level. So clear objectives and a hard struggle in the factory are the necessary pillars needed to fight harder and more effectively in general terms." It must be born in mind that to "withdraw, surrender, negotiate with the bosses, the illusion that the bosses will apply effective measures (price freeze) without struggle is sheer madness."

The *Nucleo operaio* ("Workers' Nucleus") of Lotta Continua in Magneti Marelli argued that the Coordinating Committee "has trampled on what was left of the assemblies of Crescenzago, which is the heart of the Group, the centre of the struggle." The letter from the Coordinating Committee was just about professionalism, not even a trace of money, that's why it was necessary to make the union act for the workers. Yet, reflecting the real demands of the workers, the assembly in reality supported the proposal for substantial wage increases. The assembly of the second shift almost unanimously approved these demands:

1. automatic transition from the second to the third level after six months without a professional exam or change of job,
2. automatic transition from the third to the fourth level after 18 months, without exam or job change;

---

for all workers by category and including all the elements of the company wage; seniority advancements should be biannual; inflation-linked increases must be calculated on a monthly basis. The new third monthly element will merge the third and fourth elements (a kind of production bonus per person), output pay (piecework), the superminimum, incentives etc., excluding the award of annual production bonuses. Thus we move towards the abolition of piecework. *Dibattito unitario*, "Wage framework and single classification," no. 12, September 1973.

The platform of demands was as follows: a) an investment programme and new hires, especially in the factories of the South, for the years 1974-1978, b) implementation of single framework from 1 November 1973 with the introduction of the new wage structure (third business element), c) increase in the production premium for 1973 of 65,000 lire annually, d) the price of a canteen coupon set at 150 lire, replaced canteen allowance of the same amount, direct management of all the refectories (menus, quality) and meal break for shift workers, e) holiday pay of 8 hours per day, f) other issues relating to breaks, replacements, seniority and long service bonus, older workers, student-workers. *Dibattito unitario*, "Critical moment and a turning point in the dispute," no. 13, November 1973.

3. effective fourteenth monthly salary,
4. 15,000 lire monthly increase for everyone to get through the establishment of a new business element that eliminates inequalities between workers classified at the same level;
5. renewal of the productivity bonus,
6. payment of sick pay at the full rate, as for white-collar employees.

The *Nucleo operaio* recognised that the assembly of the first shift had fallen into the "game of the union," while the votes of the third assembly showed a lot of confusion, as evidenced by the high number of abstentions. In the other Group plants there were not even meetings, while the union convened the Coordinating Committee, "that is, a very small group of people," in order to "have no opposition and to try to change the results coming out of the assembly."[106]

On 27 September, the company opened negotiations, which were immediately set back to 8 October. The Circolo operaio Karl Marx calls on the workers to not accept the bosses' logic, that wants lengthy negotiations without a struggle, and to impose objectives discussed in the workers' assemblies. On 28 September meetings are held in the workshops.[107]

On 17 October general meetings are held to discuss the dispute and the forms of struggle to be used for the future: the next day's strike needs to block movement of goods and the management offices. According to the Nucleo operaio of Lotta Continua in Magneti Marelli "we are not fighting for the application of the single framework, but to go beyond it, with automatic advances in category." The blockade of goods during the strike of 18 October served to increase the tension in the workshops so well that the factory was totally shut down the same day.[108]

---

106 Leaflet: "Today at the assembly!" by Circolo operaio Karl Marx, 9 April 1973; leaflet: "On Tuesday assemblies were held" by Nucleo operaio di Lotta Continua of Magneti Marelli, 5 Sept 1973; leaflet: "Against the manoeuvres of the bosses, against the individual advancement by qualification, for the wage: begin the fight immediately!" by Circolo operaio Karl Marx; leaflet: "Let's make it clear" by Nucleo operaio di Lotta Continua of Magneti Marelli, 11 Sept 1973; leaflet: "Launch the struggle" by Circolo operaio Karl Marx, 18 Sept 1973; leaflet: "The boss wants to demobilise us by playing for time" by Circolo operaio Karl Marx.

107 Leaflet: "'Freeze' prices, freeze wages, if that's not enough call the paratroopers," Circolo operaio Karl Marx, 10 Sept 1973; leaflet: "No! To the demobilization! No! To the wishy-washy platform!!," Circolo operaio Karl Marx, 24 Sept 1973; leaflet: "The bosses don't get in on merit, they're a bunch of shirkers," Circolo operaio Karl Marx, 28 Sept 1973

108 Leaflet "From today, during the strike, block goods," Nucleo operaio of Lotta Continua

The Circolo operaio Karl Marx and the Nucleo operaio of Lotta Continua invited the workers to take to the streets on 30 October to go to the Group's management and "to then return to the factory stronger and extend the blockade of the guardhouse as we've already begun to do, against the wishes of the union to keep the factory quiet." This slogan was accepted after the company refused to accept, for the fourth time, the key positions of the platform, an immediate large wage increase and rapid automatic advancements: "in the face of this bosses' intransigence, the union continues to negotiate calmly and deliberately goes along with the game of the management."[109] Despite the march, the company did not give in, so the Circolo operaio and the Nucleo operaio asked workers to prepare for a general strike in the area of Sesto San Giovanni to protest against rising prices and for wage increases. On this occasion the struggle in Magneti Marelli had to consolidate its role as a reference point for the area, "for the workers of Breda Termo, Ercole Marelli and Falck, as well as the struggles of students around the cost of schooling, increasingly unbearable given workers' wages."[110]

The blockade of goods continued without the approval of the unions, the management convened the Executive of Crescenzago factory and threatened disciplinary action against the workers taking part in it, the captain of the guard began to collect names of participants in the struggle. The Circolo operaio and Nucleo operaio demanded that the Factory Council and the unions take a clear position "in front of all the workers" about what is happening, because "in the factory, there are no neutral forces," "the Factory Council must take a position on the blockade of goods, on the forms of struggle on the eve of the sixth negotiation." Fim and some of representatives of the PCI were consistently "guard dogs for the productive efficiency of the factory, they are trying to keep the factory running despite the struggle!"

The Union drew up a proposal, considered as dangerous, to stagger increases over time. "Given a pittance now," "we say no to the staggered increases because prices, rent, taxes are not staggered." For the Nucleo operaio and the Circolo operaio, this was yet another failure of the union, because such proposals "have always been a weapon of the boss to stop struggles, to make us feel good at the factory," but now it is even the union itself that makes these proposals. On 12 November there was a meeting during which, for the Nucleo and the Circolo, "the union leader on duty must not make the usual speech,"

---

of Magneti Marelli, 18 Oct 1973

109   Leaflet "Go down to the streets tomorrow to break the isolation and reiterate our goals!," Circolo operaio Karl Marx and Nucleo operaio of Lotta Continua, 29 Oct 1973

110   Leaflet: "The bosses raise prices. We raise the struggle for wages," Circolo operaio Karl Marx and Nucleo operaio of Lotta Continua, 4 Nov 1973

there must be a serious discussion and we have to get to a vote against this proposal: "Today there is no escape, the Assembly must impose the NO, this is a real challenge to our wage needs." The assembly actually decided against the gradation of the increases and for the continuation of the blockade of the factory and the goods. On 22 November, during the worker march through Sesto San Giovanni, "guided in a militant way by Magneti Marelli workers," skirmishes broke out between members of the PCI and Socialist Party and the Circolo operaio Karl Marx.[111]

In Italy a new big increase in oil prices promised the usual corollary of inflation, despite the "price freeze" decided by the government in agreement with the unions, and a dramatic increase in unemployment, since "the bosses use the energy crisis to bring forward restructuring processes more decisively, expelling workers from the factories (Fiat has already stopped hiring), making demands that the bosses call labour flexibility, i.e. the ability to use as the workers as they see fit, with new shifts, increases in pace of work, change of jobs etc."

The ban on the movement of cars on Sundays affects to a greater extent "proletarians who have only this one day to escape the squalor of a dormitory or the isolation of the industrial belt villages."[112] Industrial restructuring was accompanied by renewed bosses' intransigence. With the excuse of the oil crisis, they would first wear down worker resistance and then export the same standards to all spheres of Italian society, leading to a historic defeat for the Italian working class.

This analysis applies perfectly to Magneti Marelli, where the boss broke off negotiations and denounced the prolonged blockage of production, carried out mainly by the workers of the Second Section. In addition, "the boss pushes foremen to organise against the workers, after having pushed them into a provocation against the vanguards." For some time the head of the Factory Council

---

111 Leaflet: "The management don't like the blockade so they make threats!!!"), Circolo operaio Karl Marx and Nucleo operaio of Lotta Continua, 7 Nov 1973; leaflet: "Provocations vigil," Circolo operaio Karl Marx and Lotta Continua, 8 Nov 1973; leaflet: "Today in the assembly, No!! to the gradations," Nucleo operaio of Lotta Continua and Circolo operaio Karl Marx, 12 Nov 1973; leaflet: "Yesterday the boss broke off negotiations," Nucleo M. Marelli of Lotta Continua, 14 Nov 1973; leaflet: "In the assemblies, No to the gradation, Yes to effective struggle," Nucleo operaio of Lotta Continua and Circolo operaio Karl Marx; leaflet: "Tomorrow everybody to the streets," Nucleo operaio of Lotta Continua and Circolo operaio Karl Marx, 20 Nov 1973; leaflet: "Magneti workers in struggle are not alone," Circolo operaio Karl Marx and Lotta Continua, 23 Nov 1973

112 Leaflet: "The oil measures don't 'hit' everyone the same way," Nucleo operaio of Lotta Continua and Circolo operaio Karl Marx, 25 Nov 1973

of Marelli Crescenzago had been a character who spoke the same language as the management and the Christian Democrats, Paolino Riva. He succeeded in changing the position of the Factory Council, which from then on "endorsed the boss's repression" and defended the section heads. The Circolo operaio and Lotta continua invited militant workers in the PCI to not forget their "righteous attacks on foremen" and the "police regime" of the factory.[113]

The company sacked ten workers from Rabotti in Turin, put another ten on the *cassa integrazione* at Fivre in Pavia (two companies of the Group) and suspended one in Crescenzago, while on the dispute front refused for the ninth time to consider the union proposals.

On 12 December events are held throughout Italy "as a first response to the government action." On 13 December in Milan there is a demonstration by the whole Magneti Marelli Group to strengthen the fight at the factory and for wages, linked to the fight against the use of the crisis by the bosses.[114]

Soon afterwards, the management of Magneti Marelli reduce the piece rates for female staff monitoring the line, and 800 workers march to "force the payment owed."[115] The Workers' Committee recall the episode like this:

> In the framework of the fight for the collective bargaining agreement, Magneti carried out a provocation to test the capability of reaction of the workers (men and women): it didn't pay a few hundred line workers a special bonus, the 38% of the piece rate that they are guaranteed. On the 13th, the first shift and the "normal" one got their pay, found the bonus money was missing and quickly got together to discuss what to do. When they got their pay the workers of the second shift joined the assembly. Even the workers of other departments, though not directly affected by this provocation but hearing the measure as an attack on all workers, went on strike and participated in the meeting. It was clear what to do: in all the speeches and around the tables in the canteen the proposal is made to all go in a demonstration to the Head Office in Sesto San Giovanni. The

---

113 Leaflet: "Proletarians, forward in the fight against the bosses for wages!" by Circolo Karl Marx and Lotta Continua, 3 Dec 1973.

114 Leaflet: "Against the bosses' crisis we respond with struggle," Circolo Karl Marx and Lotta Continua, 11 Dec 1973; leaflet: "Gratitude is not one of the boss's virtues," Circolo Karl Marx and Lotta Continua, 13 Dec 1973; leaflet: "The boss wants everything! Only struggle pays," Circolo Karl Marx and Lotta Continua, 18 Dec 1973

115 "Chronicle of a trial," Workers' Committee of Magneti Marelli, *History*, only issue, February 1980.

usual old peacemakers of the [union] Executive are opposed to this decision, making many excuses. The most cunning, in the face of protests by workers and fearing losing control of the struggle, came up with the excuse that it was too late (it was 4pm), and that there was no one in Sesto, trying to postpone till the next day… Containing their anger the communist workers… proposed to go to the Head Office at Crescenzago. To avoid wasting time, workers invite those who agree to go to the headquarters that is within walking distance from the canteen. 300 workers out of 800 who were at the meeting leave without hesitation… After a brief discussion with the personnel chief, who of course claims to know nothing, comrades invite him peremptorily to go with them to the factory manager. The demonstration passes in front of the canteen and the other workers join in while the Executive and some of their loyal followers discuss how to get control of the situation. The demonstration goes to the Director and meets the captain of the guard with some of his men, who are told to go back to the gates where they 'work.'

"Negotiations begin with the director. At the same time, the 'knights' of the Executive also arrive to show the workers that it is also their business, assuming grotesque postures and pushing themselves to the front. Then along came a 'gentleman' who introduced himself as a Police Commissioner supposedly responding to a telephone call to verify the serious events that were happening in the factory. The workers reassured him, noting that the only act of violence had been perpetrated by Magneti, stealing part of the wages of hundreds of workers. He left rapidly, having to go through the middle of hundreds of workers, including many women and was embarrassed to lose his hat. Seeing that the fight would not stop, the Personnel Office surrendered and retracted the theft. Three days later the workers who had suffered the cut to their wages received, in a separate envelope, what was rightly owed them.[116]

A general strike in Lombardy was called for 18 December, and on 19 December was the eleventh meeting between management and unions. Negotiations continued over the following days.

---

116   "Chronicle of a trial," "4 years of struggle, 4 years of the workers-bosses workers-union workers-justice relation," February 1980

On 28 December there was a draft agreement between the parties "in which the first thing that strikes the eye is the negation of the wage objectives which in fact were the centre of our struggle."[117]

On 4 January 1974, after more than four months of struggle, 54 hours on strike and numerous marches in Sesto San Giovanni and Milan, the Management and FLM (Metalworkers Federation – a confederation uniting the metalworkers' unions: Fiom, FIM and UILM) sign the agreement for the 12,000 employees of the Magneti Marelli Group. The signing takes place as usual at the Assolombarda Milan office, and only after the assemblies of various plants had approved it on 28 December. For the Factory Councils Coordination, the key points of the agreement, defined as successful, were the equalisation of pay for workers of various factories at the same level, a total of 4,700 advancements in category level, consolidation for everyone at 71% of the average income in the Crescenzago plant, a fixed canteen cost of 150 lire ("a step towards gaining a free canteen, wages in kind and social service"), a productivity bonus increase of 50,000 lire per year for 1973 and new investments favouring jobs.[118]

---

117 Leaflet: "Negotiation: the boss's provocation continues!" by Circolo Karl Marx and Lotta Continua, 20 Dec 1973; leaflet: "This agreement sacrifices wages and categories and divides us, we cannot accept it," Lotta Continua, 1 Jan 1974.

118 *Dibattito unitario*, "Positive agreement won," no. 14, January 1974. For the various stages of negotiation see also the leaflet: "Workers(f/m) of Magneti Marelli" by the Comitato nazionale di Coordinamento Magneti Marelli, Sesto San Giovanni, 28 Sept 1973; the leaflet: "Management has stopped negotiations!," Magneti Marelli National Coordinating Committee (CGIL-CISL-UIL)-Metalworkers Federation area of Sesto San Giovanni, undated; leaflet: "We ask the management for precise and concrete answers," Metalworkers Federation (FIM-FIOM-UILM)-area of Sesto San Giovanni and the Magneti Marelli Factory Council, Sesto San Giovanni, 1 Oct 1973; leaflet: "Workers(f/m)," Magneti Marelli National Coordinating Committee (CGIL-CISL-UIL), Sesto San Giovanni, 9 Oct 1973; leaflet: "Today an open assembly," FlM Sesto San Giovanni, 10 Oct 1973; leaflet: "The Sesto San Giovanni's FLM on the Magneti M. dispute," Executive Committee of FLM, Sesto area, Sesto San Giovanni, 15 Oct 1973; leaflet: "Magneti Marelli Workers(f/m)," Magneti Marelli National Coordinating Committee (CGIL-CISL-UIL), Sesto San Giovanni, 16 Oct 1973; leaflet: "A negative fourth meeting with the management"; Magneti Marelli National Coordinating Committee (CGIL-CISL-UIL), Sesto San Giovanni, 25 Oct 1973; leaflet: "The management avoid the concrete problems," Magneti Marelli National Coordinating Committee (CGIL-CISL-UIL) and Metalworkers Federation area of Sesto, 31 Oct 1973; leaflet: "After stopping the negotiations the management of Magneti Marelli moves them to Assolombarda," FLM-area of Sesto, Sesto San Giovanni, 21 Nov 1973; leaflet: "Wednesday 5 December 9am

Egalitarianism

In 1973, the final balance sheet of Magneti Marelli showed a profit of 610 million lire (around $US 1m), against a loss of 221 million in 1972, and the company was able to distribute a dividend of 32 lire for "ordinary" and 42 for "privileged" shares. Turnover had increased by 39.5%, exports by 23%. All this was as a result of massive investments made in the period 1971-1973, which led to increased productivity, despite the incomplete utilisation of machines, the reduction and inflexibility of working hours, the high level of absenteeism and the loss of production caused by labour unrest. The most important customer was still Fiat, which had notably increased "sales" on the balance sheet of Magneti Marelli. In terms of production, happier notes for the company came from San Salvo (close to Chieti in Abruzzo), whose facilities were put into operation at the end of 1972 and which could now be considered no longer in its start-up period, although increased production was recorded in all plants, including Crescenzago. One of the most significant improvements was in Radio-TV thanks to agreements for industrial integration and a new sales organization. The organisational structure of the company changed, with the division into 6 parts that were each a profit centre, a homogeneous product and a specific type of activity. The divisions of Equipment (sales revenue increased by 45% in 1973) Batteries (25% increase), Fivre Electronics (+13%) and Rabotti (+15%) were characterized by the execution of all processes from design to production, administration and sales. The other two divisions had more specifically commercial tasks: Parts and Service (responsible for the marketing of the four industrial divisions) and Radiomarelli (business in traditional radio and TV appliances).[119]

---

negotiations resume at Assolombarda"; Magneti Marelli Factory Council A, B, N, and Branch area of Sesto S. Giovanni, Sesto San Giovanni, 3 Dec 1973.

The agreement was signed between the Assolombarda's representative and three executives on one side and five representatives of the provincial sections of the FIM-FIOM-UILM unions (Antonio Pizzinato, Guido Laudini, Giampiero Colombo Rino Caviglioli and Donato Di Meo) on the other. Participating in the RSA (Company Union Representatives) were the Magneti Marelli plants of Sesto San Giovanni, Sesto Batteries, Crescenzago, Alessandria, Carpi, Romano Lombardo, Potenza, Turin, San Salvo and Branches. The agreement included: a) increase in the production premium in 1973 of 50,000 lire, b) increase of 5,500 lire a month for all, c) establishment of the new "third wage element," d) establishment of "single framework" with gradual mobility by second to third category for 4,400 workers, e) a good meal at a fixed price of 150 lire and a canteen daily allowance of 75 lire, gradual transition to the direct management of the refectories, f) forecast about employment investments in the southern areas and jobs' safeguard in Carpi and Alessandria plants. *Dibattito unitario*, "Positive agreement won," no. 14, January 1974

119 *Il Sole 24 ore*, "The Magneti Marelli balance sheet bounces back," 1 May 1974.

After the national agreement of 1973, one of the most debated issues among the workers was that of categories, "the contract is in fact already out-of-date because it is based on a division of workers using a parameter which only affects 80% of them. The majority position, which is expressed by struggles at all levels, is that of those who, from a proper assessment of the reality of the factory, ask for automatic progression for all workers to a higher category... Starting from the idea that women that work on the conveyor belt and the mass mechanical workers were able after a very short time to "fit" the professionalised job and that they never would have been able to do this professionalised work because the boss did not need so many, took hold in the debate as the concept of "potential" professionalism and so of automatic advancements of category... It was interesting to hear one delegate shout themselves hoarse in an effort to convince the assembly of the validity of the "existing professionalism" parameter and then to see the marches that went to negotiate the level directly and then the delegates themselves running to follow them but only with their feet (not with their heads)."[120]

Between February and March 1974, in order to enhance the production of brakes for heavy trucks, the management of Crescenzago called for the introduction of new shifts, even at night, and overtime on Saturday, and almost simultaneously asked to lay off 200-250 workers of the fifth section (windscreen wipers) and the fourth section (ignition coils) due to the lack of parts coming from ICS in Canonica d'Adda (Bergamo region). All business proposals were rejected by the Factory Council of Crescenzago "N."[121]

A general strike of metal, textile and chemical products workers was called for 7 February, with a national demonstration in Milan "for the wage, for it to be guaranteed, for political prices of basic necessities, for the reopening of the issue of pensions, family allowances and unemployment pay."[122]

---

120 "4 years of struggle, 4 years of the relation...," op. cit.
121 Leaflet: "Magneti Marelli workers(f/m)" by the Factory Council of Magneti Marelli Crescenzago, Crescenzago, 18 Feb 1974 and leaflet "Workers(f/m) of Magneti Marelli Crescenzago" by the Factory Council of Magneti Marelli "N," Crescenzago, 5 March 1974. The boss's proposal provided for the establishment of a third shift, the night shift, in the Second Section workshop and testing, two shifts in second section Assembly, third shift in Screws and Plating, and also on Saturday three shifts at the Foundry plus a fixed amount of overtime on Saturdays. Leaflet: "Management threaten *cassa integrazione* in the second section," by Lotta continua, 4 Feb 1974.
122 Leaflet: "Management threaten *cassa integrazione* in the second section," by Lotta continua, 4 Feb 1974 and leaflet: "The Foundry refuses overtime and joins the fight for strong wage increases," by Lotta Continua, 8 Feb 1974.

On 21 February, in a similar way to what had happened in the big factories in the rest of Italy, the Crescenzago workers responded to new government measures with stoppages in all departments, while the workers of the third section (assembly) "have begun to lay the foundations for immediately starting the fight against new shifts and overtime, and for strong wage increases." At the national level a new general strike for 27 February was being prepared. Strikes, meetings and stoppages continued over the following days.[123]

In the first week of March, the management announced to the union Executive that it intended to suspend 250 workers in the fifth section on zero hours, while the fourth section would provide work for a few days. The reason given by management was the blockade of goods imposed by the workers of ICS while fighting against the suspension of some workers and delegates. ICS was a company, a Magneti asset, where the Factory Council was not recognized, and could not represent the workers, indeed the company tried to turn them against those of Magneti Marelli Crescenzago with the threat of layoffs.

According to the Nucleo operaio of Lotta continua, the real reason was the intention of Magneti management to hit its workers, "and take them back to the old days, with the introduction of night shifts and new shifts in some departments, while at the same time they want to reduce production in the fourth and fifth sections." The Nucleo operaio would beat this manoeuvre "by rejecting now and in the future new shifts, night shifts and overtime, with the unity and struggle of the whole factory, including with the workers who, on Friday or Monday, can be suspended; imposing full payment of wages for today and forever; imposing job guarantees."[124]

At the end of March, the foundry entered into a struggle for recognition of significant wage increases, against the toxic working environment and for more breaks.[125]

Shortly afterwards the following staff of Crescenzago went on strike spontaneously: mechanised processing in "A," the Equipment "N" division, technicians and typists, Accounting and Planning. This was after months of the Crescenzago unions singing the praises of the "framework" and supporting individual advances in category. At the Design office, there had been only 5 advancements to the sixth category out of 130 employees on the fifth, which

---

123 Leaflet: "Let's bring down Rumor and start fighting again," by Lotta Continua, 21 Feb 1974 and leaflet: "The government robs us, La Malfa resigns, forward with the fight!," by Lotta continua, 21 March 1974.

124 Leaflet: "No to the *cassa integrazione*, let's impose a wage of 100%," by Nucleo operaio of Lotta Continua, 6 March 1974.

125 Leaflet: "The foundry opens the fight for wages in the factory," by Lotta Continua, 27 March 1974.

effectively contradicts the contracts of employment for "designers" for whom the sixth category was expected. At DM (Materials Laboratory) some workers had languished in the second category for 18 years, "while the department heads and the line-heads that do the policing in departments reach the upper fifth and the sixth level by demonstrating that they are able to terrorise and enslave workers(f/m)." As evidence for this last statement it was argued that "on the test benches, not all team leaders have gone to upper fifth and the categories were given or taken away depending on the degree of servility."

In the "A" factory the same logic applied. In the Commercial Office (which was responsible for sales in Italy and abroad) for the same job you had different levels, in the Export Sales office there were two new recruits doing the same job but at different levels, the presence of completely different wage levels "to break the material unity of workers and to encourage crawling, hostility towards strikes, to break the struggle and the very possibility of organising." In the spare parts shop everyone did the same job but with levels ranging from two to six, it was the same with typists and punch card operators.[126]

The second, third and fourth sections, mechanised plant "A" and the foundry went on strike, asking "for collective category promotions and, refusing the logic of division that management has once again put in place with the application of the unified framework," and for wage increases against high prices.[127]

The *Nucleo operai-impiegati* ("Workers-employees Nucleus") of Magneti Marelli, belonging to Lotta Continua, denounced the national government and union policy, but also that of the boss in the factory, where the most militant workers were moved from the fourth section and threatened with punitive transfers, creating divisions among workers. The use of piece rates continued to grow and "voluntary" night work, encouraged by 40% extra pay, grew – "the increase in prices and the need for greater wages are a great weapon of blackmail and intimidation, division, and the encouragement to greater exploitation that the bosses are trying to impose." For several months, the foundry workers had been fighting against exploitation, occupational hazards (saying "NO" to the proposal to monetise health – danger money – coming from the union Executive) and the "looting of wages." The workers of the Second Section at the meeting then proposed an automatic step up to the

---

[126] Leaflet: "After months and months of smoke around the classification, finally some light: more divisions, more misery for workers, more power for the managers and for the boss," Nucleo operai-impiegati of Lotta Continua, 1 April 1974; leaflet: "A framework that divides, a classification to prevent the unity of the workers when struggle resumes in the factory!," Nucleo operai-impiegati Magneti Marelli of Lotta continua, 8 April 1974.

[127] Leaflet: "From the strikes of sections 2, 3, and 4 and the foundry, objectives for the struggle of the whole factory," of Nucleo operai-impiegati of Lotta Continua, 15 April 1974.

fourth category and "disgraced the now empty theorising of the Executive on 'professionalism' and 'individual advancement'." The assembly of forklift drivers, receptionists and warehouse workers demanded an equal increase for all of 30,000 lire, the cutters went on strike over categories, in plant "D" line workers were fighting against the load on the machines and against toxicity, there was unrest even in offices "A" and "N." The factory was in ferment, overcoming divisions between workers and white-collar employees because "the looting of wages has the same effect" and because restructuring, increased exploitation and control by the boss, were happening in the workshop the same as in the office. The privileged were only the managers, those who command. The Worker-employee Nucleus suggested this "workers platform": automatic category advancements for workers up to the fourth level; reunification at the highest level of ex-third employees; automatic advancements for graduates and from the fifth to the sixth level for the technicians of "N"; an increase of 30,000 lire for all; collective breaks of half an hour on the assembly line, in the foundry and for harmful jobs; consensus agreement for moves and transfers.[128]

On the occasion of the 25 April Anniversary (of the insurrection leading to the "liberation" of Milan in 1945), Lotta continua and the Worker-employee Nucleus invited all Magneti Marelli workers to demonstrate against the fascists and the Christian Democrats in Piazzale Loreto in Milan, for the "worker programme," and to maintain the right to divorce in the next referendum.[129] On that occasion, they reaffirmed the platform, with the wage as its central objective, because they had to deal with the continuous price increases imposed by the bosses and the government. So the platform included a bonus of 150,000 lire for everyone, "that allows us to go on family holidays," an increase of 15,000 lire a month, the same for everyone, as a "minimum necessary to move forward," the advance to the third level by the end of 1974 and, finally, automatic advancements for new recruits from the second to third level within six months.[130]

The Magneti Marelli workers linked to Lotta Continua were openly in favour of squatting houses in Gallaratese (a district of Milan) and Cinisello Balsamo (a nearby suburb) and sympathised with those twenty or so squatters

---

128 Leaflet: "The government dismisses the trade unions and goes forward with the anti-worker plan!," by the Worker-employee Nucleus of Lotta Continua, 10 May 1974.

129 A referendum on the right to divorce was held in Italy on 12 May 1974. Voters were asked whether they wanted to repeal a law passed three years earlier allowing divorce. Those voting "no" wanted to retain the law and their newly gained right to divorce. The "noes" won with 59.26% of the turnout.

130 Leaflet: "Against escalating prices, start the industrial action!" by Worker-employee Nucleus and Lotta Continua, 23 April 1974.

who had been arrested. For Marelli workers, "repression cannot stop the fight for the right of all workers to a decent home at a rent equal to 10% of the salary of the head of a family" and they invited them to make the factory the organisational centre of the struggle for housing, because the strength and political consciousness gained by the working class "is the only guarantee that the struggle continues and extends outside, under the direction of our workers." The Lotta continua programme for the right to housing included the seizing of vacant properties, stopping all evictions, workers' control over the allocation of public housing and the expropriation of land required for the construction of housing.[131]

Between 31 May and 1 June, at the town hall of the Municipality of Sesto San Giovanni, the national congress of delegates of the Magneti Marelli Group took place, attended by the national leader of the FLM, Bruno Sacerdoti. His presence was important because the Congress followed the meeting of the General Council of the FLM and therefore allowed people to draw the first conclusions about the decisions taken by the highest executive body of the metalworkers' union. After a journey of 4-5 years, in the opinion of the Coordination of Factory Councils, it had finally become union policy at company level, achieving equal treatment in all plants. From now on problems were always going to be resolved at Group level. During the Congress they debated the future orientation: the delegates must participate in general, inter-category and confederal union policy, which concerned reforms, control of prices and individual increases. It would also strengthen the role of the Coordinating Committee, which would have a closer link with the FLM national and provincial union coordinators. In the final motion ample space was given to the national negotiation with the government and Confindustria – demands for more investment and employment in the South, development of public housing and rent control, political prices for basic necessities, reducing taxes on income from employment and pensions, tying pensions to wage increases. It was also proposed to change the structure of the Coordination, a change that would provide a different representation for all the delegates and representatives of the national, provincial and local FLM and FULC ("Unitary Federation of Chemical Workers" of the CGIL). It would establish a Coordinating Committee (made up of 49 delegates and national, provincial and local FLM and FULC representatives) and a Secretariat of the Coordinating Committee, with 13 members elected by the Coordinating Committee, both based in Milan. The formation of the Labour Medical Commission and the Commission on Social Questions was proposed, and the

---

131   Leaflet: "On Saturday the houses occupied by hundreds of working-class families were cleared" by Lotta Continua, 5 May 1974.

role of the Coordination magazine, the newspaper *Dibattito unitario* ("Unitary Debate"), was raised.

The activity of the Coordination was financed through the contributions of workers (on the occasion the newspaper price was increased from 200 to 500 lire), and national, provincial and company FLM and FULC branches (when they took part in negotiations).

With regard to corporate agreements already reached, the final motion was that the various Factory Councils and the Coordinations must engage in constant evaluation of the six points: transition from the second to the third level; the right arrangement for the remaining categories; the recomposition of functions and professional development; the control of investments; "continuous workers' control" over restructuring and the work environment.[132]

The conference took place immediately after the neo-fascist massacre on 28 May 1974 in Brescia, which was perpetrated in the *Piazza della Loggia* during a union demo, and left 8 dead and 94 injured. There was a mass mobilisation and demands to outlaw the MSI: "workers and unions need to modify the economic changes imposed on our country and to fight the restructuring driven by the big companies, to weld the factory struggles to the general struggles and to impose a different social and economic development. This proposal, supported by appropriate initiatives to fight, firm objectives in defence of wages and employment to lead the country out of the political, economic and social crisis."[133]

To demonstrate that among the delegates of the Group were those with positions critical of the line proposed by the national unions, a statement was issued at the conference denouncing the attitude taken by the seven delegates

---

132 *Dibattito unitario*, "Renewal of the production bonus – introduction of the holiday bonus – social contribution of 1%," n. 16, May 1974 and "Final motion passed unanimously," n. 17, June 1974, and the document "Announcement to all employees of the Group Magneti Marelli" by Convegno nazionale Gruppo Magneti Marelli, Sesto San Giovanni, 1 June 1974, in *Dibattito unitario*, n. 17, June 1974.

The Congress in Sesto decided the lines of development of enterprise bargaining for 1974. The delegates decided to open the group trade dispute with the renegotiation of the production bonus for 1974 (increase of 98,000 lire per year) and its transformation into a monthly payment, the establishment of a work bonus (the fourteenth month) and a company contribution to social services (1% of total wages). Ibidem

133 Ibid.

As evidence of greater attention paid to broader issues: number 12 of *Dibattito unitario* published an article on the recent coup in Chile ("Us and Chile"); in n. 15 there were three articles on the referendum on divorce ("Resolution of the Milan FLM, text of the law, divorce in Italy").

of the "N" plant at Crescenzago, which supported "a line contrary to the document proposed by a Congress commission," and who even left the conference declaring themselves "free to do what they see fit." These "splitters" were accused of undermining the unity of the workers and therefore "are proposing a line unrelated to the wider interests of the organised movement."[134]

On 7 June, the union platform was presented to management. Lotta continua accused the Marelli bosses of attempting to divide the workers of the Group, by dumping on the weakest factories – the locations of Potenza, Vasto and Alessandria – things that would not be accepted at Crescenzago due to the militancy of workers (struggles against increases in the pace of work, night shifts, overtime, overloading of machines), nor in Sesto San Giovanni (the struggle in the foundry), the offices (fight against restructuring) or Fivre of Pavia (a five months-long fight against the increase in workloads and the cutting of hours). These facts showed that "where there is struggle and workers' unity, the boss does not pass," and that "the boss hits the periphery to hit the centre more quickly."[135]

What did Lotta Continua propose? "100% pay when we are suspended and laid off. No to transfers and suspensions! No to new shifts and to the strengthening of existing ones! No to increased workloads! Collective breaks on the lines, conveyor belts, and in hazardous environments! Immediate non-negotiable wage increases, 30,000 lire summer bonus! Automatic progression for former first category workers, consolidation of the former third level employees and recruitment of graduates directly into the second category."

Lotta continua also provided a "general programme" which benefited all workers: dissolution of the MSI, the unification of the components of individual wages, rent fixed at 10% of income and housing for proletarians, revaluation of pensions and their indexation to wages, a guaranteed wage for young people seeking their first jobs and for the unemployed, political prices and lowered administrative and food prices.[136]

On 28 June, there was the first meeting of the Directorate-General of Magneti Marelli and the National Committee for the coordination of the Factory Councils of the Group, during which the requirements coming out of the National Conference were explained: rewards, holiday bonus and social contributions, reimbursement of Coordination costs. At the same time overtime was suspended and all Factory Councils were called on to organise the struggle.[137]

---

134 Ibid
135 Leaflet: "The boss, the bosses… and us," by *Lotta Continua*, 25 June 1974.
136 Ibid
137 Leaflet: "Workers(f/m) of the Magneti Marelli group" by Comitato nazionale

On 12 July management proposed an increase of 4,500 lire a month. The union counter-claim was 25,000 lire delayed, and that amount was deemed insufficient by Lotta Continua, given the continuous rise in the cost of living. On 15 July, the workers of Crescenzago gathered for a meeting to decide what to do.[138]

On 18 July they showed up at the management office of the Group in Sesto San Giovanni to protest against the "main attack," the preparation of restructuring and layoffs in September. For Lotta continua, the workers' answer had to be a hard one from the start, up until the summer plant closures. The march to the management prepared the events of 24 July by the engineering factories in struggle and cemented the unity of the workers of Magneti Marelli and those of Ercole Marelli, also subjected to the bosses' attack: "24 July will not be a demonstration, but a threat to the bosses' initiative in August, a bridge to the struggles to be launched after the holidays."[139]

The workforce

Returning from holiday, the Worker-employee Nucleus of Lotta continua started off by attacking the "politically criminal" behaviour of the Executive of the Factory Council, which left the departments' delegates to themselves and disoriented the workers about the company's restructuring manoeuvres: "after the holidays the Executive is even worse in this incredible political and union blindness and crookery." The Nucleus intended to continue vigorously with the proposal for a rotation in the composition of the Executive to force the union to be "for the immediate opening of the general struggle."[140]

The attacks against the Executive started up again when the women of the fifth section entered the fight against the rising discomfort caused by the transfer of their unit of production. For Lotta Continua, the meeting of the Factory Council Executive sided against the decision taken by management but then "when dealing with the boss, accepted the requests for shifts and transfers and has gone among the workers to support bogus technical reasons." Executive

---

coordinamento Gruppo Magneti Marelli and FLM area of Sesto, Sesto San Giovanni, 28 June 1974.

138 Leaflet: "The boss is thinking of sending us on more miserable 'holidays'," Lotta Continua, 15 July 1974.

139 Leaflet: "July is not over, every day is a day of struggle!," Lotta continua, 18 July 1974

140 Leaflet: "Respond to the boss's threats with debate and struggle" by Nucleo operai-impiegati of Lotta Continua, 29 August 1974.

behaviour had to change, so it was proposed to rotate the delegates and to replace some of its members.[141]

On 11 September, meetings and rallies were held in and outside the factory, and there were various demonstrations throughout Italy against the rising cost of living. On 13 September, factories struck in Sesto San Giovanni and workers marched through Milan.[142]

The management of the plant did not intend to solve the long standing problem of the canteen staff. On 12 September 1974, in Crescenzago there was a meeting about the company's agreement at the very moment that the workers in the cafeteria went on strike, over staffing levels and working conditions.

> At the end of the assembly, while the workers came in to work the day shift, those on the first shift waited in line at the counters for the meal to be served. But the meal wasn't there! The situation was a bit tense, there were discussions between canteen and department workers. The Executive decided on strike-breaking action and put the delegates in place to distribute a cold meal (salami and cheese). The workers and the more conscious vanguard stood against both of these divisive attitudes… An elderly woman worker from the fifth section Motor horns proposed that they all go together to the Head Office. Immediately a demonstration of 300-400 workers went to the factory manager with the following demands:
>
> – Recruitment of 9 people to the canteen,
> – Payment of 4,000 lire to all workers present that day for the absence of the meal,
> – Payment for hours that were not worked.
>
> After about two hours of talks with various managers who blamed each other or didn't accept the requests, we decided to cut it short and invite the managers to clarify the matter to the rest of the workers who remained in the workshops without returning to work. The demonstration thus passed through all departments, with the managers in front and we explained how things were with a megaphone. The demonstration was constantly growing so we arrived at the canteen with more than 1,000 workers. A delegation of workers went to the Factory

---

141 Leaflet: "A week of struggle, for workers' initiative!," Lotta continua, 8 Sept 1974.
142 Ibid

Council Executive who in the meantime had gathered in the "smoking" room (the union room) to discuss what to do. We invited them to participate in the meeting to share with them the things that would happen. The negotiations resumed and after a quarter of an hour the manager at the microphone in the cafeteria accepted all of our requests. The next day a communiqué was attached to the management notice board annulling the agreement made the day before, because it had been extorted by force and violence, and threatening action against the workers responsible for these deeds. Fourteen written warnings had been sent.

Meanwhile, the Executive, that had objected to the statements made by management at the meeting, only three days later "frontally attacks the forms of struggle of the Magneti workers and their vanguards." Lotta Continua argued that "the Executive have already given proof of their passivity in the face of the bosses' restructuring ... but today this stunt shows them as gravediggers of the labour movement."

The company proposed to reduce the number of layoffs, but suspended all of the 14 "guilty men" for one day. Some of them accepted this suspension as the lesser evil, others, after much debate on the shop floor, still entered the factory "in their place of work and struggle." The management sent new letters to workers who had decided to come in despite the suspension, but was forced to withdraw them because the union threatened to not ratify the workplace contract and the agreement of 12 September.[143]

In the general assembly on 12 September, the workers decided to struggle to integrate the enterprise negotiation into the broader struggle against restructuring and the increase in the cost of living: "the forms of struggle must be adequate to the level of the attack carried out by the boss; this is why the unionists denigrate the marches inside and outside the factory, which block the gates and go out to block transportation against the rise in fares, the marches which go to Sesto to enforce the area general strike or the hiring of workers."

---

143   Leaflet: "The form of struggle for waging the factory fight as part of the general struggle!," Lotta continua, 12 Sept 1974 and leaflet: "Comrades, the boss attacks" by Lotta Continua, 18 Sept 1974 and *4 anni di lotta*, op. cit. This is the company's version of the incident: "On 12 Sept 74 several officials were injured, insulted and taken in procession through the Crescenzago plant by a large group of employees." Letter of Domenico La Monica to the judge Forno, Sesto San Giovanni, 3 Dec 76, quoted in *Controinformazione*, n. 17, January 1980, p. 24. On 9 October 1974, the management makes a complaint about these matters to the Commissioner of State Police, Greco Turro.

Assemblies convened on 16 September in the third and fifth section reiterated these concepts.[144]

Workers close to Lotta Continua denounced the "exhaustion which the boss wants to lead us to" with his continuous provocations, the last of which was the letters of suspension sent to six delegates and seven workers "with the threat of dismissal next time." We must, they said, demonstrate to the boss that the workforce is intact, we must make internal demonstrations and external blockades of the gates, blockades of the transport companies SAS and ATM, self-reduction of public fares. On the basis of these initiatives a general assembly was called on 25 September in the new canteen "to fight repression, to finally decide on the forms of struggle during the negotiation, and against the increase in transport costs."[145]

On the night of 10-11 December 1974 there was a failed attempt to set fire to the car of the head of personnel of Crescenzago, Filippo Polifroni. The action was claimed by the same Red Brigade that in the same night had destroyed the cars of two Breda managers and fired shots at the workplace of some Sit-Siemens managers.[146]

---

[144] Leaflet: "They don't frighten us! Our response will be even harder" of Lotta Continua, 16 Sept 1974.

[145] Leaflet: "No to repression of the vanguard, No to repression of forms of struggle" by Lotta Continua, 25 Sept 1974. In February 1974 the government announced a sharp rise in the price of petrol and some foodstuffs, a decision which led to immediate spontaneous strikes, including protest demonstrations. In August of the same year, a new form of protest developed: some groups of commuters from Fiat Rivalta in Turin decided to self-reduce the price of public transport. Their example spread rapidly throughout the Piemonte region, spreading to Enel (power) and Sip (telephone) bills. In the winter of 1974-75, this form of protest spread to the whole of Central and Northern Italy, involving hundreds of thousands of people. These forms of "illegal" protest were supported by the peripheral structures of the union and all the revolutionary groups, while the central structure of the union and the Communist Party condemned the movement as adventurist. *Storia d'Italia…*, op. cit.

[146] After a few days the Red Brigades distributed a statement in which they claimed all the attacks. The leaflet concluded: "Even Polifroni Filippo, via Fiume 37 in Sesto San Giovanni, received a visit from a group of the Red Brigades, and even though his car was miraculously not destroyed, the warning is equally clear for him. He is the chief of staff of the Magneti Marelli Crescenzago staff and stubbornly continues his anti-worker policy despite repeated reminders that the workers have made, by going in procession to "find" him in his office." Quoted in *Il terrorismo in fabbrica*, op. cit.

The Workers Committee and *Senza tregua*

In this period Lotta continua began to take a position in favour of trade union "'entryism" and to structure itself like a party, sparking controversy from its worker members because of its organizational roots, which claimed "we are all delegates" as the unifying slogan and that unions were enemies of the workers.

Within the Sesto section Secretary Robertino Rosso was elected, reinforcing the radical wing, which was already a majority of this section.

At the end of '74 and during the Lotta continua Provincial (Lombardy) Congress, the Lotta continua militants of Marelli and Sesto announced that if there are no changes in the line about party and union questions at the national level, they would leave the organization immediately after the National Congress held in Rome in January 1975.

Meanwhile, in the Sesto section the idea took hold of the exercise of violence in a direct and self-organized way, and, after leaving Lotta Continua, many of those who were pushing for this armed hypothesis stopped playing at politics to dedicate their energy to violence.[147]

During the Lotta Continua National Congress in 1975, the Workers' Committees of Sesto San Giovanni (Falck, Breda), of Magneti Marelli Crescenzago, of Telettra of Vimercate and the Committee of the Casoretto quarter of Milan all left the organisation. Together with another group, the product of the slow dissolution of *Potere operaio*, they would create *Senza tregua* ("Without truce"), perhaps the most traditionally "operaist" of the Autonomia experiences, very concerned with the topic of the "workers' decree"[148] and prone to discourse on the "centrality of the factory." In Milan it was the second major pole of attraction, after the group close to the positions of the magazine *Rosso*.[149]

The flagship of the new cluster was formed by the Communist Committees of Carlo Erba in Rodano (Milan), Telettra in Vimercate (Milan) and the new one in Magneti Marelli Crescenzago. In a document dated April 1975 they

---

147 *L'orda d'oro*, op. cit. p. 326

148 The "workers' decree" is a global formula opposed to traditional "workers' control," put forward by political groups, and workers' committees. It expresses the capacity for workers to impose concrete measures of their own dictatorship, which are not submitted to capital and its valorisation. Thus, the systematic introduction of workers made redundant into the factory or even the imposition of a workers' command over production by the capillary destruction of the apparatus of management and boss's control. Other examples of "workers' decree" are: the abolition of overtime or of the relation between real work and the wage; the reappropriation or destruction of commodities; the conquest of control over areas against the structures of surveillance and state containment, etc.

149 Lucio Castellano, *Aut. Op. La storia e I documenti*, Savelli, 1980, p. 111

made a point about *"The characteristics of the movement of struggle and our tasks."* The rift that had formed in the relationship between the labour movement and the unions was formally identified by the unnecessary strike of 24 July 1974 and the acceptance by the unions of a big decree by the Rumor government. The Committees defined the phase as pre-revolutionary and emphasised the political continuity of the movement, even though "the working class has not yet expressed a revolutionary will."

The characterisation of the period as pre-revolutionary is based "not on an economic analysis fixed by the possibility of the expansion or recession of capital, but on the basis of the class struggle under way and the political characteristics which the proletariat has in this fight and which are growing in this fight." The high degree of autonomy "is now the practical and necessary condition where the fight takes place and develops." Struggles to which they refer are antifascist ones ("the open fight in the streets of the working class in Milan on Friday 7 March [1975],[150] against an attempted neo-fascist provocation"), but also "the struggle of the unemployed in the South because of the structure of the shipyards, the workers' struggle at Italsider and SIR, the department struggles at Fiat, the struggle for wages and category transfers in small factories, preventive struggles against the *Cassa integrazione*, the return of suspended workers into Magneti Marelli – with the far-reaching political inspiration and perspective that it carries – and, with more or less clarity and autonomy, in other factories, at Alemagna, Siemens, etc. up until the Carlo Erba, struggles against the wave of repression in the schools brought about by the division of the movement, the ministerial decrees, the social "normalisation" (parental intervention) of both students and teachers, the struggles in the neighbourhoods, the occupation of the houses." These struggles have "a

---

150 On 7 March 1975, after the announcement of a meeting of the MSI in Piazza San Carlo, in just over an hour fifteen thousand Milanese workers mobilised to stop it. Dozens of marches organized by trade unions and revolutionary organizations were concentrated in Via Mascagni, outside the headquarters of the ANPI (National Association of Italian Partisans – a partisan veterans charitable foundation), which hosted a meeting of the general secretary of UIL, Polotti. The initiative came from the factories of Leyland-Innocenti, Pirelli and Borletti. The demonstration started marching by via Borgogna, Piazza San Babila, Corso Monforte and returns to via Mascagni where the provincial president of the ANPI Tino Casali made a speech. The revolutionary organisations continued with the procession, during which there were some incidents and "punishments" of fascists. *Corriere della Sera*, "Anti-fascist demonstration in the city centre, thousands of workers walk out of the factories," 8 March 1975

character less and less about demands and are more and more political and demonstrate the determination to fight and to organise themselves."[151]

The programme for the labour movement proposed by the trade unions and Communist Party had failed, but the working class had absolutely no need of it. The Workers' Committees proposed the resumption of struggle in every sector of the proletariat as the first point of the program, together with the continuity of the struggle and the autonomy of its contents, to arrive at the "disruption of the Confindustria/unions repressive balance," against the Historic Compromise and restructuring. Therefore, preventive strikes against the *Cassa integrazione* – as at Magneti Marelli, workshop-level strikes, but, above all, all the strikes disconnected from the national and local contractual negotiation process were important.[152]

The Committees rejected accusations of being corporatist, arguing that "the only corporatist force is social democracy with its political and trade union programme" that ensures "opposition between sectors of the proletariat" (employed and unemployed, manual and intellectual labour, private and public employees, schools and neighbourhoods). Nothing can guarantee a general organisation that represents the programme of the movement, and that is why local struggles are important. The factory and the territory "are the first political domains in which the movement of struggle expresses its programme in concrete terms and therefore enriches it."

The political framework in which the movement had to fight was conditioned by the national and international bosses' objective "to politically destroy the levels of consciousness and organisation achieved by the working class." This plan was carried out by "the encirclement of the big factory" via the attack on employment in small factories, the massive use of overtime, political sackings, division between workers and non-workers, tax increases, the reduction of wages and the division of the working class through the use of the *Cassa integrazione* (a sort of "State wage"), but also "thanks to the practice and the repressive interventions of social democratic functionaries, within a union that you can no longer even accuse of 'treason' because it acts only as a counterpart of the boss, as a partisan of the logic of repression and informing."[153]

The Communist Party proposed the "Historic Compromise," but it was an illusory proposal, since it was based "on the possibility for the planning of capital, on its balanced development, on the cooperation of the working class

---

151 "Linea di condotta," *Documento*, only edition, 1975
152 Ibid
153 Ibid

in the normalisation of the capitalist crisis, through its further sacrifices, its further divisions, the increase of exploitation."[154]

According to the Communist Committee for Workers Power, *"the centre of our initiative is the factory,"* so their job is to *"create workers' power in the factory, to extend workers' power from the factory to the territory."* From this it follows that the focus of the workers' programme is the refusal of restructuring, while the privileged form of struggle is the autonomous and preventive strike. The organisational forms must be the Workers' Committee of the department, with its levels of autonomy, its overall political tasks, and the Communist Committee of the factory as a revolutionary organisational structure.

Territorial worker activity ["attivo" (meeting)] was the political and organisational model proposed by the Communist Committees as a unitary venue for discussion and joint action.

At the heart of their initiatives, the Committees placed militant anti-fascism *"in the rejection of parliamentary and constitutional mediations."*[155]

> The principles and the practice of workers' power in the territory will be extended based on the already practiced initiatives in autumn (against overtime, closed and occupied factories, external expansion of the fight against restructuring) and already seen in this new powerful tool of the masses and the vanguard that is the 'workers' patrol.' Territorial patrols and squads, external demonstrations, mass picketing, will expand and organise themselves, but the territory will be the ground for new experiences of struggle and new levels of political organisation. Anti-fascist militancy and the prevention of state attacks, the attack against the centres of provocation, the unification of the weak sectors under the political hegemony of the class, new goals such as political prices, new matters of urgency such as those posed by the school and neighbourhood struggles. Factory platform, workshop platform, territorial platform.

Mobilisation against "the state, the fascists, the laws on public order, internationalist mobilisation, all these struggles are part of the same programme that defines struggles for wages, for categories, against restructuring and against the suspension of workers."[156] The Committees do not favour any political and organisational point of reference in the current situation, but want to open

---

154 Ibid
155 Ibid
156 Ibid

the debate *"on the national and international situation, the concrete process of formation of the party."*[157]

The composition of *Senza tregua* was heterogeneous and therefore destined to fragment. The Committees gained more weight in the political reality of Milan's factories (Magneti Marelli, Carlo Erba, Sit Siemens, Telettra, Falck, Breda), neighbourhoods (Ticinese, the southern part, Romana, Sempione), hinterlands (Rozzano, Gratosoglio, Cinisello Balsamo, Cormano), up to Desio, Sesto San Giovanni (the *Senza tregua* office was in Via Marsala), Bergamo and Brescia. From here, the area was expanding to reach other parts of Italy, especially Turin, Florence (the Committee of the Architecture Faculty), Bologna, Rome, and Naples (where there were two poles: the group of Pomigliano d'Arco coming out of Lotta Continua and the Workers' Collective of Aeritalia). Initially there was also Genoa, with part of the student movement, but it did not adhere to the project.[158] But the place of greatest strength of the Workers' Committees was undoubtedly the Magneti Marelli Crescenzago.

Corporate restructuring

In those years, the company went from being an "independent" factory to being "integrated" into the related activities of the Fiat group, with a swirl of people at the top of the company. Since 1974, the company had tried to implement in all of its plants a deep restructuring "by resorting to the traditional means of employers: *Cassa integrazione*, hiring freezes, transfer of whole departments, increasing pace of work. But the boss was facing a working class characterised by a high degree of political consciousness and militancy which (especially in the Crescenzago plant) was implementing a wide and constant mobilisation against these manoeuvres. These were the workers who, rejecting the concept of union delegation, were the protagonists in the forefront of all struggles and who recognised as their real vanguard those comrades who know how to give their organisations a concrete synthesis of demands and politics."[159]

The process of restructuring, long studied by Fiat, served on the one hand to gain global market share for automotive components and the other to

---

[157] Ibid

[158] Guicciardi, *Il tempo del furore*, Rusconi, 1988, p.10 and Procura della Rapubblica di Milano, *Requisitoria del pubblico ministero Armando Spataro dell'11 luglio 1981 relativa ai procedimenti n. 921/80 F G. I. e n. 228/81 F G. I.*, p. 833 and Interrogation of Roberto Sandalo in front of Ufficio istruzione in Turin, 21 May 1980

[159] "Gli operai e la giustizia," *Lo scontro di classe investe l'istituzione giudiziaria* ("The class struggle invades the judicial institution"), 12 Nov 1976

destroy the strength of the organised workers in Crescenzago. "The boss tries to increase productivity wherever the opportunity arises. It does not matter if the market demands it or not, the important thing is that the amount of output per worker increases. This applies both to the workshops and the offices." Hiring was frozen. In the office sector, "terminals, recording and mechanised processing of information were the order of the day. But ultimately that means a drastic reduction of staff." It also assists the relocation of work (with consequent strong increase in productivity) from one part of the company to another: for example, high voltage coils went from the Crescenzago plant to that of Alessandria, starter motors going to Potenza. To protest against these methods, the workers of the Committee blocked a truck leaving from Crescenzago to go to the Potenza plant, the workers not only confiscated the material from the truck, but also ensured that the office was not ready to send other material.[160]

The main card that Magneti Marelli played, however, was the *Cassa integrazione*. The Workers' Committee began to raise awareness among workers against the procedure of *Cassa integrazione*, defined as a complementary tool to the redundancies that take place in small factories and seen as an "instrument of exhaustion of factory workers that reduces them to simple individuals and not a collectivity."[161]

At the end of 1974, the Magneti management "offered a long non-working bridge [layoff period], except for a hundred or so workers who had to come to the factory and do overtime," a form of work abolished elsewhere by hard struggles in the factories in Milan. The provincial trade union signed the agreement on the bridge, but in the factory it was rejected. For the workers of Lotta Continua these "bridges" were "*Cassa integrazione* that workers pay for with their own money (in anticipation of the holidays of '75 and using the holidays falling on Saturday and Sunday)."

In this way the bosses propose:

1. using the days when the factory is closed for immediate restructuring (relocation, new machines with fewer workers, getting rid of machines and jobs), and
2. producing as they require: in winter we produce less, then we close; in spring we produce more, and then work on Saturday and Sunday with time off in lieu, and

---

160   Document: "3 years of fighting at Magneti Marelli Crescenzago," by Communist Workers Committee of Magneti Marelli, 1977, in *Lotta Continua*, 30 July 1977, p. 8 and *4 anni di lotta*, op.cit.

161   *4 anni di lotta*, op. cit.

3. emptying of factories for several days to allow the new government room for manoeuvre and perhaps, with the workers out of the way, to enable it to put forward a new Decree;
4. leaving room for internal conflicts within the Christian Democrat and social-democratic military hierarchies who continue with the threat of a coup.

For Lotta Continua it was logical to extend the struggle against the "bridges," accepted by the Factory Council, and against overtime: "workers of the big factories must be in charge of organising 'workers' patrols' and picketing on Saturday morning in front of the small and medium-sized factories where perhaps work is subcontracted by Magneti." It was also necessary to think about the practice of political prices, which, for example, meant "going mass shopping at the supermarket, paying for basic necessities at last year's prices." On 16 October, at Assolombarda, the company and unions reached a possible settlement of the Magneti Marelli dispute. For Lotta continua there was too much disparity between what was demanded by the workers and what they obtained: increases of production bonuses and summer bonuses were reduced and staged in over two years, and not in the current year as the workers wanted.

The workers of Lotta continua challenged the agreement, especially because, as they said, "our strength and our unity are growing, the fight is getting harder and more acute." During the strike in the Milan factories on 17 October, the workers of Lotta Continua at Magneti Marelli called for: the rejection of the *Cassa integrazione*; guaranteed wages for the unemployed; the indexing of pensions to wages; the consolidation at the highest level for all categories; political prices of essential goods and services. On 22 October in the Marelli Group there were strikes, demonstrations and meetings against the *Cassa integrazione*, against the fascist murderers, for the outlawing of the MSI and against the arrests of proletarians involved in imposing price reductions in a supermarket in Via Padova in Milan.[162]

To win it was crucial to find unity between workers and white-collar employees, equally affected by the restructuring of Magneti Marelli:

---

162 Ibid. and Leaflet: "No to the instrumental use of government crisis – No to the Cassa integrazione. General struggle!," Lotta continua, 8 October 1974, and leaflet: "No to the bridges! Against overtime! Workers' patrol on Saturday!," Lotta continua, 14 October 1974, and leaflet: "The struggle must pay!," Lotta continua, 17 October 1974, and leaflet: "Against the boss's blackmail of *Casa integrazione* and early elections," Lotta Continua, 15 October 1974, and leaflet: "Relaunch the struggle," Lotta Continua, 22 October 1974

We can appreciate right now, in every office, the productive vision of the bourgeoisie:

- surveillance by a swarm of big and little bosses thanks to the restructuring in every office,
- the militarization of the hierarchy that today no longer has the task of "guiding production and work," but that of pressure, control and denunciation,
- the daily threat of *Cassa integrazione* in the workshops and offices, and the threat of unemployment hanging over those looking for work,
- control of sickness breaks, constant reminders at work, control even during the supposed 'physiological breaks' from the workbench.

Although the strikes had been taking place in a diffuse way for years, the company level struggle began to draw in employees in plant "A" (blocking the gates, overtime ban, participation in the mobilisation on the streets) and those in the offices of plant "N" around category issues.[163]

For Lotta continua the boss's restructuring plan also went via the "bridges" demanded by Fiat, which became a way "to remove the workers from the factories every three months, sending them on a political vacation," to break their programme of struggle and destroy their organization, "dividing teams and departments with transfers by the thousand." Lotta continua's workers complained that the main targets of the bosses' attack were the Magneti Crescenzago second and third sections:

> the ongoing repression in the second section, where a dozen letters of suspension have already arrived, is not the initiative of the reactionary leaders who are raising their heads again. It is a clear choice from the head office of Fiat which, through Polifroni [Head of Personnel, see above], decided on a mass repression to launch the more decisive attack that aims to reimpose work and discipline on the workers, giving the power back to managers over deciding categories, and to deploy more machines, but especially to subdue the young workers who were the protagonists of the previous struggles.

---

163 Leaflet: "A general struggle and a factory fight, of all workers!," Lotta continua, 29 October 1974.

This was compounded by the goal of drastically reducing the size of the workforce by a hiring freeze and the expulsion of female labour through the imposition of shift working and shifting traditionally female work to other plants.

For 10 December the workers of Lotta continua proposed a work stoppage with a march inside the factory to protest against the agreed framework between boss and unions (which provided for the "bridge"), and against the letters of suspension: a march of the "vanguard" as well as internal demonstrations for each shift which "have swept the factory and visited the management... Now the boss knows that we can, we want to and we know how to move and fight. The revisionists know it as well." Lotta Continua workers were aware that the boss's plan was the same in all the factories, in all industries, "they want the dismantling of entire sectors of workers," the workers' defeat was the real goal of the industrialists. Before Christmas, the company imposed the *Cassa integrazione* at the Crescenzago plant while guaranteeing 93% of the wage, unleashing the first attack on the plant, relying on the fact that "at this time it's easy for everyone to be at home for a few days." The Lotta Continua Workers' Nucleus rejected the calls for *Cassa integrazione* so as to "ensure workers' vigilance in all departments against restructuring. With the factory empty it is easier for the boss to push ahead with restructuring with the movement and transfer of other work from the factory, attempts we have already seen in every department with the increase in the pace of work, work on several machines, work on the assembly line for the transition to the fourth level or wanting workers to work on 30 machines as in the third section, the dismemberment of the Regulators department and the introduction of shifts in the fourth section." On 15 December, a demonstration took place inside the second section against the *Cassa integrazione*.[164]

The Workers' Committee decided to put forward workshop platforms for "humanisation of work" that offered: reduced pace of work, more breaks, category promotions for women and the fight against toxic working conditions. In January initiatives in this area began: the female workers on the lines took breaks, all departments decreased performance, workers carried out an extensive analysis of dangerous machinery. ENPI (national accident prevention body) inspectors were taken by the workers to all departments and "their

---

164 Leaflet: "Against the Agnelli bridges and Magneti restructuring and repression, let's resume the initiative" , Lotta Continua, 1 December 1974, and leaflet: "Restructuring and repression shall not pass!," Lotta continua, 10 December 1974, and leaflet: "Continue the fight, organize the fight: this is the only guarantee!," Lotta continua, 12 December 1974, and leaflet: "Reject the *Cassa integrazione!,*" Nucleo operaio of Lotta Continua, 15 December 1974

formal visit turns into a week of workers' power. Self-organized groups of workers take the inspectors to the factory entrances, lead them into the workshops, and make them record all the deficiencies of the workplace and succeed in imposing new protective measures for their health. The results were not long in coming: heavy fines on Marelli, investment of hundreds of millions for safety, improved workers awareness."[165]

"Drive the delegates out of the 'bosses' palace'!"

The management attacked, announcing *Cassa integrazione* for twenty days for the two departments employing women in Crescenzago, for the plants in Vasto (automotive), Alessandria, Turin, Pavia and five days for the rest of the Group. For the Communist Committee in Magneti, *Cassa integrazione* "is a weapon in the hands of the bosses to secure division, uncertainty, and to threaten workers, while laying them off, blocking recruitment, increasing exploitation." The bosses "give us a bit of money today in exchange for isolating workers (starting with women workers), the destruction of our strength in the workshops, the opposition between the employed and unemployed, the division between large and small factories (the latter just close and *basta!* [enough]), then they reopen with homeworking, with the artisan's workshop."[166] There was no room to negotiate on *Cassa integrazione* as indeed was demonstrated by similar struggles of workers from the nearby factories Ercole Marelli and Falck. While the Crescenzago workshops had been fighting for a week, the Factory Council remained in the Assolombarda office to negotiate with management instead of appearing on the assembly lines and in the workshops: "What are we dealing with? On *Cassa integrazione* there can be no discussion! Drive out delegates from the "bosses' palace"! Out of the Assolombarda and inside the factory to address the workers' debate!" The Communist Committee organised a demonstration on 7 February inside the factory and prepared a general assembly.[167]

The provincial trade union organisation accepted the proposal from the management, but worker opposition was total, and for the Communist Committee "whoever supports the boss's discourse of dismantling struggles and dividing the workers is exposed as fully opposed to the very growth of

---

165 *4 anni di lotta*, op. cit.
166 Leaflet: 'No to Cassa integrazione/ unemployment! No to the boss's attempt to destroy the workforce!," Magneti Communist Committee, 27 Jan 1975
167 Leaflet: "Continue and extend the workers' struggle against the boss's provocation of *Cassa integrazione!*," Magneti Communist Committee, 3 Feb 1975, and leaflet: "Prepare the General Assembly! For the unity of the whole factory," Magneti Communist Committee, 7 Feb 1975

the struggle itself." Workshop assemblies had to transform themselves into one big general meeting to stabilise the new forms of struggle. The struggle must leave the factory and join the Crescenzago fight to similar struggles, such as at Falck Unione where the bosses had suspended dozens of workers and wanted to impose Saturday working in the rolling mill while demanding the *Cassa integrazione* for the same workshop. The Committee intended to "visit" the management offices in Sesto San Giovanni to see "how they are made, these offices which are planning unemployment for the workers and the dismantling of our strength" and to respond directly to requests for *Cassa integrazione*.[168]

The fight got tough, and for the first time women organised themselves to get re-entry into the factory (management had suspended a thousand of the 1,800 women who worked in Magneti), and their demos snaked around the factory. The first day of *Cassa integrazione*, 900 suspended women organised themselves without union leaders and delegates and, at 8 a.m., entered the factory. "The joy of overcoming their fear and the bosses' threats was written on their faces. They walked around the factory in procession, a hundred or so workers who had not been suspended joined the others. 2,000-strong they invade the offices: the managers (pigs and cowards) had fled." The first assembly without the union took place inside the factory.

> The management cannot help but take note of the worker response and consequently withdraws the *Cassa integrazione*. This worker response was despite the fact that the union had already accepted it at the provincial level. The return into the factory had been preceded by numerous marches on the management offices, demonstrating that the strength that the bosses had wanted to break was organised and had fed the debate in the workshops on a few points: you don't discuss the *Cassa integrazione*, the agreement that the union signed on restructuring goes against the interests of workers, and the only way to counter it is to fight it before it is introduced. Then, when the boss tries to implement it, the strength which is capable of opposing

---

168   Leaflet: "Put the bosses in *Cassa integrazione!*," Magneti Communist Committee, 10 Feb 1975, and leaflet: "Go directly to tell the boss that the *Cassa integrazione* is not happening!'," Magneti Communist Committee, 13 Feb 1975, and leaflet: "Exit the factory and hit the management at Sesto! Exit from the affected areas and unite the workforce!," Magneti Communist Committee, 17 Feb 1975, and leaflet: "Reject the union compromise on layoffs," Magneti Communist Committee, 3 March 1975.

it is already formed and sufficient to repel it. The leaders remained invisible in those days.[169]

On 13 February, several revolver shots were fired at the garage and the car of the director of the Crescenzago plant, engineer Franco Tacchini. The attack was claimed by the Red Brigades.[170]

The Communist Committee of the factory exalted the "preventive offensive mobilisation" of the working class in Milan that took to the streets on 7 March, with 30,000 workers showing what had been built in the last month in the factories, schools and neighbourhoods,

> against the overall plan of capital... by workers' patrols (to unite and open up factories isolated by scabs and Saturday working), by the refusal of the *Cassa integrazione*, by the refusal to abandon the struggle and to increase profits behind the bosses' and revisionists' 'guarantees' on the new economic development and new political balance. The struggle is prepared, is organised, has built up its strength, and now comes naturally to the streets against the gangs of capital, against the bosses' state![171]

On 13 March, three hundred workers (men and women) of the fourth and fifth departments enter the factory despite being put on *Cassa integrazione*. As had happened the previous week, a march of 500 workers went into the streets of Crescenzago and nearby neighbourhoods, taking their demands beyond the factory gates. The *Cassa integrazione* was seen as justified by the crisis in the automotive sector and was accepted by the National Coordination of the Factory Councils in the Magneti Marelli Group but rejected by the Factory Council of the Crescenzago plant, which called on the workers to mobilise against the use of job replacements to control breaks and the pace of work in workshops where *Cassa integrazione*, control of machines and investment had been proposed.[172]

---

169 Document "Workers and the state," Magneti Communist Committee, 1977, and *Controinformazione*, "Marelli: The Red Guard tells its story," no. 17, January 1980, p. 24 and "Four years of struggle," op. cit.
170 *Terrorismo in fabbrica*, op. cit.
171 Leaflet: "From the factory to the square: 30,000 workers in Milan against the new level of the boss's attack!," Communist Factory Committees, 10 Feb 1975.
172 *Quotidiano dei lavoratori*[Workers' Daily], "Exemplary mobilization at Magneti M.," 14 Feb 1975

On 14 March 1975, there were "acts of vandalism and destruction against the office of the director of the Crescenzago plant."[173]

On 17 March there was a general strike in Sesto San Giovanni to boost the fight in the streets and in the factory. The workers responded to the attacks of the bosses and the class "practiced arming itself in the indoor demonstrations, in worker patrols, in pickets, in the destruction of the fascist headquarters, in big mass mobilisations." The slogans were:

1. the 12,000 lire of personal increases that the infamous union-boss agreement (attendance bonus) has brought has divided us over pay, creating a dangerous precedent,
2. the return of all suspended workers (Magneti Falck, Arduini, Camptel, La Fiaba, etc.), preventative strikes against any bosses' demand for suspensions,
3. workers' organisation in the workshops against transfers, suspensions, hierarchy,
4. territorial worker organization. The resumption of the struggle around wages and against production in subcontracted workshops and small factories,
5. the refusal of the laws on order, weapons and preventive detention.[174]

In the early months of 1975 the work of consolidation of the Communist Committees for Workers' Power (a group coming out of Potere Operaio founded in 1975) aimed at a "proletarian expropriation" of the UPIM (a department store) in Cologno Monzese ("we invited people there to leave with goods without paying, we also brought out our shopping cart to show that some people were openly taking goods so that the people following would take stuff without paying"). "Political" events like these had already taken place in 1974, at Quarto Oggiaro and in Via Padova, Milan.[175]

---

[173] Letter from Domenico La Monica to the judge Forno, Sesto San Giovanni, 3 Dec 1976, quoted in *Controinformazione*, n. 17, January 1980, p. 24. These facts, along with two attacks by the Red Brigades, were reported by the company on 28 March 1975 in a complaint to the Commissioner of Greco Turro.

[174] Leaflet: "At the Sesto general strike, on Friday 7 March, we bring the worker programme to the streets," Communist Factory Committees, 17 March 1975.

[175] Guicciardi, *op. Cit.*, p. 62 testimony of Costa. On the morning of Saturday 19 October 1974, there were two incidents of "political shopping" in the supermarket SMA on via Padova and the Esselunga in Quarto Oggiaro, two neighbourhoods in Milan. In the supermarkets, once at the tills, the customers met "young men determined to impose

At the same time a nationwide struggle around the self-reduction of transport tickets achieved a notable success, and even the support of the union, which activated a series of territorial networks for collecting self-reduced tickets.[176] This form of struggle created a broad debate about the meaning of legality within mass struggles, on how to determine which behaviours are necessary and desirable to obtain concrete results. At the same time "patrols" against overtime were organised in the factories in Milan.

---

the old prices of the goods, inviting people to self-reduction." Outside the supermarkets other youths, women and workers of the district put forward slogans like: "If prices go up, let's take the goods and not pay more." The discount was 10-15%. The police were called and a patrol of 30 cops arrived, followed by *Carabinieri* and other forces of repression. "This time not even the system's press could deny it, the extremists were all women sick from fatigue and poor nutrition, young immigrants affected by unemployment and poverty, adolescents which capitalist welfare has subjected to child labour and absolutely insufficient food." There were numerous injuries and arrests, and the value of the goods expropriated was about four million lire. A leaflet distributed in Quarto Oggiaro reads: "the goods that we have taken are ours, as is everything that exists because we have made it with our exploitation. This is a political lesson that should be recorded, understood and perfected. This is not civil disobedience, not 'getting by,' not sub-proletarian rage, but an active embryo of political struggle against exploitation, parallel to that of the factory."

This initiative was part of the contemporary self-reduction campaign that took place throughout the national territory against the dramatic increase in the cost of living happening over the previous year, a campaign organized by FLM and concerned with various bills for public services (electricity, gas, transport, rent). In Via Padova 11 people were arrested, including a member of the executive of the Factory Council of Clement, a representative of the Factory Council of Magneti Marelli, another four workers, three employees and two housewives. A committee was created to free the arrested people, and it placed itself at the head of the popular struggles that, on 27 October, organised a popular assembly at the Liberty hall in Largo Marinai d'Italia in Milan to prepare for the day of action on 29 October, the day of the summary trial. The promoters of the assembly were numerous Factory Councils, Struggle Committees and Collectives in the Milan area. *Controinformazione, La spesa politica* ("Political shopping"), no. 5-6, November 1974.

176 This practice was initiated by the base committee of ATM (the public transit network in Milan), in liaison with other Workers' Committees in the region. The principle was that workers must not pay for going to be exploited. Concretely, when the workers took the bus or tram they paid half price, with the agreement of the conductor, a member of the committee of ATM. The CGIL was not hostile and supported its generalisation to the whole of Italy, issuing "self-reduced" tickets which it would collect afterwards from the conductors to assess the scale of the phenomenon.

The "April Days"

In this period, the most important politico-military action was represented by the so-called "April Days": three days of very hard fighting throughout Italy, especially in Milan, where there were numerous attempts to storm the city headquarters of the MSI, with enormous mass mobilisations.

During the protest demonstration against the murder of Claudio Varalli, a day on which Giannino Zibecchi also died, the militants of the committees that had left Lotta Continua were able to take the extremist workers with them. The worker left, grouped behind the banner of the Sesto factories, managed to gather workers from other factories, thus encountering other experiences that already identified themselves as belonging to *Autonomia operaia*, such as the militants of the Workers' Political Collectives or the workers of the autonomous assembly of Alfa Romeo. It was the proof that the worker left in Milan existed as a political subject.[177]

---

177 The "April Days" in Milan: in Piazza Cavour, near the police station at about 19:30 on 16 April 1975 the fascist Antonio Braggion shot dead seventeen-year-old Claudio Varalli, a militant of *Movimento lavoratori per il socialism*. "He returned, with a group of his comrades from a protest against the eviction by the police of occupied houses on Corso Garibaldi (the Casa albergo)... The fascists in a car, a Mini minor (but there was another car nearby, a Volkswagen) accosted the comrades. There were three of them, with a Doberman dog. They yelled something... A most vulgar provocation, which the comrades, including Claudio, responded to by surrounding the Mini. Some glass was shattered. Suddenly they heard the first shots. The fascist who was driving, Antonio Braggion, shot the first time from inside the car, putting a hole in a door, but without hurting anyone. Then he got out and, coldly, with a big 7.65 calibre revolver, shot Claudio who was right in front of him in the head. The comrade falls. ... After a few moments of uncertainty, many people rushed to help Claudio, who was lying on the ground... Then they loaded him into an ambulance that went at full speed to the *Fatebenefratelli* hospital, just around the corner. But Claudio Varalli was already dead on arrival." *Quotidiano dei lavoratori*, "The murder of Claudio Varalli," 18 April 1975.

After *Il Giornale nuovo* came out, reporting a distorted version of the facts, comrades carried out a raid on the "Same" printers in Piazza Cavour, and stopped vans carrying the papers, broke windows, damaged machines and put the lift out of service. *Quotidiano dei lavoratori*, "The death of Claudio Varalli," 18 April 1975.

On the morning of 17 April in Milan, as elsewhere in Italy, there was a big student and worker demo with the participation of 50,000 people. The march went from via Larga in Piazza Cavour, through the city centre. There was a brief rally, after which there were two separate marches, one that went to the *corso XXII Marzo*, the other to the State University, then to the courthouse to be reunited with the other march. "The comrades attacked the Milan Federation of the MSI several times. Police and *Carabinieri* stationed on one side of via Mancini, tried to contain the people's anger by firing tear gas canisters that were picked up off the ground by comrades and immediately thrown back. The fascist head office suffered extensive damage: large plumes of black smoke rose ... At this point, from the beginning of Corso XXII Marzo, on the side of the piazza Cinque Giornate, a deadly carousel conducted by the police started [the *giostra* (carousel) is a common tactic used by the Italian police, consisting of driving vehicles in a circle to break up a crowd]... Almost immediately jeeps and trucks stormed into the street with sirens blaring, the lights on, at full speed... The soldiers fired wildly through the windows at the side of the road at the comrades who, to avoid the carousel, were forced to run along the walls." It was in this situation that 27-year-old physical education teacher and activist of the Antifascist Vigilance Committee (Ticinese district) Giannino Zibecchi was run over and killed by a police truck. In via Caminadella the MSI lawyer, Cesare Biglia, was beaten. In Viale Premuda the secretary of CISNAL, Rodolfo Mersi, was beaten up. There were attacks on the office of "Lo Specchio" and the Alemagna pub was burned, in Via Manzoni, on the corner of Via Croce Rossa. The windows of the stationery shop belonging to the fascist Carlo Sala were broken. The offices of the MSI in via Murillo and in via Guerrini were attacked. The windows of the Iberia airline were broken. Molotov cocktails were thrown at the fascist bar *Gin rosa* and another one in via Borgogna, the bar *Doria di Città* "needed complete renovation." Six Molotov cocktails were thrown at the social housing office in Viale Romagna, and also at the Rusconi bookshop in via Turati, at the bar Rallj in Sesto San Giovanni ("known to be a meeting place for fascists").

On the evening of 18 April in Turin, a comrade of Lotta Continua, Tonino Miccichè, aged 23, was killed by the security guard Paolo Fiocco. The guard was a sympathiser of the right and wanted to use the abandoned garage of a squatted house, while the Housing Struggle Committee wanted to use it as its headquarters. That day a violent argument had broken out between the security guard and a group of members of the Committee, during which Fiocco pulled out a gun and fatally shot Miccichè in the left eye. Immediately he ran away.

Protest rallies were held throughout Italy, but the most violent ones were once again in Milan. "Dozens of demonstrations, big and small, moving from the early hours of the day flowing into Piazza del Duomo, where the gathering was expected to take place. From there goes a procession that winds for hours through the hot spots for two days. During the procession they broke into the Moquito bar, where the police go, at the corner of piazza Fratelli Bandiera and via Pisacane, where they smashed up the furniture and set it on fire. They threw Molotov cocktails at the armoured door and on to the balcony of the apartment of Senator Gastone Nencioni, in corso di Porta Vittoria 32. They broke down the door and set fire to the office of the lawyer Benito Bollati, MSI deputy. They broke the windows of a car belonging to Mondialpol, the company which the murderer of Miccichè worked for. The broke into the office of CISNAL on the fourth floor of via delle Erbe, where Francesco Moratto was injured, and the office was set on fire. They

The comrades who followed Sesto and the Communist Committees understood the rapid evolution of the protests, and many of them joined the order service and got ready for confrontation. The comrades of the Committees were at the forefront of the fighting in those days in Milan. For them it was necessary to deal with the antifascist issue, to fight for possession of the streets and accentuate the political confrontation in the factories. On this occasion, the Committee's workers led the fight to launch the strike in the factories at Magneti Marelli and Sit-Siemens, and to go out into the streets in a determined way.[178]

For the occasion, a single issue of the magazine *Comunismo* came out, in which the editorial pointed out "the profound unity between the great mass mobilisations and the attacks carried out against the sites and offices of the fascist organisation": only newspapers such as *L'Unità* (the PCI daily) did not mention the events of 16 April, so as to avoid "digging a deep furrow between workers and police." For *Comunismo*, the position of the "revisionist" newspaper repeated the theory of the "extremists on both sides," which went back to speeches by Fanfani and Berlinguer, but had no basis in truth because "the violence of the proletarian and the communist cannot be in any way equivalent to the violence of the fascists, the bosses, the State!"[179]

The paper then analysed the long process of struggle that led to those days, similar to the guerrilla warfare and the insurrectionary wave which followed the attack on Togliatti in 1948, the occupation of land and the strikes in the fifties, the Genoese revolt of July 1960 (violent clashes with police during protests against the holding of an MSI Congress in the city) and Piazza Statuto in 1962 (the site of important confrontations between police and striking workers in Turin). All these struggles were able to "block the road to an authoritarian

---

destroyed another bar in Via Modena. The provincial headquarters of the PSDI [Italian Social Democratic Party, a split from the right of the PSI in 1948] on via Dogana 4, was devastated and the action was claimed by "Armed struggle for communism." There was another arson attack on the PSDI office in via mar Jonio, in the San Siro district, the most important one in the city with more than 1,200 members. At 23.00, during a similar protest march in Florence, the police killed a 28-year-old worker, Rodolfo Boschi, a member of the PCI.

The facts of this story are mentioned in: *Controinformazione*, "Internal war or class war?," N. 7-8, June 1976 and *Quotidiano dei lavoratori*, "Popular anger explodes in Milan against the fascists and the DC" and "Crushed under a police truck," 18 April 1975, "Milan: a flood," 19 April 1975 and "Florence: a comrade killed," 20/21 April 1975.

178 Leaflet:" "More ahead than on 7 March!," Communist Factory Committees, 21 April 1975, and "For the First of May," *Compagni* (Comrades), 29 April 1975.
179 *Comunismo*, "In the space of a week…," only edition, April 1975.

model of the management of the economy and capitalist society" based on confrontation with the workers and the harsh repression of class conflict. Thanks also to the post-war reconstruction, paid for entirely by the workers who had given permission to restart capital accumulation, there began in Italy the era of the "centre-left" and the reformist project that was to rationalise the Italian development model: "a certain wage dynamic, a certain social development, a higher standard of living of the mass of workers and the popular layers could be an element in the revival of their economy" through the development of domestic consumption. Conflicts were not repressed but regulated. The working class grew in number, but its strength to make demands, seizing an always bigger share of the wealth that it produced and attaining an always greater social weight, imposed its own "political threat over the whole of society." But in 1968-69, this process "spilled over": "the working class comes to the fore as a political general subject, unified, increasingly aware of its own strength, conscious of its ability to make material and political gains, of the possibility of imposing its own autonomous needs, its own independent point of view in the face of the productive, social, institutional machine of the bosses." Militants that emerged in these struggles forced the unions to institutionalise this new social power.[180]

The response to this worker attack was the crisis, "created as an anti-worker terrorist operation, trying in the short term to break the insubordination of the class with the threat of unemployment and to make workers' autonomy respect the norms, and – if that's not enough – then it uses restructuring, as the deliberate destruction of productive forces and the seizure of wealth by the capitalists, in order to reduce the production base, create unemployment and have a profound effect on technical composition and the political structure of the working class. For capital it is a matter of shifting the balance of forces in its favour, thus overturning the workers' threat to the economy and capitalist power."

In this crisis, however, the deep gap between the economy and the needs of proletarians becomes obvious. For *Comunismo* this announces the "maturity of communism" because the mechanism of capital is broken, "its laws of operation no longer satisfy the demands of social development of the vast majority of people. There is no sense in making the vast majority of people pay the horrifying costs."

Capitalism is now in everybody's eyes "reduced to its nature as a machine dedicated to command over labour." Today everything can finally be called into question, inverted – "the slogan of the struggle against labour, the refusal of work, is beginning to mature. It offers the chance to break free from

---

180 Ibid

the compulsion to provide labour for wages, to freely express our needs, as a possibility to replace the production of goods in exchange for wages with the social production of all useful goods." What prevents the Communist victory? – "the existence of a subordinate aspect of the working class (the working class as labour power, as part of capital, as acceptance of the relationship of domination-profit) and thus the functioning of the social structure of its institutions of power, its political and military instruments." The task of communists therefore is to fight against these two elements that relate to the question of political power and its various forms: "Today the working class of the metropolis needs to build an intelligent and coordinated instrument to affirm their own needs, to exercise its dictatorship over the whole of society. Workers' autonomy today must become workers' power, as the process which progressively puts the communist project into practice."

We must build "a mass movement of the working class, entirely political because it seeks at the same time the destruction of its own power and the dissolution of the power of its adversary" a movement which "systematically re-appropriates social wealth and establishes the conditions that make it possible." It is not a matter of episodic acts but the consequence of "a new legality which consolidates itself, which organises itself in stable forms of power, armed against the enemy power, a process of civil war in acts and organisation through an organised structure, an internal hierarchisation, the existence of forms of direction of its action."

We pour scorn on the reformist organisations "who have had the task of defending the historical conditions of labour power in the capitalist mode of production and of containing conflicts within the framework of the general conditions of survival and reproduction," the working class must regain the offensive: real wages, working hours, prices, are the immediate objectives which imply the slogans of guaranteed income for all workers, organized self-reduction of working hours, the imposition of political prices, decided by the workers. To do this it is necessary to find appropriate forms of organisation: "the construction of a fighting party of workers for communism, an organisation capable of anticipating the determined and decisive path of disintegration, of breaking the machinery of the state and affirming the proletarian dictatorship, a network of political and military leadership of the movement on the terrain of revolutionary civil war, that can and must take place within a process of construction and organisation of a political class movement that contains these new features, which consolidates itself thanks to forms of the exercise of proletarian power which – so as not to grow as a subordinate appendage of the capitalist state – must assert itself as an armed force, with the systematic ability to launch attacks against the entire institutional articulation of capitalist power."[181]

In line with this hypothesis, some factories were building and strengthening organisational forms (workers' patrols, worker teams to maintain order, offensive marches) that were "able to challenge the control of the boss in the factory and the political and military control of the State over territory." It's now, they said, the time to build the "communist committees of worker and proletarian power in the factories, in the neighbourhoods."[182]

The "April Days" gave a new impetus to the extra-parliamentary groups in crisis, while accelerating the development of the area of Workers Autonomy, more and more structured. The Communist Committees in the factories published a journal that invited people to demonstrate on 1 May 1975 and analysed the events of April. For them, the murder of Claudio Varalli had triggered a chain reaction that the "groups" ended up submitting to, not being able to master them. In the Italian streets conflicts which had been maturing for many months exploded in an open, clear and violent manner. Anti-fascism was only one of its components. "These confrontations carried into the street the battle between the working class and capital over restructuring; between the proletariat and the state over prices and rents; between the movement of struggle and the political power of the bourgeoisie. All this accentuated the crisis of the traditional mediations of bourgeois political power, with the DC [Christian Democrats] at its head, and developed contradictions between the reactionary components, the use of fascist provocation and parallel bodies, and the authoritarian project, on which was founded the social and political area of the 'historic compromise'."[183]

---

181 Ibid

182 Ibid

183 The leader of the PCI, Enrico Berlinguer, published a long article in the weekly journal of the Party, *Rinascita* ("Rebirth"), entitled "Reflections on Italy after the events in Chile," in which he mentioned for the first time the "*compromesso storico*" ("Historic Compromise"). The proposal for compromise was confirmed and improved in his report to the Central Committee of the Communist Party in preparation for the XIV Congress in 1974. It concerned the analysis of the crisis of world capitalism, the problem of relations between the Italian political parties, and the Communist proposal for ending the crisis. *Rinascita*, 28 Sept 1973, 5 Oct 1973 and 9 Oct 1973 and *Relazione al Comitato centrale per il XIV congresso del PCI*, Rome, 10 December 1974 and *Relazione al XIV congresso del PCI*, Rome, 18/23 March 1974. Berlinguer had already anticipated the search for a new political relationship with the DC, see his *Relazione al XIII congresso del PCI*, Milan, 13/17 March 1972.

With the "revisionist control" chains broken, the PCI "behaved in a contradictory and uncertain manner that went from the commitment to repression assumed in 'Red Tuscany,' which it dared to express, in terms which could certainly be defined as social fascist, in the face of the murder of one of its own activists, Comrade Rodolfo Boschi, to the stupefied passivity with which it met the combative Red wave in the streets during the general strike."[184]

The phase that opened had no historical precedent, except that of July 1960, because "it served to push back a reactionary attempt by the bourgeoisie, but also opened up a new balance and a new regime of the bourgeoisie itself." On the contrary, the clashes in April 1975 marked the highest point in a confrontation lasting several months in which the workers' offensive was consolidated. The capitalist crisis deepened, while no new institutional and international equilibrium appeared. Faced with the power of the Christian Democrats there appeared to be no credible institutional alternative to the "historic compromise." The movement had an even less clear orientation, but it was hoped that it wouldn't fall into the hands of the reformists, as it did in 1960. During the general strike of 22 April "the reformists tried to use the workers' mobilisation as a moment of democratic solidarity, of support for the institutions of the republic founded on work," but "wide layers of workers made their slogan 'Arms for the Workers!'"

For the Committees, the "April Days" demonstrated to the working class the perspective of power, which necessitated some critical thinking about what had happened: "the workers' strength organised in the factories possessed a fighting capacity which was much less than that expressed in the struggles and mobilisations of recent months," despite the massive participation of some of the most militant factories in the protests in Milan. The battles of 17 and 18 April demonstrated that trade union demonstrations were a thing of the past, "the quality of the clashes went beyond all sectoral divisions. In the streets it wasn't factory or school nuclei which confronted the bosses' state but the advanced sectors of the working class and the entire proletarian movement."

This did not mean abandoning political work in the factories, but rather marked a qualitative leap, so that "the political battle with the crisis state and anti-worker violence" placed the workers at the head of the most significant struggles. The workers' strength, which had expressed itself in the workshops, must have "a class combat strength." Over the past years the most militant factory workers had dominated and directed the struggle during the contract renewal negotiations, which "determined the objectives and then generalised them to the whole movement to the point that even the unions were forced to take them up. In those struggles we have almost always seen the effective

---

184 "For the First of May," *Compagni*, 29 April 1975.

majority of workers in those factories showing a capacity for mobilisation with internal and external demonstrations, pickets, street mobilisation, blocking movement of goods, blocking the streets, deploying an accumulated strength in the daily battle against the organisation of work and for wages."

The Communist Committees asserted "the relevance of a leap forward in the strength and organisation of the class based on an attack on the factory hierarchy and the power of the boss, capable of conducting hard fights in the factory towards a worker hegemony over territory constructed on the basis of the communist programme and organisational implements to support and impose it on the struggle for the affirmation of the exercise of workers' power." The engine room of this must be the large factories. The Committees opposed the occupation of small factories against their restructuring and, on the contrary, wanted workers to get out of them. Here were the signposts for the struggle: "impose the withdrawal of any *Cassa Integrazione*, launch autonomous struggle, strikes, marches in the factory in response to any request for reduction of hours, wages or jobs; organise territorially the return to the factories of suspended workers and unemployed; eliminate all areas of provocation in the factory by neutralising the hierarchy; use the factory as an organisational base for outlawing the fascist centres of attack and provocation against the proletariat in the territory, and their organisational networks."

The crisis of governance of the bourgeoisie affected above all the Christian Democratic Party and its political initiative groups. The article concludes: "to the state respond with the appropriate weapons; to the revolutionary trend, to the will to power and communism living in the workers' and proletarian' struggles, give them the tools and the concrete programme. The capacity for attack and combat of the movement at this point is central, as is the transformation of traditional workers' strength into a deployed revolutionary force." This is why it was necessary to build Communist Committees for workers' power.[185]

The demonstration on 1 May 1975 coincided with the victory of Vietnam against US imperialism. The Communist Committees made a comparison with the previous Mayday which had been marked by the Chilean coup. On the one side there was the "massacre of proletarians and Chilean communists, disarmed by the reformist leadership," on the other "the realism of the 'criticism of weapons' has imposed itself as the only sure way to communicate with the class enemy!" The Communist Committees drew attention to the armed unity of proletarians and Portuguese soldiers against the two coup attempts following the revolution of 25 April 1974.[186]

---

185   Ibid

186   "For the First of May," "Class struggle, proletarian internationalism, in arms for communism," 29 April 1975. On 25 April 1974 the Armed Forces Movement (MFA), formed

The struggle spreads to other workplaces

At Magneti once again the restructuring plans aimed at the dismantling of the Klaxons workshop, the displacement of the Third section (to Potenza) and the Aeronautics workshop. Over the past year the company had already transferred a hundred or so workers from the Fourth section and the Regulators to other workshops. But, in the first days of May, they decided to reactivate the workshops and therefore to redeploy 50 women from the Klaxons workshop to the Fourth section and Regulators. In addition, the boss annulled the *Cassa integrazione* and wanted to transfer the whole of the Third section to the South. For the Communist of Magneti Marelli, this was a declaration of war:

1. No transfers in the workshops;
2. No movement of shifts;
3. The boss must not close or suspend lines, workshops or sections;
4. Our struggle is against restructuring, against the infamous laws, against the law "on weapons," because the working class must organise itself in an effective way against fascist provocation, police attacks, attempts to divide us, and the authoritarianism of the bosses;
5. Our struggle is preventive, we respond instantaneously, we do not isolate ourselves in the workshops and sections immediately affected, we unite Magneti with the other factories in Sesto.[187]

On 7 May, in the Klaxons departments and the Third section a sort of exhibition was prepared with signs illustrating the boss's plan, as well as banners, puppets and flags. "The 8 did not work because of the holiday; when the 9 was back, the first shift was surprised to find nothing left of this material. Immediately discussion began: we asked ourselves who could have done that and how to respond to this affront. There was no doubt that the perpetrators were the security guards at the factory because they were the only ones there, and that they had acted on management orders: so it was necessary then to all go together to the management and make them understand that at Magneti for several years we

---

by a number of officers and troops under the command of the various branches of the armed forces militarily occupied Lisbon and other major cities in Portugal, ending one of the oldest European dictatorships, that of Antonio de Oliveira Salazar who came to power in 1932. The military uprising went down in history as the "Carnation Revolution," as it was supported directly by the people who cheerfully invaded the streets and gave the soldiers red carnations.

187 Leaflet: "From department transfers to layoffs! From the *Cassa integrazione* to the closure of entire sections!," Magneti Marelli Communist Committee, 6 May 1974.

had conquered by force political spaces and habits that we had to preserve. So at 8 a.m. when the day shift came in, almost all of the two hundred workers present in that workshop, along with two hundred others from various workshops, went in demonstration to the office of the captain of the guards (Palmieri). He replied that he knew nothing about it. But, at the same time, the workers there found hidden bundles of posters, leaflets, banners, the fruit of years of spying on the workers." The blacklist files were burnt in the street. The workers, after warning that this would no longer be tolerated, returned to the department.[188]

The management submitted complaints to the police against ten workers, for assault, kidnapping, verbal threats and criminal damage. The workers in question were also suspended for three days, but the magistrate later dropped the charges. Of the suspended workers, four belonged to the Workers' Committee, four to *Democrazia proletaria* (an electoral party formed in 1975 as an alliance of several leftist parties and groups) and two were delegates of the PCI. According to the management: "on 9 May a group of employees invaded the office of the chief of security of Crescenzago; acts of violence were carried out against the same head of security and the chief of staff of the plant; part of the documents kept in the office were destroyed, either burnt or stolen by the protesters... on 13 May 1975 Mr. Tamburrini Giuseppe, a car-transporter train driver from Potenza, was attacked by unidentified employees."[189]

On 4 June, the car of the chief of personnel of the Crescenzago plant was set on fire. The action was claimed by the Red Brigades.

The summer of 1975 was characterised by the closure of many small factories in the area that were then occupied by the workers. Inside Magneti Marelli a cleaning company, Svelto, worked on a subcontract. Its workers went on strike for three days for the national contract and to be directly employed by

---

188   Document: *Operai e Sato*, Magneti Workers' Committee, 1977.

189   "Chronical of a trial," *Cronistoria*, February 1980 and letter "Domenico La Monica to the judge Forno," Sesto San Giovanni, 3 Dec 1976, in *Controinformazione*, n. 17, January 1980, p. 24. The facts were reported by the management on 16 May 1975 with a complaint sent to the Public Prosecutor of Milan at the beginning of the proceedings no. 15308/75 sec. I of the criminal court of the District Court of Milan, then passed to the PM 10713/75 and then given criminal case no. RG 3235/76 Inst. Following a union agreement reached with the Ministry of Labour with the mediation of the Secretary Mrs Tina Anselmi, Magneti Marelli sent a letter of 6 December 1975 to withdraw, "where procedurally possible," the facts presented, not to bring a civil lawsuit and to annul the complaint. Concerning the alleged assault on the driver during the confrontations, 16 May 1975, the management made a complaint to the Commissioner of Police of Greco-Turro.

Marelli. Already the workers' assemblies had discussed putting this demand into the platform of demands for the workplace.

> Finding the canteen more and more dirty the workers of Magneti direct their protests and their anger against the management which threatens the cleaning workers, and take action against the management of Magneti that, despite the strike, was able to get scabs to come at night to clean the offices, but not the two canteen halls. On 6 June there was a demonstration of cleaners with bags full of rubbish, joined by a hundred or so Magneti workers and all headed for the management offices. In each office, according to the quantity of waste that the management had had removed by the scabs, an equal volume of rubbish was put back, when it wasn't done according to quality. Magneti sent the usual letters to 5 workers. This demonstration was very popular and approved of by the majority of workers. It was transformed into a demonstration to management with all the delegates of the Factory Council. The letters were dropped, despite the Secretary of the PCI branch having grassed up the most active protesters.[190]

During the summer, taking advantage of the closure of the big factories, the bosses tried to forcibly evict a whole series of small occupied factories. The workers of the Magneti Marelli Workers' Committee participated actively in the meetings and the assemblies of the Struggle Committee of the occupied factories, particularly in the *Porta Romana* area of Milan. The first objective was to organize the resistance up until September, when the factories reopened. Fifty Magneti workers helped out with the strike in the Porta Romana area, during which a demonstration went to the Marino palace (seat of the Municipality of Milan) to demand financial support for the workers in struggle, especially those laid off from Pini metalli. They organised collections at a toll station on the motorway.[191]

In the autumn the Communist Committees applied the "workers' program" to the workers' struggles in the occupied factories, the fight against layoffs, the refusal of the *Cassa integrazione* and the relaunching of workers' demands at workshop level. This was the answer to the closure of small factories one after the other and to the mass layoffs announced at Innocenti, Imperial, Farma, Philco, SNIA, Alfa Romeo and Pirelli, where "the unions are trying to

---

190 *4 anni di lotte, 4 anni di rapporto*, op. cit.
191 Ibid

isolate struggles, and do dirty deals around restructuring and closure of plants. This happens in the small occupied factories, where the union guarantees the evacuation of the factory, and control of the finished product and goods in stock that workers want to sell to fund the fight. This happened at Philco in Bergamo, as at Pini in Porta Romana, and it is happening and will happen in Imperial and Innocenti."[192]

On 21 July, a delegation of Pini metalli workers presented themselves at the gates of Magneti, where they were greeted by dozens of workers on strike. They entered the factory and went into the workshops, collecting hundreds of thousands of lire. During lunch in the canteen, short meetings were held. "At 14.00, escorted by the workers of the first shift, the workers from the small factories left the factory, protected from any provocations by the guards and the police."[193] This political legacy "will remain in the workers' consciousness and will reproduce itself in militant support given to struggles in the years to come, a political heritage which first of all belongs to the workers, without delegation or institution." Management suspended (for two or three days) three workers of the Committee for trespassing and unauthorised demonstration and report them to the police. They do not accept the suspension measures and appeal to the magistrate who considers that the behaviour of the company violates trade union rights and cancels the suspension.[194]

Political layoffs

In September 1975, the company decided on a new tactic to downsize the Crescenzago plant. They re-proposed the transfer programme already rejected by the workers and the use of total *Cassa integrazione* for 800 workers, with the aim of preparing the ground. "They considered it necessary to eliminate first of all these vanguards so as to intimidate the entire workers' collectivity."[195] Provocation kicked in on 5 September 1975, at 14.00, when ten men of the second section were called to the office of the Director of Personnel,

---

192 Leaflet: *Comitati comunisti di fabbrica*, 21 July 1975.
193 *4 anni di lotte*, op. cit.
194 *Operai e Stato*, op. cit. And *4 anni di lotte*, op. Cit. The three suspended workers were Enrico Baglioni, Sergio Folloni and Antonio Reale, defended by the lawyers Giuliano Spazzali and Alberto Medina. In sentencing, the Milan magistrate, Massimo Trois, also stated that "the purpose of the visit, definitely of a union nature, was also socially commendable, since it sought to bring comfort to many workers at that time who were layed off." Cited in "Chronicle of a trial," annex no. 1, February 1980.
195 Leaflet: *Gli operai e la giustizia* ("The workers and justice"), "Class confrontation besieges the judicial institution," 12 Nov 1976.

Bertinotti, "for direct worker-management negotiations. Among the 10 there were also two delegates not present as delegates, but as comrades of the workshop concerned with the questions being discussed. Direct negotiation is a practice established in recent years by the workers that the management calls into question every time, but each time is forced to accept it. The question was banal: the withdrawal of a letter of reprimand for poor performance sent to a worker in the second section of the piece rate shift. This is the team where all the workers, turners, milling machine operators, tappers and adjusters were organised to overcome piece rates and self-organised production collectively. The comrades entered the office of Bertinotti where there is also Mr. Isella, his direct superior. They raised the question, but Isella refused negotiation in that form. The comrades do not give up and demand to negotiate with Bertinotti, the signatory of the letter. Things drag on. While the negotiations were in progress, Mr. Bàllatore from central personnel management burst in and, at one point, screams that they are seizing the managers. After the altercation, the comrades return to the workshops to report back, new issues having emerged, notably the refusal of direct negotiations by the management. For collective piece work you cannot speak of poor individual performance. On 9 September, 5 p.m., management delivered a letter of dismissal for manager kidnapping against two comrades [Enrico Baglioni and Giovanni Spina], others would be delivered to two other comrades the next day [Raffaele Chessa and Giuseppe Mazzariello]. The news circulated, the union was informed. The two comrades organised a meeting for that evening. At the meeting they put forward a precise position: they will enter the factory and then discuss with the workers, and also with the Factory Council if it wants."[196]

The Autonomous Collective[197] and the Communist Committee, which the first two dismissed workers belonged to, distributed a leaflet calling for a strike at Crescenzago from 8 a.m. on 10 September with a demonstration to bring the layed-off workers into the factory. They accused management of having turned a normal union negotiation into kidnapping. But they thought that the company wanted to hit harder through suspensions, provocation and aggression, dismissals, transfers and the *Cassa integrazione*. It was trying "to destroy everything the workers and vanguards have built in recent months – in the workshops and in the factory – against restructuring, the guards and the factory hierarchy, against the isolation of small factories which is used by

---

[196] Letter of Domenico La Monica to the judge Forno, Sesto San Giovanni, 3 Dec 1976, quoted in *Controinformazione*, n. 17, January 1980, p. 24, and Document *3 anni di lotta*, op. cit.

[197] Many and various names of committees and collectives appeared on leaflets, but we can assume that they were often the same people "wearing different hats."

the bosses." Magneti Marelli Crescenzago became the first Italian factory to reject the *Cassa integrazione*, the workers' struggle continued there "destroying powers of bosses' control, building self-organisation in the workshops, uniting men and women workers, pushing back against the transfer of the Third [section], destroying the boss's ability to repress."[198]

On 10 September at 7.45 a.m. the gate was occupied by around a hundred workers. A procession with the two sacked workers at its head came into the factory helped by a team of workers from the day shift who had watched the gate since 7.30. The factory stopped work, three hundred workers marched through it, the others did not work and warned the union.

"The delegates do not know which way to turn, and play for time... The demonstration crosses departments and goes to the Director of the plant, engineer Tacchini... All the offices were full, people were tense and angry, but, strangely, they did not want violence... The workers took possession of the factory and held a meeting to take stock of their strength and to decide how to proceed. It was decided to continue to impose the return of sacked workers to the factory, and to do that every morning, to organise a march... A team of workers would accompany the comrades leaving work to prevent provocations by the guards. At 11 a.m., the meeting ended and the sacked workers went to their department to speak more calmly with their immediate comrades. At 2 p.m., during the entry of the second shift, there was a new strike with a new internal demonstration and an assembly... Assemblies in every department. In the afternoon the Factory Council meets and proposes no struggle, at a maximum the Factory Council would take on legal defence. The break was clear and definitive. It was the delegates of the left of the PCI that made this break, the same ones who for years had been at the head of the struggles, organising them, including by violence. The party and the union indicated that they were ready for dismissal letters for them and the management quickly denounced them to the courts. The management had also told them that the national union accepted dismissal for the 'autonomous terrorists'."

There was in fact a meeting between Trentin (secretary of the CGIL) and the management representative of Magneti Garino, in mid-July, where the redundancies were agreed. "The council ended in a brawl between comrades and the PCI. The fight went on the next day on the gates. On 11 September, there was a demonstration, assemblies, and squads to escort the sacked workers."[199]

---

198 Leaflet: "After a series of provocations, the boss's attack arrives: 2 vanguard militants fired! *Cassa integrazione* from 1 October!," Autonomous Collective and Communist Committee, 10 Sept 1975.
199 Letter of Domenico La Monica, cit. and *3 anni di lotta*, op. cit.

A Committee of Struggle Against Redundancies was formed that combined all the revolutionary forces of the factory. At the same time the company announced complete *Cassa integrazione* (zero hours at work) for three months for about 800 employees of the Magneti Marelli group, especially for the Pavia, Turin and Potenza plants. For the new-born Struggle Committee, the crackdown long planned by Magneti Marelli had arrived. The redundancies were considered political. They could be added to the trial which began on 3 October relating to "the Palmieri actions" and to a request for piecework in plant D from 16 December. "The objective of the boss is increasingly clear: to eliminate the most combative vanguards to crush the strength of the whole factory, with the direct help of the repressive organs of the bourgeois state. In the face of all this, the position of the union is absurd and suicidal, its silence in the face of the restructuring of departments, the denunciation and slander against some delegates during confrontations, the total lack of mobilisation against the *Cassa integrazione* leading the workers to defeat." The only way to prevent divisions between workers was to unify the struggle to keep layed off workers in the factory with the mobilisation against the *Cassa integrazione*.[200]

On 16 September the letters of dismissal came and removed all doubt that "the precautionary suspension was really intended to permanently eliminate from the factory the four vanguard militants." That same morning 500 workers accompany the layed-off workers into the workshops, "after touring the factory, the workers have a short meeting at which the decision emerged that the comrades would continue to be brought into the factory until the trial. Then the demonstration breaks up and goes to the Factory Council's room, to demand that the Council take clear positions. In fact, the Factory Council had not yet taken up a clear defence of its sacked comrades nor had it launched initiatives to combat the *Cassa integrazione*."[201]

---

200 Leaflet: "Watch out boss!! Today the sacked comrades are at their posts of struggle!," Committee for Struggle against Layoffs, 15 Aug 1975.

201 *Quotidiano dei lavoratori*, "*Big* demonstrations in Magneti. Sacked workers in the factory," 18 Sept 1975. The Red Brigades also reacted to political redundancies in Magneti Marelli with an article in their underground newspaper ("Armed struggle for communism"), with the title "Political layoffs: trade unions and workers' autonomy," published in September 1975. For BR the situation of struggle in the factories in Milan is characterised by two "bad" examples, that of Alfa Romeo ("The workers went in to work, not to fight, so the newspapers could show them as brave boys and not as absent from work") and Innocenti (where "the workers seem to stir more for the nation than to fight against redundancies"). The struggle at Magneti Marelli, on the contrary, had to be taken as an example, where the workers decided to put the layed off workers into the factory "at their post of struggle," despite the union being against all mobilisation ("The role of the union

So it goes until 8 October, the day of the trial at the Palace of Justice in Milan for the lawsuit filed by management against the four workers. Meanwhile, the dismissed are reported for trespassing and called to the Greco Turro police station, where they are warned about continuing with the alleged offense. During this period, "the fired comrades also receive almost a whole wage, the product of worker self-taxation and of taxation of some managers, 1,600,000 lire over three months." On 8 October, there was the first meeting between workers and Justice. To the District Court of Milan came a horde of Magneti Marelli workers led by a banner declaring "Magneti workers against political dismissals," while the Factory Council had still not yet ruled on the harsh company crackdown.

The worker initiative surprised the police and the "trembling" magistrate Buonavitacola. The workers demanded that the trial be conducted in open court and also in the largest room of the courthouse. A worker took the megaphone and said "we are in their den but we are not afraid. There is a trial against the redundant workers and they want to do it behind closed doors, this is democracy in Italy." At 1 p.m. the chief magistrate De Falco consented to the completion of the trial in the main hall but on condition of "absolute silence" and with the presence of an armed police guard. Inexperience lead workers to accept that the first part of the hearing be conducted behind closed doors. There was a demonstration along the staircases of the court and front door of the courtroom in which the hearing was held and slogans were chanted. At the end a workers' march returned the sacked workers to the factory with the slogan: "layoffs are fought out in the factory."[202] The judgment was pronounced

---

in this phase is as the manager of bourgeois legality in the factory"). The experience of the Struggle Committee was considered by the Red Brigades as a real novelty, being "perhaps the first time that an autonomous structure succeeds in conducting a struggle with continuity by counting entirely on its own resources. What's more, it's a political and not an economic battle." This struggle "has become a mine of clarification for the political debate both among the masses (as is shown by the new participation of women) on the role played by the bosses and the right of the MO [traditional "Workers Movement," that is, the unions], as well as in the vanguards on the problem of new forms of organization." The stakes are high and even the "neo-revisionists" of Avanguardia operaia are already "beginning to publish texts in which they distance themselves." *Lotta armata per il comunismo, Licenziamenti politci: sindacato e autonomia operaia,* September 1975, in *Controinformazione,* n. 7-8, June 1976

202 *Quotidiano dei lavoratori,* "Today, everyone to the trial of the Magneti Marelli comrades," 8 Oct 1975, and *Quotidiano dei lavoratori,* "The Magneti Workers march into the Court," 9 Oct 1975 (with photos), and letter from Domenico La Monica, op. cit. and *3 anni di lotte,* op. cit. 3 October 1975 was to be the trial date for the disturbance in the office of

only after five days. The comment of the Communist Committee of Magneti was that "the only justice is that of the proletariat." In effect the court could not tolerate that the workers were passing from being the accused to being accusers. The strength shown by the 400 workers must be transposed to the factory because "the fight against layoffs is won in the factory."[203]

On 13 October, the judge rejected the layoffs. "A worker demonstration with the sacked workers at its head confirms to the management that the layoffs will not happen, and then launches a sort of 'hunt the manager' operation."[204]

In the days that follow factory assemblies approve the fight against lay-offs. The delegates from the Left of the PCI also declare themselves in favour of this struggle. Things change after the worker march in Innocenti on 29 October, when part of the protesters clash with the order service of the reformists. The Factory Council of Magneti Marelli convened a "secret" meeting to which only the faithful of the union and the "revisionist" left were invited, excluding the delegates of the Workers Committee and the undecided. In essence, the trade union left was given the choice between changing their combative line or being expelled by the governing bodies of the union. The result of this encounter lead to the acceptance by the union of the transfer of the assembly line of the third section, without having obtained in exchange the withdrawal of judicial complaints against workers, as promised by the management.[205]

> In all that time, the discussion in the Committee and in the factory was the meaning to be given to the presence of former employees in the factory. The comrades did not enter the factory to work, but as 'officials' of the workers' organisation that was being built in the course of the struggle against layoffs itself. The comrades in the factory released from work could move around the departments, putting all their time and their expertise at the disposal of the workers. They organised themselves and guaranteed that they would be on the side of those earning a wage. The factory was seen first and foremost as a place of struggle against layoffs, but, starting from there, against

---

guard captain Palmieri, but it was postponed to a later date.
203 Leaflet: "The only justice is proletarian justice," Magneti Communist Committee, 10 Oct 1975. In the first two months after the layoffs 700,000 lire were collected from the workers of plant B at Crescenzago. Leaflet: "Workers of plant 'A'" by Struggle Committee against Redundancies, 12 Nov 1975.
204 "Chronicle of a trial," *Cronologia*, February 1980
205 *Senza tregua*, "How to build the formation of revolutionary workers," 14 Nov 1975, and the paper *Operai e stato*, op. cit.

forced labour. The sacked workers imposed their presence as leaders of this struggle. In this climate the autonomous struggle came from places where there were comrades and became general, laying the foundations for the fight against restructuring. Laying off the four workers was the beginning of a more general offensive against the workers of Crescenzago to dismantle two departments and to make massive use of the *Cassa integrazione* to create flexibility for all the workers. The destruction of the self-organisation of the workers was a necessary condition for the start of the general offensive by the bosses. The autonomous organisation in Magneti was born in the struggle, but above all by taking positions in defence of the most advanced sections of them… It strengthened itself… in the practice of direct negotiations… and vigilance teams during the struggle against layoffs. These groups organised and consolidated what was created over four years of direct negotiations… Groups of workers in direct relation with a single head, with a single manager.[206]

With this cycle of struggles against *Cassa integrazione* and redundancies and everything that followed, a direct relationship was built between the vanguard and the masses, without delegates or contractual and institutional mechanisms born from a political logic, founded on the sale of workers' interests; a relationship in which the vanguard always puts itself forward, every day, in person, it does not take its directives from anyone other than the formation of the masses, representing itself starting from this strength.[207]

For "Senza tregua," the obvious position that union and workers' interests were opposed was born from the need to promote workers' interests. Certainly "there is a given 'contractual' relation today whereby the living conditions of workers are stable for some time, while they are constantly in play in the class struggle." The discussions that took place in Marelli concerned "building an organisation that imposes the workers' objectives, which prevents the formation in the factory of a bosses' power capable of destroying the organisation and gains of the workers, not a workshop guerrilla, made up of a homogenous group opposed to negotiation in the factory, but a self-organised behaviour opposed to the sell-out of workers' interests. Transforming each bosses' attack into an affirmation of power – as it was for redundancies – attacking the basis

---

206 Letter Domenico La Monica, op. cit. and *3 anni di lotte*, op. cit.
207 *Operai e stato*, op. cit.

of the bosses' organisation, raising the initiative in the factory against every anti-worker element to defend the most immediate class interests – the fight against relocation, for less hours, for the wage in all its forms."

Such united political and economic struggle "cannot exist on the basis of union demands." The fight against political layoffs at Magneti Marelli "created the conditions for a political debate more advanced and practical for the whole working class. It showed workers the existence of two sides between which it is necessary to choose, it went from the fight against repression that, for a while, united all the workers, to the union that allows redundancies, which also indicates – as at Innocenti – who to sack. It showed what the vaunted 'neutrality' and 'democracy' of the labour courts meant when *Confindustria* brings out into the light of day clear and coherent attacks on autonomous organisation in the factory, when the PCI becomes the left of the courts. The sense of these democratic institutions is clear: on the one hand they are proof of partiality and ratify the power relations that are established in the class struggle – and fixed at a limit compatible with the social domination of capital. But on the other hand, in periods of capitalist counter-attack, when the management of the crisis restricts possibilities and pushes for the defeat of the workers, they become a tool of deception – because they conceal their true nature as an anti-worker tool behind a 'legitimacy' that stems from their apparent 'neutrality,' from the 'democratic credentials' that are artfully constructed." The fight against political redundancies showed on the contrary "the existence of an independent force in the camp of the left."[208]

Meanwhile in Rome, the Ministry of Labour and the trade unions signed an agreement on Magneti Marelli, the negotiations having gone on for ten months, initially held in Assolombarda Milan, but then shifted to Rome. The main points of the negotiations concerned turnover, transfers of work and staff, and the defence of jobs, following the resort to *Cassa integrazione* in the Potenza, Pavia and Turin plants. The union's demands were almost completely disregarded: during 1976 100 new jobs would be created (60 at Crescenzago, 40 in the rest of the group), but this did not conform to any workers' requirements. Some manufacturing at Crescenzago would be transferred to Potenza, dismantling the Third section, the most combative section in which the revolutionary left was most implanted.

On 10 December, meetings were held to evaluate the agreement in various sections of the plant in Crescenzago. There was a lot of disagreement and grumbling, but the agreement was approved. In the afternoon there was a meeting of the Third section which called for the 200 workers affected by transfers to meet all together and deny the right of other assemblies to decide

---

208 *Senza tregua*, "How to build the formation of revolutionary workers," 14 Nov 1975.

the fate of the other sections.[209] Soon after this the company proposed overtime from 2 to 6 January 1976, but the Magneti Communist Committee did not agree: "We will not take it lying down, we communist workers, we will not sell ourselves, we are not willing to submit to the crisis and blackmail, we have not submitted to layoffs, we reject the sell-out of the Third section, of the Regulators, of the struggles of the last few months around the pace of work, breaks, piecework, we refuse the union sell-out of the workforce."

The Committee proposed to fight against overtime, to form a "direct workers organisation" to prevent the dismantling of the Third section and the Regulators, and to continue the fight against the pace of work, and for breaks and the abolition of piece rates.[210] In the factory, things were moving towards a clash between those who supported the union which "called for unity in poverty" and those not prepared to give an inch. The climate in the factory was extremely tense. Confrontation broke out in the screw-making shop which saw "on the one hand, the workers who've been at the head and in the struggle for 5 years, the comrades who've rejected the bosses' agreements signed in Rome, workers who struggle every day against layoffs, and on the other those who, having reached the fifth level, being control operators, or wanting to become one, stand against the open political battle, stand against freedom of speech, stand against those who fight for the abolition of overtime, stand up for the bosses and the bosses' plan."

A provocative sign put up by the union opposed "the workers for the boss's line with union amendments" and those who see "the distant prospect of communism living in everyday acts."[211]

The fight against the dismissals at Marelli continued. For the Communist Committee it was part of the larger struggle against sackings and industrial restructuring that were affecting all the big and small Italian factories, Pirelli, Imperial, Innocenti, even Fiat. There were two possible solutions: "Either we think we can get by with individual solutions, staying calm, accepting the workloads, suffering aggressive foremen, staying at home when there is a *Cassa integrazione,* hoping not to be dismissed, as it is at Innocenti. Or we start to say to the foremen that they should quieten down if they want to last, to reduce the pace of work, to fight the attacks made by the management in Turin, Potenza and Pavia, to prepare the mass mobilisation against our enemies with demonstrations in court for the trials still to come." On 18 November, the trial

---

209 Leaflet: "At what point is the Magneti situation?" by Magneti Communist Committee, 19 Nov 1975, and *Quotidiano dei lavoratori*, "Negative agreement for Magneti," 11 Dec 1975.

210 Leaflet: "It is not stocktaking but only overtime and as such must be rejected!" by Magneti Communist Committee, 19 Dec 1975.

211 Leaflet: "Comrades, workers in glazing and cutting!," 22 Dec 1975.

began of "the worker in the march who discovered and destroyed the centre of anti-worker filing in the office of Palmieri," then on 16 December there was the one concerning "the reduction of output where the boss thinks he has legal authorisation to reduce workers' pay and then switch to direct repression."[212]

On 6 December 1975 in Rome there was an agreement between management and the union under which Magneti Marelli was committed to withdraw the complaints relating to the episode of 9 May of that year. On 23 December management accused the four sacked workers of aggravated burglary and called for urgent action in order to remove the four from the factory by force. This complaint was forwarded to the Public Prosecutor of Milan, but the judge Pescarzoli did not accept it.[213]

On 19 January 1976 the workers found themselves in front of the judiciary a second time, "but this time they had learned their lesson." Six hundred workers marched into the court, "where there was a state of siege." The workers forced the hearing to take place in a room large enough so that all could attend. Among the proposals to help reach a conclusion the management offered 40 million lire "for the laid off if they don't return to Magneti." The sacked workers refused any negotiations of this kind. At two in the morning the judge Muntoni revoked the layoffs.[214]

The rehired went back to the factory "victorious, as true communists, with their political reliability, their will to transform this society, to eliminate the boss, to build communism." On the next day in the factory the 8 a.m. march was not demobilised, the vigilance teams remained at the gates. "It is well known that the decision of the magistrate is certainly not enough to return the comrades. The boss doesn't countersign their cards, does not pay the comrades, but cannot prevent them from entering the factory. Wait for the appeal. At this moment management is going on the restructuring offensive. In Rome the union accepts the dismantling of two departments, and at Crescenzago redoes the blackmail of the left unionists to make them accept it: denouncing the violence exercised over 8 years of struggle, which left delegates also participated in."[215]

At the end of January, the consequences of the "Rome Agreement" began to be felt in the dismantling of the Third section. The workers of the section

---

212 Leaflet: "Enough of the boss's platform. Let's discuss our objectives," Communist Committees, 10 Nov 1975.
213 "Chronicle of a trial" op.cit.
214 Leaflet: "Tonight at 2 a.m.," Giustizia proletaria, 20 Jan 1976, and article in *Controinformazione* no. 17, "*Marelli: La guardia rossa racconta*" ("Marelli: the Red Guard tells its story"), Jan 1980.
215 Ibid

remained idle, in spite of the agreement providing for their reintegration into the Second section, because the company knew there were problems of excess staff. In the Fifth section, Klaxons, the first transfers began and "already a few women had refused to move so as not to break the unity of struggle." The company had to guarantee jobs by the availability of workers on the night shift and reduction of the workload in the Second section. The Communist Committees pushed the struggle to stop the bosses' threats and to not end up like Innocenti.[216]

In February 1976, two significant events showed the development of the political initiative in Magneti:

1. a woman worker fired for absenteeism was accompanied every morning by a worker demonstration to the personnel office. The demonstration demanded that her card be stamped and that the sanction be withdrawn. This sort of attempt at dismissal was taking place in similar manoeuvres in all the other factories: "At Magneti they decided to attack the mass of workers after they'd found that it was impossible to attack the vanguard as such. It is the second attempt after the *Casa integrazione*, also withdrawn."[217]
2. On 12 February management announced that, following a strike of the employees, they could not pay all of the wages for February, but only 50,000 lire to each worker. "A management provocation to test the ground and the union reaction – it is a traditional tactic of the bosses that we've seen several times at Breda siderurgica." Three hundred workers spontaneously went on strike. On 13 February the union called for a symbolic demonstration under the windows of the management office in Sesto. There 1,500 workers broke through the union lines and, led by the comrades of the Committee, occupied the office and imposed direct negotiation, which, after two hours ended with the payment of 150,000 lire for all, even though a member of the executive of the Factory Council, a member of the PCI, proposed asking for 100,000 lire. For many, this was more than their salary.[218]

The boss wanted to make a police presence in the factory normal, as had already happened at Pirelli, thanks to the "provocative behaviour of the order service of the Communist Party" and the violent press campaign about the

---

216 Leaflet: "Monday to Magneti, the workers begin to be made unemployed, without any job," Communist Committees for Workers' Power, 23 Jan 1976.
217 *Operai e stato*, op. cit.
218 "The Red Guard tells its story," cit. and *3 anni di lotte*, op. cit. and *Operai e stato*, op. cit.

ungovernability of Crescenzago. The Workers Committee was not afraid of the use of police: "they do it against us because they are afraid, because we are strong. According to workers' principles, the police must not enter the factory, so we need to develop stronger and stronger fights against the boss's plans, must be always more attentive and organised to neutralise the spies and enemies in our midst and to impose more and more workers' power in the factory."[219]

On 17 February, the case brought by the company against ten workers suspended for taking part in the demonstration in the office of the chief of security, the "spy" Palmieri, was heard in front of the Civil Court of Milan. On this occasion the criminal proceedings were suspended, which was an important first victory in the trial. "They want to criminalise the workers' struggle. Every worker is a possible offender for the boss and for the state, because they can become unemployed or laid off or because their wage is not enough. So the crisis becomes worse, the boss tries first of all to isolate the vanguard before they can develop ever more incisive struggles for the defence of material and political interests, before the workers no longer accept mediators and, as they did on Wednesday, negotiate directly. Any effective fight directly against the boss and the state, from train blockades by the unemployed, to pickets against scabs, to hard-fought strikes like on Wednesday in Sesto, is attacked as a provocative action and those promoting it as thugs."[220]

The expulsion

The union was put in difficulty by the successful initiatives of the Workers Committee and tried "the big stick" with the expulsion of three workers' delegates (Baglioni, Reale and Folloni): "the Factory Council, after the withdrawal of cards by the union, threatened to verify their relationship with the shop floor by means of a new extraordinary election of delegates, something that it did not in any way have the courage to do."[221]

The occasion for the expulsion was 2 April 1976 when the head of the guards of the Magneti Marelli Crescenzago, Matteo Palmieri, was wounded.

At 15.15 two men entered the workers' reception at Magneti Marelli by via Adriano 81 claiming to be lawyers who had to talk to Palmieri. The three guards let them pass and one of them accompanied them into the office

---

219 Leaflet: "New strength, new organisation, new perspective comes from the struggle of these months in Magneti," *Per il potere operaio* ("For workers' power"), 13 Feb 1976.

220 Leaflet: "Tuesday 17th at 11.30 am at the court of Milan," For Workers' Power, 16 Feb 1976.

221 *Operai e stato*, op. cit. and *3 anni di lotte*, op. cit.

where Palmieri was working. Immediately they pulled out pistols and ordered Palmieri and the attendant to lie face down on the floor, took possession of the keys to the locks of two shelves and three small safes on the wall and asked where the weapons of the security personnel were kept. Before leaving, one of the "lawyers" shot Palmieri in the right leg (it took him 5 months to recover). Meanwhile, two people came out of a red Alfa Romeo Giulia 1300 waiting outside armed with a machine gun and a pistol and began to shoot in the direction of the guardroom as covering fire for the two coming out of Palmieri's office.

On the night of 4 April 1976 individuals armed with rifles fired at the windows of the Magneti warehouse in via Clerici. On the spot the police found copies of a leaflet in which a "communist armed commando" claimed responsibility for injuring Palmieri. Other copies were found a few hours earlier in a phone booth not far from the site of the shooting. The purpose of the action, the flyer said, was "to strike Palmieri, who is directly responsible for the systematic work of denunciation of workers' struggles and in particular the communist vanguard. The working class and its communist armed vanguards are developing a systematic work of counter-information and surveillance against the anti-worker role of the armed factory guards and we know how to impose this first warning by force of arms. Against the armed vigilantes, organised by the bosses to impose militarily the laws of profit, we impose the revolutionary law of the armed workers vanguards." The text ends by calling for the building of "the armed power of the working class."[222]

The union declared a strike of solidarity for the wounded, but the Workers Committee proposed a separate demonstration and assembly "for worker objectives." The Workers Committee boycotted the one hour protest strike called by the unions and they explained their reasons in a leaflet entitled "*Neither one minute on strike, nor one tear for the guard chief Palmieri!*" To call a strike for Palmieri "is a provocation." The Marelli workers had already been on strike for Palmieri "when the workers threw him out of the assemblies where he was doing his job as an informer trying to identify the vanguards – when a demonstration of hundreds of workers(f/m) went to flush him out in his office finding those files where thousands of notes, denunciations and profiles of simple female workers, of struggle vanguards, of communists had been compiled for

---

[222] *Corriere della Sera*, "A mysterious commando breaks into Marelli and injures the head guard with a pistol shot," 3 April 1976, and *Il Giorno*, "Years of Lead: new arrest warrants," 12 Aug 1984, and announcement from Magneti Marelli Management, 2 April 1976, and Court of the Republic of Milan, "Referral to justice of Baglioni Enrico+17," 23 Dec 1977, and Sentence no. 24/86 of the Third Court of Assizes of Milan of 20 March 1986, and *Il terrorismo in fabbrica*, op. cit.

the management. A huge amount of policing material was revealed and, on this occasion, set on fire."[223]

On the day of the strike the "two opposing sides faced each other in the factory, the workers continued to debate without expressing any solidarity with the boss." The union official and PCI member Egeo Mantovani,[224] in an interview with the newspaper *Corriere della sera* appealed to the management and the state to intervene directly, complaining about the presence of an excessive number of subversives among the workers.[225] On 6 April, the Factory Council and the FLM notified the personnel management that "the FLM and the Factory Council have decided to expel Baglioni Enrico, Folloni Sergio and Reale Antonio from the union. Therefore they invite the management to suspend from the current month forward any union delegation or representation for the above named."[226] In the public statement, the Crescenzago Factory Council argued that "as a result of what happened the FLM and the Factory Council have decided on the expulsion from the Federation of Metalworkers of the delegates Enrico Baglioni, Sergio Folloni, Antonio Reale and to verify that they really have been excluded from the Factory Council. In effect, these individuals declare themselves to be for the elusive 'Communist Committees' and 'Workers Committees,' supported by some workers. They are opposed to the union in struggles and theorise that the events taking place at Magneti serve the labour movement. The grave economic situation and the hard contractual confrontations are elements of the bosses' strategy which is trying to ensnare the union and the labour movement. The objective of the strategy of tension, which is part of such a design, is to target the factories, considered as a decisive element for a conservative and reactionary political change in the country. Faced with this, maximum unity, firmness and discipline is necessary to isolate the provocateurs and those who theorise these types of action, at

---

223 Leaflet: "Neither one minute on strike nor one tear for the guard chief Palmieri!," Marelli Workers Committee, 5 April 1976, cited in *Senza tregua*, 14 July 1976, p. 3

224 Egeo Mantovani (1921-) was a WWII Partisan in the Monza-Brianza area and a PCI member. Hired at Magnetti Marelli in 1946 he was elected to both the Internal Commission and the Factory Council from 1954 to 1970, and was an official of the FIOM up to 1977. He was a staunch bureaucrat of the PCI section in the factory, systematically countering workers autonomy with his brain and his fists. The villainous Stalinist is still not dead at the time of writing.

225 *Operai e stato*, op. cit. and *3 anni di lotte*, op. cit.

226 Statement "to the Personnel Management of Magneti Marelli," FLM and the Factory Council of the Crescenzago plant, 6 April 1976.

the same time as implementing the decisions of the Union to win contractual objectives and reforms."[227]

The Workers Committee's response was very strong. It accused the Factory Council and the FLM of being informers, since they fed the three expelled comrades to the company and the police. But "the Communist Party, the Socialist Party and their supporters have done more: from now on they are recruiting from the scabs, the kind that we all went to throw out from the workshops during the strikes. They are recruiting from the foremen, the operators of the fifth level, on the basis of anti-communism, on the basis that the crisis is the 'ruin of the workers,' the resumption of mass exploitation and unemployment for most of the workers, will bring to them, the scabs, foremen, fifth level people, new advantages." This union attitude started a long time ago, since "they always declared themselves for restructuring, have sold out the workforce and workers' wages in exchange for investments in the form of new machines that will put dozens and dozens of workers(f/m) out of a job." This is what happened with the Third section and Regulators, when management fired the leading militants. The union stood aside, "after trying to openly endorse layoffs, because the incessant workers mobilisation defeated them." Reformist parties called for a strike against injuring the captain of the guard, but did not say a word, did not strike for an hour for those who were killed in the streets. As for the Reale Law, the PSI voted for it and the Communist Party let it pass. These political forces are trying to sell at a low price the strength and perspective of the Italian workers movement and "are furious with us who stop them from doing it easily."

The Workers Committee, on the contrary, is made up of those who personify "firmly and concretely the path of workers towards communism, who affirm that we must destroy this economy, this bourgeoisie, these repressive structures, exploitation, and that the workers are the ones who must direct, decide, distribute goods, decide who and how to tax, define prices, decide which production, of which goods we need."[228]

---

227   Statement of the Factory Council of the Magneti Marelli-Crescenzago plant, 5 April 1976.

228   Flyer: "Who we are, who they are. Who is in the workers' movement. Who is with the boss," Magneti Workers Committee, 8 April 1976. The Reale Law (No. 152 of 22 May 1975 – from the name of the Minister of Justice, Oronzo Reale, who wrote it) extended the situations where the use of firearms by the police is considered legitimate, made it possible to search people's homes without the permission of a judge, extended the definition of offensive weapons, forbade participation in demonstrations "with the face fully or partly covered by any means in order to prevent identification," and restored the fascist institution of exile for political reasons.

At the end of April, a new court ruling went in favour of some sacked workers, but the company refused to return their employment cards. The battle inside the factory Crescenzago flared up again. On one side the company and the unions accused those from the Committee of being provocateurs and terrorists, on the other the workers of the Committee had no intention of falling "into the sleazy game" of those who become hysterical because they "see their society threatened, their domination in peril":

- the bosses are hysterical because, despite the sense of responsibility of the union, they still face workers who are absent, who do not accept transfers, who do not accept the pace of work, who want lower prices, who go to the supermarket and shop for free, who occupy housing;
- the cops are hysterical who shoot and kill more and more;
- the rulers are hysterical because they have taken to embezzlement and graft;
- the trade unionists are hysterical because the chemical workers reject the rubbishy contract, because "absenteeism increases," because the pace of work is smashed, because they sell cigarettes in the factory [smuggling], because Palmieri is in hospital, because instead of making sacrifices the workers begin to do free shopping.

The accusations did not end there. "In their stated positions the union and the Communist Party invite the authorities, the police and *Carabinieri* and judges, not to let us enter the factory anymore. They forget that it is the bourgeois court that we don't believe in, but that Mantovani and his accomplices do believe in, that has proved us right."[229]

On 20 May the Magneti Marelli Workers Committee called for a strike against the high cost of living which mobilised 60% of the workers. On 21 May, at around 6.45 p.m., about fifteen young people entered the Esselunga supermarket on Via Pellegrino Rossi, in the working class neighbourhood of Bovisa in Milan, and expropriated various goods from the shelves, while one of them cut the telephone wires and spoke into a megaphone about the high cost of living. Outside, members of the Workers Committee held a rally against rising prices and urged people not to pay.[230] The campaign against rising prices

---

229 Leaflet: "Who provokes who?," by Magneti Workers Committee, 26 April 1976.
230 Interrogation of Enrico Baglioni in front of the Assize Court of Milan, 1 Feb 1984, quoted in the acts of the trial of PL. Milan no. 921/80 and *Il Giorno*, "Robberies, bombings and kidnappings," 24 Feb 1984 and Court of the Republic of Milan, *Requisitoria del*

in big retailers was called by the Communist Committee for Workers Power: the expropriation of foodstuffs was a new line of struggle to follow, especially with price increases of 40%, "today it is no longer possible to fight just for the objective of defending the real value of wages." Fighting against speculators to have fair prices must be accompanied by a fight against the state, "because most of the industrial and commercial network in the food market is in the hands of large multinational companies." Inflation is one of the most important repressive rings tightening around the Italian working class. "It is not the law or reform which counts because, by means of taxes and prices, the bosses want to take back what they say they pay as a 'cost of labour'."

In the view of the Committees, the measures taken in some supermarkets in Milan, such as moderated prices, were ridiculous. A particular discussion took place around the initiative of the "red markets" set up by *Democrazia proletaria* in working class neighbourhoods. To have food at affordable prices is obviously nice, but it must be remembered that "there have always been alternative sales channels in factories and neighbourhoods" such as smuggling. The issue is political because these markets do not affect "the profit of the great owners of the retail trade but, above all else, this is a turn away from the victorious struggle which could constitute proletarian re-appropriation and the use of proletarian force imposing its own laws against those of capital and all its lackeys." From this point of view, "the red market is a by-product of struggle" while "today the imposition of political prices is closely linked to the organised expression of proletarian strength. We must impose by our organised force on the directors of supermarkets in our area the lowering of prices according to a norm that we decide. We need to establish a control over the network of merchants, against the profiteers and speculators. The delinquent is not the one does free shopping but the one who today still intends to raise the cost of food, who throws away tons of fruit and vegetables to increase the price."[231]

After the 20 June elections, in which the DC got 38.7% and the PCI got 34.4% of the vote, the Communist Committee was convinced that it was at the beginning of a long showdown in which the masks would come off. The "DC-PCI-unions-Confindustria" agreement talked about sacrifices to be imposed on workers. Already Agnelli had called for the blocking of the *scala mobile* (index-linked wage increases), while the secretary of the UIL, Benvenuto,

---

pubblico ministero Armando Spataro dell'11 luglio 1981 relativa ai procedimenti n. 921/80 F G. I. e n. 228/81 F G. I., pp. 843-844 and Court of Milan, *Sentenza-ordinanza del Giudice istruttore Elena Paciotti relativa al procedimento penale n. 921/80F del 3-6-82 contro Antonio Achilli ed altri.*

231 Leaflet: "Comrade workers, comrade proletarians," Communist Committee for Workers' Power, 18 May 1976.

was also prepared to block automatic increases. Meanwhile, in Milan, workers' struggles continued against redundancies and the closure of workshops at the Carlo Erba and Innocenti plants, against the *Cassa integrazione* at Motta, and, at Pirelli, for the staffing levels and wages of workers in the canteen. At Magneti Marelli the fight resumed in Stamping, Contacts, at Samas and in the Fourth and Fifth sections. The boss tried to limit the wage demands of workers on piece rates, thus guaranteeing an increase in production and profits and attempting to divide the workers. According to the Communist Committee, in this operation the company was helped by the PCI through a character like Di Stefano ("this Executive member who does not work (!), who enters and leaves the factory in a suit and tie with his management briefcase"), who in two meetings at the canteen tried to get across the principle of higher productivity and greater discipline in the workshops.[232]

The verdict of 15 July

In the factories in Milan, the pre-holiday period was marked by the trial against the four laid-off workers from Magneti Crescenzago, the dismissal of other leading worker militants at Carlo Erba, Fiat OM and Alfa Romeo, but also by new struggles like that of workers in the Pirelli canteen, the workers at Breda Termonucleare[233] and at Breda Fucine (Breda Forges in Milan), along with those at Marelli and Carlo Erba. The Magneti Marelli Communist Workers Committee and the Carlo Erba Communist Workers Committee described the situation like this: "at the Carlo Erba factory in Rodano they threaten six layoffs prepared jointly by the boss, the unions and the PCI workplace cell against the historical vanguards of the factory who have rightly responded to provocation by scabs by systematically expelling them from the factory. OM-Fiat lays off four worker vanguards for absenteeism when in fact what

---

[232] Leaflet: "After the vote, we return to the struggle!," Magneti Marelli Communist Committee, 30 June 1976. The "scala mobile" ("escalator") is a mechanism that determines, by means of trigger points of living costs, a link between wages and rises in the cost of living. The *scala mobile* therefore serves to defend, albeit partially, the purchasing power of wages. After a series of struggles, the workers' movement got the application of the *scala mobile*, the result of agreements signed with Confindustria between 1945 and 1968. The mechanism of the *scala mobile* is divided into two phases: the first is the calculation, on the basis of average variations of some consumer goods, of the increase in the cost of living based on the consumption of a "family" of four (two spouses of average age and two children of 9 and 14); the second phase is the transformation of the percentage of change in average prices into cost of living and therefore into wage increases.

[233] A plant producing metal parts for reactor vessels used in nuclear power plants.

the boss wants to prevent is the fight against dangerous working conditions, a struggle which gave rise to the first post-election strikes at OM-Fiat and stimulated working-class resistance to super-exploitation and permanent restructuring. Fighting pickets were organised on Saturday against the 600 cops in the coach shop. In one year OM-Fiat had already fired 50 other workers. As far as Magneti Marelli is concerned, on 15 July there is the appeal judgement against four comrades who Magneti-Fiat tries in vain to fire from the factory."[234]

On 15 July 1976, the appeal trial of the layed off workers took place at the Labour Court of Milan. For the Magneti Communist Committee, the Labour Court had already been revealed as "a real anti-worker special tribunal, which defends managers, foremen and scabs, is ruthless in applying the bosses' rules on the workers in struggle, is attentive to declare 'criminal' every workers' struggle." The union at Magneti Marelli didn't just keep quiet about layoffs, "but prepared them at the boss's table." That is why the Labour Court "represents their last hope to chase out of the factory the four workers that the union also considers as irredeemable enemies, because these workers represent years of struggle, autonomous platforms, who have achieved victories and an organisation in the factory."[235]

On 15 July, the last working day before the summer break, "the court is empty of people and full of police." A few hundred workers came to attend the trial despite everything. At 4 p.m., in the hall of the tenth civil division of the court, Labour section, on the third floor of the Palace of Justice, Magneti Marelli presented its appeal against the decision of the magistrate who had declared the dismissal of the four workers (Enrico Baglioni, Giovanni Spina, Giuseppe Chessa, Giuseppe Pazzariello) illegal on 9 September 1975. Company lawyers Gullotta and Trifirò called for an annulment of the decision which legitimated the presence of the 4 sacked workers in the factory, "guaranteed daily, for ten months, by the strength of a worker demonstration."

The President of the tribunal, Vittorio Emanuele, briefly describes the behaviour of the workers outside of any context. The company lawyer Gullotta says that "this has nothing to do with politics." The intervention of Gullotta is interrupted by slogans, whistles and shouts and "some voices from the audience asked that they talk about the struggles that these workers carried out every day in the factory." After this interruption, the President declared

---

234 Leaflet: *Compagni, compagne!* ("Comrades(f/m)!"), Marelli Communist Committee, 5 July 1976, and the leaflet: "Workers struggle and mobilisation against the dismissal of the vanguard militants in Carlo Erba, Om-Fiat, Alfa and Magneti Marelli!," Magneti Marelli Workers Communist Committee and Carlo Erba Communist Committee, 9 July 1976.

235 Leaflet: "Against the dismissals of the vanguard: in the factory, in the court, it's struggle which decides!," Magneti Communist Committee, 15 July 1976.

that the hearing was definitively suspended and left. "In front of hundreds of workers(f/m) from Magneti Marelli and other factories in Milan, the judges of the Court attempted to unleash direct repression," and the hall was evicted by force. The President called on the four laid-off workers and their lawyers (Giuliano Spazzali, Luigi Zezza, Alberto Medina, Francesco Piscopo and Anna Perosino) to follow him to another room on the third floor. Once they were inside the doors were closed and the President announced that the hearing be held *in camera*.

"The fired comrades decide that they do not intend to submit to the judgment if their comrades are kept out. They declare that they were dismissed for struggles that are not their personal property, but belong to all the comrades of Magneti Marelli and the entire working class, and they invite their lawyers to give up their defence brief if the case takes place in those conditions. The defence for the fired workers, faced with this sneaky manoeuvre, renounce their functions because it is impossible to assume their task." A worker and the lawyer Medina leave the courtroom to announce their decision to the others, but they again find themselves surrounded by *Carabinieri*, while the judgment in favour of dismissal is made behind closed doors, in front of just the company lawyers. Outside the hall the police "unleashed a frantic manhunt" down the stairs and corridors of the court, where all exits had been closed.

Many were wounded, and the same lawyer Medina was hit on the head with a rifle butt and left bleeding on the ground, while the lawyer Luigi Zezza was threatened with a gun pointed to his chest. The police fired canisters of tear gas at head height. Outside, in via Freguglia, there was wild firing of tear gas, and police charges. A Fiat 500 caught fire because of a smoke bomb. At the end there were 12 injured, including 7 of the police.[236]

The Milan section of Workers Autonomy produced a leaflet in which it accused the judges of the tenth section of the Labour Court of being "well known to the working class in Milan for their infamy and their open links, theoretical and practical, with the employers." This trial was a real "anti-worker provocation" obedient to the objectives of the company management, from

---

236 "Workers and Justice," "Editorial" and "Class confrontation besieges the judicial institution," 12 Nov 1976 and *3 anni di lotte*, op. cit., and announcement by the Defence Committee of the sacked comrades, 16 July 1976, and *Corriere della Sera*, "Violent clashes at the Palace of Justice, courtroom invaded by ultra left," 16 July 1976, and *Corriere d'informazione*, "Justice and violence," 16 July 1976, and *Corriere d'informazione*, "Protagonists speak about the incidents," 16 July 1976, and *Il Giornale di Milano*, "Clashes in the Palace of Justice between police and hundreds of extra-parliamentarians," 16 July 1976, and *Corriere della Sera*, "The intervention of thirty extremists was enough to provoke serious incidents in the court," 17 July 1976.

the fixing of the trial date to the choice of the three judges (Vittorio, Marzorati and Gargiulo). To this had to be added the unprecedented deployment of police and the "treacherous" attack against workers and lawyers, "but there was nothing good to expect from bourgeois justice. The workers know this because for a year they have taken their sacked comrades into the factory." An assembly at the State University in via Festa del perdono was announced for the afternoon of 16 July.[237]

> All the efforts of repression are coordinated: all the press incites the lynching of the workers and comrade lawyers; trade unions condemn the 'trouble' and call on the police to do what they cannot do at the factory – liquidate and destroy the worker vanguards – and the PCI justifies and supports the iniquitous law and the infamous judges; the 'honourable' deputy of the DC, De Carolis, a lawyer himself, standard-bearer of petty bourgeois reaction in Lombardy, speaks about the facts, with names and surnames of the accused, in the city council; Marelli prepares new provocations, which it will try to put in place after the August break.[238]

L'Unità (the PCI daily) wrote that:

> the exceptional seriousness of the incidents is above all due to the fact that they were clearly planned in advance, if not by the mass of the participants, certainly by the promoters of the action. As we have said, they were previously announced by the newspaper *Lotta Continua* in the context of provocative statements. As for the precedents of the trial, it is worth recalling that the four dismissals occurred at Marelli after a series of adventurist episodes put in place in the big Crescenzago factory. The protagonists of these actions were members of a group going under the name 'Circolo operaio,' grouping, from time to time, individuals adhering to the various extra-parliamentary formations. It put forward exclusively wage and corporatist

---

237 Leaflet: "The sacked comrades re-enter the factory again and it will continue!," Magneti Marelli Struggle Committee against Redundancies, Communist Committees for Workers Power, Coordination of Autonomous Organisations of the Factories and Neighbourhoods, Communist Committee (marxist-leninist) for Unity and Struggle, Italian Communist Party (m-l), 16 July 1976.
238 "Workers and Justice," *Editorial*, 12 Nov 1976.

demands and led in reality a relentless action against the trade unions and their factory sections.[239]

The Justice section of the PCI took a stand by denouncing "the inadmissibility of actions which disrupt the normal course of judicial activity, produce negative reactions in public opinion and lead to effects that are incompatible with the aim of making workers more and more aware of the justness of workers' interests and the harsh requirements of their struggles." Furthermore, "provocative and adventurist actions do not fall within the traditions and practices of the labour and democratic movement, that, on the contrary, today searches for a new and constructive relationship with the judicial world, with the aim of more and more putting into practice the values and principles of the Republican Constitution. The groups which provoked these incidents advance the idea that the working class defends its own interests through intimidating judges and denying their independence. This utopian idea is aberrant and must be strongly condemned."[240]

On the morning of 19 July, there was a meeting in the canteen of the Crescenzago factory about "what really happened in court," with the presence of the lawyers from the Defence Committee: "the illusions have fallen, those who believed in good faith in law, in the impartiality of Justice, have seen their petty bourgeois illusions vanish. But the workers' reply has not been absent: the sacked comrades continue to march into the factory. The price paid by the bourgeoisie to eject the four comrades from the factory has been high. In fact the democratic mask of justice has fallen away, the mask with which the bosses and the PCI covered its face to better trap workers and proletarians."[241]

> Now the battle is harder, to restore the comrades to the factory requires an act of force without any legal covering, against the law. The 'Red Guard' organises itself, at 7.45 a.m. it occupies the lodge of the guards, places two pickets at the side of this lodge, and allows the sacked workers to enter, while a group of day shift workers accompanies them. The team accompanies them also outside the factory, because the comrades can be stopped at any time.

---

239   *L'Unità*, "Serious accidents at Palace of Justice caused by certain extremist groups," 16 July 1976, and *L'Unità*, "The Palace of Justice disorders provoked by elements of 'Autonomy'," 17 July 1976.
240   *L'Unità*, "Unacceptable actions," 17 July 1976.
241   Leaflet: "This morning at 8.30," Workers Committee, 20 July 1976.

On 12 August a young magistrate decided that the sacked workers could enter the factory until the Court of Cassation made its judgment. On 8 September, "the boss returns to the fray: he deploys at the lodge an 'army' of guards brought from other plants." After three minutes, clashes break out between the workers' pickets and the guards, but in the end the sacked workers get in. Ten guards were injured, while the management suspended for three days five workers who fought with the guards, a measure that will be declared illegitimate by the magistrate in December of the same year. The next morning, "the Red Guard is strengthened, the comrades enter the factory, hold meetings, organise the struggle against restructuring. The Red Guard lines up every morning in the lodge as a clear form of workers' counter-power, as an organisation hostile to the social and productive organisation of capital."[242]

The Workers Committee makes an analysis of the role of guards, foremen, spies and trade unionists against the strength and organisation of the workers. It was normal that in the present crisis the boss could buy the complicity of certain workers and that they would fight on his side, because it was a real war between workers and capital. After the "scrap" of 9 September, the boss put pressure on some guards "to be more violent attackers of our comrades." The union had "also officially known from Domenico La Monica [company manager] on Wednesday [9 September] that Crescenzago guards reinforced with those from A and B plants were going to attack comrades to provoke incidents and to be able to hit other workers with disciplinary actions. The union did not warn comrades and so gave its blessing to the boss's action and the subsequent repression." Benefiting from the union cover, management sent threatening letters to six people, including Reale and Folloni. The trade union officials must now assume their responsibilities towards the workers. The workers' organisation must continue to control the lodges to prevent further provocations and be heard in the workshops where the foremen raise their heads. "The Committee declares its opposition to punitive transfers, it calls upon the workers not to accept individual interviews with managers and intends once more to close the harmful and dangerous plants."[243]

On 11 October, a small group of workers marched out of the factory and blocked the east ring Milan motorway to protest against government measures. For the Workers Committee it was necessary "to attack the foremen, guards, spies, to control them, make them harmless, along with those who, among the workers, make themselves the voice of the boss. Workers' patrols must restart in the factory and continue to check the guards at the gate. We have to leave

---

242   *La Guardia rossa racconta*, op. cit. and *3 anni di lotte*, op. cit.
243   Leaflet: "Force and workers' organisation – Guards, bosses, spies and trade unionists," Magneti Marelli Workers Committee, 14 Sept 1976.

the factory in an organised way and block the roads and railways to impose the withdrawal of the measures, to impose political prices on merchants, if they want to continue to sell."[244]

The workers linked to the Workers Committee decide, "through the strength and organisation of the workers, to continue to play on the contradictions of the enemy." They present a complaint to the judge requesting the intervention of the police for the enforcement of the provisional judgement. The manager Domenico La Monica receives notice of proceedings no. R.G. 15924/76/930 instructed by the magistrate Di Lecce of the Fifth section of the Milan court which reminds him that he has committed an offence under Article. 388 of the Penal Code. In effect, he did not reinstate physically, but only legally and economically, the four sacked workers. The same judge decided to mobilise the police force to accompany the four workers to their places of work and immediately instructed the *Carabinieri* of Crescenzago to provide for reinstatement. After five days the police had still not appeared, so the comrades went to their barracks to demand an explanation. Ten days after the magistrate's order, "a period during which the sacked workers are protected by the Red Guard, we met with the sergeant of the *Carabinieri* at the guards' lodge." At ten in the morning on 18 October, "the sacked workers came out of the workshops accompanied by 70-80 workers to 'take' the Sergeant of Carabinieri to carry out the orders of the judge, and they accompanied him to 'avoid any provocation by the guards'." The Sergeant stood in front of the chief of personnel, immediately followed by a worker demonstration shouting slogans such as '*the only justice is that of the proletariat*'." The union, "the guardian of justice and democracy, had once again lost an opportunity to gain ground."[245]

This episode marked "a new stage of political initiative. It is no longer a question of an advance in the struggle against layoffs, but a step forward in the global clash between workers' organisation and the initiative of the boss… The 'worker Red Guard' thus takes possession of the lodge to protect itself from attack, taking away from the guards any possibility of action. It is an explicit political occupation, the substitution of the workers' will for that of the hierarchy. The new phase of the conflict with the guards continued in October with the re-election of delegates, in which Baglioni got twice as many votes as previously [179], according to the numbers he is in first place in his department,

---

244 Leaflet: "Against the government measures and their supporters – Impose proletarian interests – Strength and workers organisation," Magneti Workers Committee, 12 Oct 1976.

245 *La Guardia rossa racconta*, op. cit. and *3 anni di lotte*, op. cit. The company appealed to the Supreme Court against the magistrate's decision, but the appeal was rejected.

and second throughout the factory." This highlighted the mass influence that the Workers Committee had achieved in the factory.[246]

In October, the Council of the Order of Lawyers and Magistrates in Milan opened disciplinary proceedings against the lawyers Giuliano Spazzali, Francesco Piscopo, Anna Perosino, Luigi Zezza and Alberto Medina who had defended the four sacked workers at the hearing on 15 July 1976: "The corporatist Order [of the lawyers] progressively drops, like waste paper, all the mystifications of professional conduct and launches disciplinary proceedings against lawyers who defend their clients so "faithfully" that they were physically attacked by the police." This way of doing things on the part of the Lawyers' Order had already been used by the Order of Doctors when it opposed the struggles of the hospital and Polyclinic workers. "A social machine of anti-working class cooperation has long been set in motion, in an attempt to radically shift the burden of the crisis onto the shoulders of the proletariat." Capital's state's tries to legitimise and justify its anti-worker repression by large social and political forces: from professional organisations to the union confederations, from the Catholic movement *Comunione e liberazione* (a Catholic youth organisation created in the mid-1960s in explicit opposition to the student leftist movement) to the PCI's order service.[247]

---

246 *Operai e stato*, op. cit. and *3 anni di lotte*, op. cit.

247 "Workers and Justice," *Editoriale*, 12 Nov 1976 and idem, "Class confrontation besieges the judicial institution," and the leaflet: "Workers and Justice," Communist Committee (marxist-leninist) for Unity and Struggle, Communist Committee for Workers Power, Workers Political Collective, Italian Communist Party (marxist-leninist), Anarchist Struggle Organisation, Alfa Romeo Autonomous Assembly, *Lotta continua*, Workers Movement for Socialism, *Avanguardia comunista*, Milan, 12 Nov 1976, and "Workers' Voice," no. 296, 20 Nov/3 Dec 1976. The text of the disciplinary proceedings states: "The defenders did not disassociate themselves from the crowd who wanted to intimidate judges and lawyers on the opposing side, and did nothing to try to curb such intimidatory activities. Indeed they showed by their behaviour that they approved of them. They then abandoned their mandate as defenders to polemicize in such a fashion that the judges had to continue the trial behind closed doors. They finally, in a manifesto, in a press release and in a document addressed directly to the *Consiglio dell'Ordine* itself, set out the facts in a manner contrary to reality." "Workers and Justice," "The 'compromise' bypasses the articles of law," 12 Nov 1976.

The Italian section of the International Committee for the Defence of Political Prisoners in Europe published a statement:

"They try therefore to stifle any contestation of the untouchable role of the institutions, to affirm, once again, that those who want to oppose the rules of the game have no right to sit at the table of bourgeois justice, with the aim of rendering completely ineffective any

Their enemy is the workers' struggle. "Its irreducible character was once again demonstrated in the last few weeks, its will and non-spontaneous character that continually emerges and affirms itself in active minorities of workers." The five "comrade lawyers" respected "the policy discussed with the vanguard of the factory, in line with the workers' interests. This lucid respect took account of the tasks and problems of this phase of the class struggle, and showed itself very critical of the mystification at the centre of the Statuto [Statute of Labourers] and the Labour Court." The comrade lawyers responded well to the letter from their Order in these terms: "we have to immediately remove any doubt about the nature of this disciplinary procedure: it has nothing to do with the crimes arising from the exercise of the legal profession, but is overtly political." It was a blatant attempt at intimidation. The lawyers had not been subjected to disciplinary proceedings "for 'unfaithfully' defending or cheating their clients, but because they have never refused to put their 'knowledge and consciousness' at the service of the immediate interest of workers." Magneti Marelli seems to have power even outside the walls of the factory. The lawyers of the sacked workers say in the strongest terms that they are not politically part of the bourgeoisie and "never fail to fight it. This lack of class solidarity today leads the undersigned of this letter to disciplinary proceedings."

On 12 November, a worker meeting was held on the subject, called by the extra-parliamentary groups at the State University of Milan. Approximately 300 people attended. Magistrates and lawyers denounced the "fascist" intervention by the Lawyer's Order of Milan and the restrictions set out by the Court of Cassation regarding the Statute of Labourers. There were also workers

---

defence of proletarians and militants. It is not therefore a question of a repression directed only against lawyers, but against the very right of an accused to be defended. Everything now seems even more serious if we see it in the framework of the general tactics of the class enemy. In Germany there are laws prohibiting the formation of colleges of defence lawyers, which in practice prevent political defendants from choosing lawyers that they trust, and excluding from public office those who are suspected of having communist ideas. In the same way, in Italy, with less overt methods, a few dissident voices have been allowed to express themselves but they suppressed those voices when they gave concrete expression to the class struggle. The defence of rights is formally allowed but its exercise on a concrete and substantive plane is prevented. It pretends to open up institutions and sectors to more democracy, but this is only done with the aim of hiding contradictions. Everywhere, in Italy as in Germany, the ruling class thus attempts to strengthen its power and its control to reconstitute, without opposition and in full 'freedom', its public and economic order, once again making the working class pay the whole price."

"Workers' Voice," "Disciplinary proceedings against five lawyers who have defended militants of the revolutionary left over the years," no. 296, 20 Nov/3 Dec 1976.

who denounced repression in the factory and the support of the PCI for anti-worker manoeuvres.[248]

For the comrades of the Marelli Workers' Committee, the trial against the workers of Alfa, Alemagna, Zambeletti and Magneti Marelli, recently held at the courthouse in Milan, showed that the working class had decided to abandon its defensive and wait-and-see attitude and that it wanted to counter-attack on the institutional level. The judiciary in the trial in the Labour Court only "perfected its class power, acting on the basis of an abstract justice that does not take into account the real inequality that pits the two parties against each other." Workers were directly intervening in the trials to highlight this inequality, throwing into crisis the false neutrality of the authorities and the judges. The labour court "is in reality only a new tool to weaken the workers' capacity for struggle, to soften and castrate the workers' rebellion against the regime of wage labour, to liquidate the vanguard."[249]

---

248   Ibid.

249   "Workers and Justice," "Justice is increasingly short of breath," 12 Nov 1976. In this article there are some examples of workers' behaviour towards the justice system. The first is that adopted in May 1975 following the dismissal of three workers and the suspension of more by Alfa Romeo "for having participated in an internal march of more than 1,000 workers against the presence of the US Ambassador at the factory, the putschist John Volpe." The first to condemn them are the unions, and then the PCI in its daily *L'Unità* which defines the worker procession as "a racket." In these conditions layoffs are not long in coming. On the first day of the trial the workers mobilised, invaded the court and obtained a declaration that the layoffs were illegal. At the courthouse 4-500 factory workers in struggle arrived, marching into the building "with banners, red flags and chanting slogans against the bosses and their lackeys, against class justice, in front of the stupefied faces of the mummies of justice." The "big snake" of the procession winds through the building, and all the proletarians who have suffered, in those gloomy rooms, the sinister liturgy of justice, get a feeling of relief and liberation. The sordid agents of the judicial apparatus grind their greenish teeth – from the President of the Court, Trimarchi, who disappears for the afternoon, to Pomarici who attacks a worker from Alfa Romeo. Caught in the act – he does everything so that his face is struck by a hail of blows from a group of proletarians. The demo ends with an assembly in the hall, which melts into the singing of the "International" and the "Red Flag." Over the following days the judge Cecconi is accused of having favoured the "active presence of worker comrades" during the trial. Immediately the Alfa workers organise a press conference and distribute a leaflet outside the court in Milan for two days: "Today, the system tries to patch up the contradictions appearing between those known as the administrators of "justice," exercising pressure and repression against judges and lawyers who have made a specific class choice. Yesterday and today, the bosses want to eliminate any kind of "tear" in the fabric of the capitalist

When divisions occurred within *Senza tregua* in the summer of 1976, the Marelli Committee came closer to the "hardliners" than to the "intellectuals."[250] A strong opposition appeared between a current accused of "intellectualism" (the editors of the journal *Senza tregua*, Scalzone and Del Giudice), a current which had turned more towards direct, local and effective action (represented by Maurizio Costa and Piergiorgio Palmero), and a third which supported the necessity of arming itself for offensive purposes (Segio, Gottifredi).[251]

Among these three currents, in the summer of 1976, it was the most radical fraction which prevailed, which wanted to create "proletarian combat groups," while Scalzone and Del Giudice were removed from the running of the newspaper, which after some time resumed publication as "*Senza tregua – seconda serie*" (second series). This episode, which happened in Milan after the holidays of 1976, was considered as the "coup by the sergeants" (Galmozzi, Laronga, Libardi, Stefan), that is to say of comrades inserted into the base structures. They criticised the "politicians," wanting a different form of organisation, complaining of having to carry out actions whose political sense had not been previously collectively discussed. The comrades who had a position more linked to the centrality of the factory, such as Maurizio Costa, Franco Gottifredi, Ernesto Balducchi and Piergiorgio Palmero, did not side with the "sergeants."[252]

---

apparatus. The bosses and their state try to strike at ever more skilled categories of the working class. Along this road there are no half-measures: either you are with the working class or against it, the proletariat has a good long memory," Document of the Alfa Romeo Autonomous Assembly.

The second example is that of 23 March 1976 when the tenth civil division of the Court of Milan was to hear an appeal against a decision to reinstate 48 seasonal Alemagna workers, a decision taken by the magistrate Stanzani. The company lawyer Prisco, president of the Lawyers Association of Milan, did not turn up, causing the judge to postpone the hearing. The workers protested by organising a meeting and a march into the Palace of Justice. The *Carabinieri* intervened and clashed with the workers.

The last example was on the first of April when there were clashes and arrests during the trial against Pietro Di Gennaro, accused of throwing Molotov cocktails against a branch of *Comunione e liberazione* (a Catholic organisation). The trial ended with a sentence even harder than that sought by the prosecution and without the sentence being suspended. The comrades in the courtroom did not accept the verdict and screamed their protest against the decision of the judiciary: "once again they don't recognise the right of a bourgeois court to use the criteria of judgement of the established power."

250 *L'orda d'oro*, op. cit. p. 326
251 Guicciardi, *op. cit,*, p. 10
252 Guicciardi, *op. Cit.*, p. 115 testimony of Baglioni and *Requisitoria Spataro, cit.*

Among the accusations against the former editors of the newspaper was that of workers linked to the Marelli Committee that criticised the intellectual drift of *Senza tregua* and the lack of attention to the "propagandist characteristics of autonomous struggles that were already in the factories. These struggles, which had a violent character, were led, supported, coordinated through the journal," and it was therefore necessary to write in a more understandable way, closer to the needs of the workers.[253]

In Milan, the "worker cadres," the comrades of Marelli and Falck and those in the Porta Romana district, sided with the Communist Committees for Workers Power that then made up *Prima Linea* ("Front Line"), while comrades from Carlo Erba and Telettra defended the positions of Scalzone and Del Giudice and formed the Revolutionary Communist Committees. In Bologna, the situation remained blocked until after the convention on the repression of 1977, with the Ducati Workers Committee standing with the "sergeants" and the sympathisers of the journal *Corrispondenza operaia* with the Revolutionary Communist Committees. Turin, Naples and Florence militants sided with the "sergeants."[254]

The worker component and the "sergeants" met after the purge to talk about the "inevitable character of the choice, in the future, of the exercise of violence, including armed violence." The hard wing proposed the creation of structures ("assault groups") who would have the capacity of self-initiative. Magneti Marelli, however, never constituted an armed "assault group."[255]

Repression and restructuring

In 1976 the PCI abandoned hope of taking power by winning elections, but more discerning entrepreneurs such as Gianni Agnelli, then at the head of Confindustria, realised that the PCI seemed eager to help save the economy following the usual rules of capitalism. They thought of a possibility of collaboration that would serve to stifle worker activism by praising the advantages of sacrifice and austerity.[256]

In the Fifth section where the women workers were, "the foremen (and therefore the management) are attacking again." For the women comrades of the Fifth section, the continuous transfers demanded by the foremen had no technical logic, "but only serve to give back to these people the taste of

---

253 Ibid

254 *Requisitoria Spataro cit.* and Office of Instruction of the Court of Turin, Interrogation of Marco Donat Cattin, 9 April 1981.

255 Ibid

256 *Storia d'Italia...*, op. cit.

commanding us, the exercise of threats, of dividing us, first making us afraid and then making us servile, and soon bringing them a cup of coffee. Tomorrow, who knows?" When someone was injured, the foremen only cared "to clap their hands to send the other workers back to the line." Or they decided that some workers can do shift work because it is "humanly" possible for a seven year old child to stay home alone! The most militant women workers were promised a quiet job in the Sesto San Giovanni plant in exchange for "respectful and opportunistic behaviour." Only direct organisation in the workshops could seriously address these issues, "ten women workers are enough, organised and determined, to neutralise the foreman and his collaborators."[257]

On 12 November, a report of the *Carabinieri* accused all participants in internal marches from 9 May and 10 September 1975 of participating in an armed band – the file was sent to the judge Pomarici. On 16 November, the judge asked to see the files but, on 18 November, Pomarici told the district court to hold on to them because, in criminal proceedings, crimes requiring a higher jurisdiction had appeared, given the "subjective and objective connection between those cases and those pending for [participation in] an armed gang." The judge asked for the formalisation of the criminal proceedings and asked the investigating judge to issue arrest warrants for all participants in the demonstration in Palmieri's office on charges of aggravated robbery, aggravated private violence and aggravated burglary and destruction of goods. He called once more for all to be charged with involvement in an armed gang. The investigating judge Forno, on 26 November, asked Dr. Lombardi for a copy of the proceedings, and on 29 November he interviews La Monica and, on 30 November, Palmieri. The same day he rejects the request for the issuance of arrest warrants, so the court cannot apply its order.[258]

---

257 Leaflet: 'Force and Worker organisation against the young bosses who want to make a career on our backs," Some Women Comrades of the Fifth Section, 23 Sept 1976.

258 "Chronicle of a Trial," *Cronistoria*, Feb 1980. The management of the factory had filed several lawsuits related to these events: against the "abusive" introduction of the four fired workers into the factory (complaints of 1 Oct 1975 and 5 Nov 1975 of the proceeding no. 16893/75 before the Criminal Court of Milan, then joined to the proceedings no. RG 3235/76 Inst.); against the repeated introduction of the four into the factory (15 Oct 1976 lawsuit giving rise to the proceedings no. 17061/76 before the fifth chamber). The court case continued on 17 Dec 1976 when the police sent a new report with the cross-examination of Palmieri and copies of documents found in the home of Walter Alasia in Sesto San Giovanni. Between January and February 1977 the workers under investigation presented themselves spontaneously in front of the investigating judge, while Palmieri in a Labour Tribunal exonerated the accused for the events of 9 May.

On 16 November 1976, a group of armed men, after having bound and gagged the four people present, threw petrol bombs into the garage of Magneti Marelli reserved for executives of the Crescenzago plant. Thirteen cars were destroyed, and the group left leaflets saying: "Take the attack to the heart of the state; break up the project of building the Imperialist State of the Multinationals; build armed proletarian power in the Fighting Party. Armed struggle for communism." The action was claimed by the Red Brigades.[259]

A month later, a very important act "shakes" Sesto San Giovanni. On Wednesday, 15 December 1976, at 5 a.m., a council house in via Leopardi is surrounded by a massive deployment of security forces. In this flat, with his parents, lived the twenty year old Walter Alasia, a Red Brigades militant. A violent shootout broke out, at the end of which there were three dead: Alasia and two police officers. The parents of Walter Alasia were two well-known Sesto communists, his mother worked at Magneti Marelli. Walter Alasia was active in Lotta Continua in Sesto but he quit before the Congress of 1975. Immediately the union called a strike of two hours in memory of the two policemen and to condemn terrorism. The following day the Magneti Workers Committee and the Falck Collective distributed a leaflet against the proposal by the union. The Communist Workers Coordination of Breda Siderurgica, of Breda Fucine, and Termomeccanica put up a poster with similar content in the workshops. The call from these workers was to not participate in the union strike, advice that some departments in Magneti and Breda followed.

On the contrary, *Avanguardia operaia* and PDUP (*Partito di Unità Proletaria*, "Proletarian Unity Party"), both groups on the parliamentary extreme left, went to the trade union march, while Lotta Continua and Lotta comunista went on strike without participating in the demonstration.[260] In the leaflet of the Communist Committees for Workers Power, workers were invited to mourn their own dead and not those of others. It stated that the real terrorism is "the economic terrorism of the bosses, of the press, of the 50 police armed with machine guns who were present in Sesto in the streets of Rondinella yesterday morning at 5:30 threatening the workers going to work."

---

259 *Terrorismo in fabbrica*, op. cit.
260 *Senza tregua*, "Three days of ideological, psychological and police terrorism against the working class in Sesto San Giovanni," January 1977; *Corriere della sera*, "Blood shed in Milan too: Red Brigader kills a sub-prefect and a sergeant of the Carabinieri, then he is killed," 16 Dec 1976; *Corriere della sera*, "Twenty year old man slept with guns under his bed," 16 Dec 1976; *Corriere della sera*, "City in mourning and protest strikes in Milan and Sesto against the ferocious murder of the sub-prefect and sergeant," 16 Dec 1976; *Corriere della sera*, "'It was terrible' said Bazzega before his death," 16 Dec 1976; *Corriere della sera*, "5 a.m., the radio cries: 'Ambulance'," 16 Dec 1976.

True terrorism against the workers "is that which uses strikes like today, which brings together workers and bosses to defend the whole of power and those who possess it and the cops who defend it, that is, those who in the past and today killed workers and peasants in struggle."[261]

The union demonstration was a failure. There were 5-600 workers (out of 2,500 PCI members), 28 FGCI students and 4 teachers one of which was a member of Avanguardia operaia (AO). Only 67 workers from Magneti Marelli (PCI members) went to the demonstration (out of a total of 380 members) and 7 who were close to AO. On their return to the factory the PCI cadres reacted violently, but they were few in number and avoided physical confrontation. It was the same at Breda. "Two minorities confront each other. The tough guys of the PCI return from the demo and are wound up and… go to the comrades who are holding a meeting of 50 people in the Screw-making department." The Secretary of the PCI wanted to chase the comrades of the Committee out of the factory, but "only 12 strong men" are willing to follow him.[262]

The next day, Friday 17 December, was the day of the funerals. The union participated in those of the two policemen, while the Workers' Committees decided to go to Alasia's with a wreath saying "To Walter, from the communist revolutionary workers of Sesto." "There is fog. Slyly, the red municipality delays the funeral for nearly an hour. Despite this, 300 comrades manage to be present, including 80 from Marelli, and some from Sesto Lotta continua."[263] When the hearse arrived, "the Magneti comrades, who were many, and us, from Breda, were arranged in two wings. Everyone had a red carnation, fists were raised and we sung *The Internationale*." After a quarter of an hour of

---

261 Leaflet by Communist Committees for Workers Power, 16 Dec 1976, quoted in *Senza tregua*, January 1977, p. 4; *Corriere della Sera*, "Today in the St. Ambrose basilica, the funeral of the assistant chief and sergeant of the Carabinieri who were killed," 17 Dec 1976; *Corriere della Sera*, "The dead Brigader participated in the raid on the 'New Democracy' office," 17 Dec 1976; *Corriere della Sera*, "Three hundred law enforcement officers demonstrate in the courtyard of the police station," 17 Dec 1976; *Corriere della Sera*, "In Milan and Sesto S. Giovanni all the shutters were lowered," 17 Dec 1976; *Corriere della Sera*, "The great silence of a crowd moved," 18 Dec 1976; *Corriere della Sera*, "The city PCI's ultimatum to the ultraleft groups," 18 Dec 1976; *Corriere della Sera*, "The Milanese judges are entrusted with the investigation into the shooting in Sesto San Giovanni," 18 Dec 1976; *Corriere della Sera*, "The Brigader's funeral in Sesto San Giovanni," 18 Dec 1976.

262 *Senza tregua*, "Three days of ideological, psychological and police terrorism against the working class of Sesto San Giovanni," January 1977, and *Controinformazione*, "Marelli: the Red Guard tells its story," no. 17, January 1980.

263 Ibid

silence, the worker Enrico Baglioni said: "There is only one way to remember Walter: reinforce our struggle against the bosses, for communism, starting from our factories." At the end of his speech, one of the attendants shouted "Comrade Walter?" and everyone present replied "Present!"[264]

The murder of Walter Alasia, like that of Martino Zicchitella in Rome, served to further increase the distance between the Area of Autonomy and the ex-extra-parliamentary groups such as PDUP and AO: "These rascals are prepared to defend, for example, people like comrade Ulrike [Meinhoff] murdered in German prisons, while Anna Maria Mantini, 'Mara' [Cagol], Martino Zicchitella and Walter [Alasia], who died for the same ideas in Italy, are for them provocateurs."[265] Criticisms were also made against the Red Brigades – "I do not think you can have the PCI card in your pocket and be revolutionaries, like the Red Brigades comrades in the factories" (*Senza Tregua* did not agree with the choice of clandestinity made by the BR) – and the Armed Proletarian Nuclei (NAP) – "brave comrades but who too often pay with their lives for

---

264   *Senza tregua*, "What is the vanguards' judgment on the facts of Rome, Sesto and Brescia?," January 1977.

265   Ibid

On the morning of 5 June 1975, a patrol of *Carabinieri* raided the firm Cascina Spiotta Melazzo of Acqui Terme (Alexandria province). Inside were two Red Brigades militants with their hostage, the industrialist Vittorio Vallarino Gancia, kidnapped the previous day. A firefight followed in which three *Carabinieri* were injured, of which one died six days later. A fourth policeman captured Margherita Cagol who was slightly wounded – she was killed with her hands up. See: *La mappa perduta* ("The Lost Map"), *Sensibili alle foglie* Bookshop, 1984, p. 285.

In Rome, on 8 July 1975, Anna Maria "Luisa" Mantini, a militant of the NAP (Armed Proletarian Nuclei), was killed by a pistol shot to the face by the vice-brigadier of anti-terrorism Antonio Tuzzolino, as she returned to her apartment, which had been located by the police. On 9 February 1976, militants of NAP in Rome intentionally injured Tuzzolino so that he was left with his legs paralysed. *La mappa perduta*, p. 288.

On the morning of 9 May 1976, the guards of Stammheim prison found Urlike Meinhof of the Red Army Faction hanged in her cell. Defence lawyers and relatives of the victims were not allowed access to the place of death and were not allowed to see the body of the deceased or to participate in the autopsy. That supposedly excluded action by a third party, and so confirmed the theory of Meinhof's suicide. In Rome, on 14 December 1976, the NAP militant Martino Zicchitella died during the attack against the head of the security services in Rome and Lazio, Alfonso Noce. In the shootout the cop Palumbo Prisco died, while Noce and another cop were injured. *La mappa perduta*, p. 291.

errors that have long term consequences, bad luck does not explain anything," in addition to being fairly isolated.²⁶⁶

In the same period Magneti Marelli reorganised the company into divisions changing its pyramidal structure into one organised "by column," according to the type of manufactured product. With the divisions created, the Crescenzago factory was ready for "worker decimation." Marelli also started producing abroad (in Nigeria, Venezuela, Brazil, Taiwan). The transition to a multinational structure was supported by all the trade unions, as workers realised the implications for employment and the inability to conduct struggles that had an impact on production. Contrary to what was imagined by the reformists of the PCI, the restructuring into divisions only served "to identify areas of the factory to be dismembered, and where the technology used is transferable to the black economy."²⁶⁷, ²⁶⁸

> In the following months, the worker minority organised in the Red Guard is involved in the preparation of the workers' response to the *Cassa Integrazione* and the dismantling of two departments, the Contacts and the Regulators, in which the Workers Committee does not even have one sympathiser. Every morning, after entering the factory, the Red Guard held rallies and meetings in these two departments.
>
> In this way they build the *return* to the factory in the days of the *Cassa Integrazione*, which the union also relies on to curb any possible autonomous initiatives. The first day of technical unemployment, the women workers of the Regulators department re-enter *en masse* with the comrades of the Workers Committee who have launched an autonomous strike and are marching around the factory with 400 workers. The union tries to divide them by making a strike of its own lackeys 'independently,' especially those in the PCI, and offers the suspended women a demo outside the factory with distribution of leaflets in the neighbourhood. With the 10 suspended women

---

266   Ibid
267   The term "black economy" could have a lot of meanings. In general, in connection with the car industry, it meant some sort of unregulated outsourcing of production of components used in production within the Fiat group of companies. In many cases the suppliers used Fiat employees, working in their "spare time," as the workforce! The workers were willing to do this as a way of obtaining a second, tax-free, income. See: Giorgio Garuzzo, *Fiat – the secrets of an epoch*, Springer International Publishing, 2014, pg 39.
268   *4 anni di lotte*, op. cit.

and 60 lackeys, the union leaves the factory, while 300 workers demonstrate inside.

In the same week management announced that in the Second section (the department of the four sacked men) there is a surplus of 40 workers and threatens to lay them off. The workers' reaction is very determined, having been prepared by agitation of the Red Guard for two days. On the third day the Workers Committee declares an autonomous department strike with an initial rally with the sacked workers. Out of 200 present, 150 go on strike and their procession collects workers from other departments, made aware by the Red Guard. First they go to the Factory Council to explain things to its members who had refused the proposal from the management. A delegate of the PCI ends up in the company infirmary. The workers force the rest of the Factory Council to discuss and join a march to the management offices. The next day, management takes back its decision: there are no longer any surplus workers in the Second section.[269]

Birth of the Autonomous Workers Coordination of Milan

On 20 October in Milan a provincial general strike was called by the unions. According to Autonomia Operaia's analysis, this was a means for the union to recuperate workers' struggles against the government measures that had developed independently. The previous week' strikes and road blockades had shown that the situation in the factories had not normalised. In Milan the perspective of building a workers' coordination, promoted by the various components of Workers Autonomy – the Workers' Political Collectives, the Communist Committees for Workers Power, the Communist Committee (marxist-leninist) of Unity and Struggle and the Italian Communist Party (marxist-leninist) – was discussed. The result was a unitary manifesto with the strike in mind that defined the meaning and development of the conflict: "the capitalists struggle to overcome the crisis and revive their profits." The union and PCI policy was adequate for this operation but the plea for sacrifices had to confront "the response of the workers, their refusal to share responsibility for recovery of the 'national economy,' and their willingness to fight for their own interests," as shown by the previous days' strikes at Alfa Romeo, Magneti Marelli and OM-Fiat. The general strike was called not to widen the worker initiatives, but

---

269   *La Guardia rossa racconta*, op. cit.

on the contrary was an attempt to contain their protest. It was not directed against the substance of the government measures, but only aimed at obtaining some minor modifications.

To counteract the project of the DC, the PCI and the trade unions, "who are the corner stones of this regime (…) we must organise in all the factories, offices, neighbourhoods and streets to break with the logic of 'sacrifices' and class collaboration." That day, the union demo divided into several successive marches.[270]

The Milan Workers Coordination was formed at the end of 1976, when the forces of Workers Autonomy in Milan (Workers' Political Collectives, Communist Committees for Workers Power) and some Marxist-Leninist groups (PC(m-l)I and CoCo(m-l)UL, pronounced "Coculo"[271]) successfully managed to organise part of the radical elements of the working class in Milan. The draft platform for the establishment of the Milan Workers Coordination stressed the first common points between the PC(m-l)I and the Workers Political Collectives with the agreement of the Communist Committees for Workers Power and CoCo(m-l)UL. The platform was divided into four parts, and it was discussed and perfected over the course of several workers' assemblies.

The first part of the document analysed the domestic and international situation. For the authors, the economic and the political ruling classes have used the economic crisis for one purpose: to obtain on the international level the maximum availability of labour, imposing a maximal mobility on the chessboard of multinational investment, achieving – with these resources – a qualitative step forward in the general intensification of worldwide exploitation. This is a direct consequence of the results obtained by workers' struggles in the advanced capitalist countries in the 1960s. The instruments used for this capitalist counter-attack are: "The unification of the financial market under the dictatorship of the dollar, the terroristic use of the instruments of international credit, the determination of the norms and limits of development (and/or of crisis) starting from the imposition of parameters aiming at

---

270 Poster: *Nessun sacrificio! Non collaborare!* ("No sacrifice! Do not collaborate!"), Workers Political Committees, Communist Committees for Workers Power, Communist Committee (Marxist-Leninist) of Unity and Struggle, Italian Communist Party (Marxist-Leninist), October 1976, in Recupero Nino (ed.), 1977: *autonomia/organizzazione*, Pellicanolibri edizioni, Catania, 1978

271 "CoCuLo" was a small group coming out of Maoism and retaining some of its ideological references, but it supported grassroots initiatives in factories, neighbourhoods and schools. It was founded in 1970 and dissolved in 1979. It was opposed to "armed struggle" but not to violence.

increased productivity." To these old recipes is added the attempt by the new social democratic block trying to "make credible the programme of capitalist restoration." In this context Italy is a weak link because of the presence of a strong working class.

The second part of the draft raised the question of the role of coordination as a tool to incite "the area of insubordination" to turn the situation towards revolutionary political action. The Coordination should put forward:

1. the struggle for wages (sliding scale, qualifications, against union collaboration),
2. the fight against work (against exploitation, against the increase of production, in defence of absenteeism, against mobility, for labour rigidity),
3. the fight against the factory command (against the foremen and the organisation of work, against the stratification and division of the working class, workers' patrols against black economy employment),
4. the fight against the State ("resistance to state provocations and its repressive forces and special corps, denunciation and intervention against the management of social exploitation – monetary, fiscal, welfare policy etc. – and against the imperialist actions of the state").

The forms of struggle over the indirect wage must be adapted, notably those concerning "reappropriation." In the factories, on the other hand, the document called for boycotts, wildcat strikes and sabotage.

The third part proposed, alongside the platform of resistance, a platform of agitation and attack. The long-term objectives were:

1. "100,000 lire [276% increase, to around $US120[272]] per month, to be able to survive and reproduce as a class,"
2. 35 hours paid as 40 hours as the maximum working week ("free time to organise ourselves politically and to be able to live better"),
3. because exploitation now affects the whole of society, it is necessary from now on to demand a "social wage" ("Why does the woman who stays at home not get paid when she works

---

272 See: https://www.poundsterlinglive.com/bank-of-england-spot/historical-spot-exchange-rates/usd/USD-to-ITL-1976 for exchange rates. In the US average earnings in 1976 were around $770 per month.

every day and suffers to reproduce labour power? Why does the student who works to gain the capacity to be exploited in the factory not receive a wage? Why should the unemployed, who have certainly not lost their jobs voluntarily and haven't found another one, not be paid?"),

4. social benefits are indirect wages so they must increase, and social services must be free.

Multinational companies are not only the direct cause of many of our daily misfortunes in terms of wages and excess working time sold to the boss. At this point they have also become instruments of destruction of our life. The Workers Coordination cannot forget the daily experience of death imposed by the boss in the factories, the pollution caused by the boss in the surrounding area, the poisoning and continual attempts at genocide to assure profits. It cannot forget the daily work of degradation, of cultural repression, of cretinisation that the boss organises, thanks to his instruments of power. We must not forget that revisionism not only participates in, but is a crucial inspiration of, the current political structure. This is why the fight against all the agents of social-democratic repression is both a slogan and a mass policy.

The fourth part of the draft concerns the orientation of the Coordination, in the sense of "worker centrality" over the entire urban network of struggles.[273]

On 18 December 1976 at the Student Residence in Milan a workers' conference for the city was held, which was in fact the first public meeting of the Milan Workers Coordination. Among the workers' groups who participated were the CPOs (Workers Political Committees) of Siemens and Face Standard, the Magneti Workers Committee, the Falck Workers Collective, Telettra Communist Committee, Carlo Erba Workers Committee, Montedison Struggle Committee, and the CTP Siemens Communist Coordination. Around 150-180 leading worker militants in total participated, discussing from morning until late at night and developing proposals. On the one hand were the workers of the PC(m-l)I persuasion and the CPOs who fully supported the draft platform, presented as a prelude to the construction of the

---

273 Document "Draft platform for workers coordination," PC(m-l)I and Workers Political Committees with the agreement of the Communist Committee (m-l) of Unity and Struggle and Communist Committees for Workers Power, Milan, end of 1976, in "Workers' Voice," no. 297, 11/12-25 Dec 1976.

workers' front in order to promote unity in struggle of the working class, on the other side was the position of CoCo(m-l)UL and that of Communist Committees for Workers Power. The first current wanted "organisations to start by agreeing upon a political and ideological platform, giving priority to the unity of the worker base." They favoured a kind of intergroup coordination. The second current, the area of *Senza tregua*, emphasised "the exercise of proletarian strength as a concrete manifestation of counter-power towards the factory command and the various levels where the capitalist attack affects society." The Coordination of Revolutionary Communist Workers of Breda also made a contribution. A committee consisting of representatives of the various factory and neighbourhood experiences was formed at the end of meeting.[274]

At a national level the Andreotti government implemented the first "big decrees." They envisioned increases in prices for public services, the blocking of the *Scala mobile* and a reduction in public holidays. In response, the Marelli Workers Committee proclaimed a political strike against the measures, and 200 workers marched towards Viale Palmanova (the main road from Crescenzago to Sesto Cologno Monzese) to block the road. The agreement between the government and the union left "only Magneti workers able to respond with strikes and roadblocks. Starting from these initiatives the comrades of the Workers Committee acquired the authority to impose a debate in Milan on the strike as a fundamental political tool of revolutionary initiative at this stage." The Magneti Workers Committee developed links with other areas of struggle such as hospitals and small factories, but did not succeed in creating a centre that organised and planned general struggle.

Despite everything, it proclaimed an autonomous strike on 18 March 1977, characterised "by an explicit worker direction, with slogans against the social democratic orientation of the PCI and the unions, and against the bosses' command."[275]

During a city-wide meeting held on 3 February at Bocconi University, over 300 "vanguard" workers in Milan discussed the need to build as soon as possible a coordination capable of organising a mobilisation in the factories. The debate touched on "the central points of the class struggle in Italy today, the role of the Andreotti government backed up and actively supported by the PCI and union leaders, the intense activity of the state's repressive bodies, the role

---

274 Manifesto "The autonomous struggles must be organised," signed by Workers Political Collectives, Communist Committees for Workers Power, Communist Committee (m-l) of Unity and Struggle, Italian Communist Party (m-l), "Workers' Voice," no. 298, 15/28 Jan 1977, and "Workers' Voice," "The beginning of the political work of 'coordination'," no. 298, 15/28 Jan 1977.

275 *Operai e stato*, op. cit. and *3 anni di lotte*, op. cit.

of fascists who once again act openly." Some departments of factories in Milan (Alfa Romeo, Magneti Marelli, Borletti, Fiat-Om, Tibb) went on strike immediately against the signing of the *Confindustria*-unions pact, following a new attack by the government: "crookery over seniority, abolition of seven public holidays, increase in shift work and overtime, imposition of mobility and repression of absenteeism, increase in VAT, increase in petrol prices, blocking of the *Scale mobile*." Many workers' assemblies opposed this agreement: Face Standard Milan, Italsider Naples, Alfa Romeo in Arese, OM-Fiat Milan, Fiat Lingotto Turin, Auto Body Mirafiori, Sant'Eustachio Brescia.

"Against the union-government-Confindustria social pact"

The first opportunity to verify the possibility of coordination of the different autonomous groups in Milan was the city demonstration on 5 February "openly in opposition to the union-government-Confindustria social pact," organised by various Milan autonomous groups. It was called by the Coordination of Struggle for the Alfa Romeo Occupation and the Coordination of Workers Delegates for the Porta Romana Area. The demonstration gathered at 15.30 in Largo Cairoli (a big square in west central Milan) and marched through the downtown streets led by worker Coordinations and ended with a rally outside the offices of Assolombarda, home of Confindustria in Milan, during which an Alfa Romeo worker made a speech, along with a representative of an unemployed organisation and a comrade of the Porta Romana area Coordination.[276]

In the Milan factories the mobilisation grew and workers demanded the calling of a provincial strike of the engineering sector, which took place on 11 February. In Sesto San Giovanni there was a march of 10,000 people in which

---

276   *Lotta Continua*, "Demonstration in Milan tomorrow," 4 Feb 1977, and *Lotta Continua*, "Develop the organized workers opposition," 8 Feb 1977. The demonstration was supported by the factory Committees of Magneti Marelli, Siemens, Carlo Erba, Face-Standard, Soilax, Breda and Falck, the Hospital workers Coordination of Milan, the Public Sector Workers Coordination of Milan, the Struggle Committee of Binda, the workers of Imperial, the Communist Organisation (m-l), the Revolutionary Communist Groups (Fourth International), the Communist Committees for Workers Power, the Communist Committee (m-l) of Unity and Struggle, the Committee of the Organised Unemployed of Milan, the Assembly of all Housing Occupations in Milan, the Coordination of Circles of Proletarian Youth, the Workers Movement for Socialism and Lotta Continua. "Once again opportunist forces such as AO and PDUP have ignored this event, the first going to a meeting of no more than a thousand, and the second trapped in discussing their internal squabbles." *Lotta Continua*, "Develop the organised workers opposition," 8 Feb 1977.

the "lion's share" was made up of Magneti Marelli workers, around 1500, but there was also strong participation by Breda Siderurgica and Falck, "with an almost total absence of the union and the PCI." At the end of the demo about 150 workers block Viale Monza for half an hour. Another demonstration of 3,000 workers took place in the area of Porta Romana, with a large number of workers from small factories, and ended up blocking the roads.[277]

On 24 February, the Milan magistrate, Dr. Cecconi, dismissed charges against ten workers. Magneti had suspended them from work for a period of one to three days, accusing them of taking part in the demonstration in front of Palmieri's offices.[278]

On 18 March 1977 the CGIL-CISL-UIL unions called a national strike. In Milan two demos were organised to meet in Piazza Duomo, where, at 10:30 a.m. the secretary of the UIL, Giorgio Benvenuto, made a long speech. At the same time, the autonomous demo took place with many thousands of people (20,000 according to *Lotta Continua*), demonstrating the presence of a duality within the workers' movement in Milan, and also the political and social force of the area of Autonomy.

The political leadership of the demonstration was represented by workers from Magneti Marelli (where women workers were being suspended on a daily basis), from Breda (where they organised internal marches), from Falck (where they organised the first autonomous strikes), but also from Niguarda, from Carlo Erba, from workers patrols around Vimercate (a suburb north east of Milan, where the headquarters of IBM in Italy was), from Telettra in San Siro (and close to Siemens). The march left at 10 a.m. from Piazza Fontana, and then crossed Piazza Duomo during the Benvenuto speech, interrupting it. At the head of the demo were banners of various trade unions of hospital workers, and of the Factory Councils of Telenorma, OM-FIAT and ENI.

The slogans were "*Sacrifices, sacrifices!*" or "*We are the real criminals, Gui and Tanassi* [a Minister involved in a bribery scandal] *are innocent.*" The demo continued to Largo Cairoli, where a worker from the Porta Romana area and a student spoke. From there four marches set out for different destinations. One of these was led by Milan Workers Autonomy, which, with workers' banners waving, went to the courthouse where the appeal case against the dismissal of the four workers from the Marelli Workers Committee was being held. The demonstration arrived in Piazza Cinque giornate, advanced along Viale Bianca Maria and went back to the centre. Shortly after 11 a.m., as the demo crossed via Francesco Sforza, on the corner of Corso di Porta Vittoria, four groups

---

277　*Lotta Continua*, "Milan: 3 demos today," 11 Feb 1977, and *Lotta Continua*, "Milan: 10,000 march in Sesto," 12 Feb 1977.
278　"Free our imprisoned comrades," motion signed by 470 workers, 5 Jan 1978.

left the march: one blocked the traffic on piazza Augusto, a second placed itself at the entrance to Via Guastalla, the other two carried out two actions. Outside the headquarters of Magneti Marelli at 2 via Guastalla, a group of about 30 armed men entered the premises of the company, threatening the people present, who were robbed of money and ID cards, tied up two employees and locked them in a room. Then they threw Molotov cocktails and fired guns, causing a fire. After the action, the two groups went back into the demonstration.

At the same time another group attacked the Bassani Ticino (electrical construction company) premises at 9 Corso di Porta Vittoria: the door was closed, a few shots were fired at the windows of the first floor and six Molotov cocktails were thrown. In the meantime, a security guard on duty was disarmed in front of the Banco Ambrosiano at 7 Corso di Porta Vittoria.

The bulk of the demonstration continued on via Francesco Sforza, where another group left the march to raid the offices of the Ca'Granda (university head office) which were covered in graffiti. Around noon, the demo ended in Piazza Vetra. This autonomous march of two thousand people "concluded a whole phase of debate demanding a political break with revisionism." The objectives aimed at during the event represented "political centralisation and formalisation, under the direction of the factory vanguards, of the political paths and goals that express themselves in the building of proletarian organisation," isolating the workers "co-opted by capital which offers them overtime and pushes them to act as scabs." It meant organising young proletarians no longer against the *Scale mobile*, "but against the thousands of centres of black work," identifying and targeting "social hierarchies that represent the enemy command body which rules over the labour of proletarians today… The ability to hit the centres of black work and hierarchies is becoming an extensive and almost spontaneous field of initiative," but that's not enough.[279]

---

279 *Lotta Continua*, "Countless processions of comrades," 19 March 1977, and *Senza tregua*, "Milan: the workers' struggle goes out on to the territory," April 1977, and minutes of the trial of Prima Linea in Milan no. 921/80 folder 23, volume 5 and Office of the Prosecutor of the Republic of Milan, "Closing speech of the representative of the Public Minister Armando Spataro, 11 July 1981 relating to the proceedings no. 221/80 F G. and no. 228/81 F G.," pp. 864-865 and Court of Milan, "Sentence-ruling by examining magistrate Elena Paciotti concerning the penal proceedings no. 921/80F of 3 June 1982 against Antonio Achilli and other people."

These are the slogans of the autonomous demonstration on 18 March:
1. *35 hours – guaranteed wage – profit to be abolished!*
2. *The Communist Party is with the boss – this is the real provocation!*

The story of the Workers' Committee

The Workers' Committee confirmed that "sacked comrades went into the factory at 7.45 a.m. on 19 March. A worker patrol, bigger than usual, 70 workers with flags occupied the guardhouse and let their mates come in. Autonomous meetings were held in the Second section and there were *ad hoc* meetings in the other departments. This happens every morning." It will be the same up until 22 April 1977. On 15 April, the Workers Committee meets to discuss the situation: "This fight has lasted 20 months and has been positive... The principle that it is the law that decides our life has not gone, but it's workers' organisation that decides our life." At the guardhouse, workers no longer found the guards but the police instead, while "in Milan there are no other situations in which to widen the confrontation." For the Workers Committee "we will leave the factory when we decide." The discussion continued for a week between all those who directly participated in the struggle.

---

3. *Social democracy = repression – Long live class struggle for revolution!*
4. *No to restructuring and the social contract – Proletarian front against capital!*
5. *Against the bosses in cahoots with the union – let's organise absenteeism!*
6. *Union bigwigs – technocrats – whoever it is – chase out the new cops!*
7. *Unpaid housework – no to state attacks on women!*
8. *Black work – unemployment – restructuring – women have had enough!*
9. *Feminism, yes! Pacifism, no! Class struggle against capitalism!*
10. *Tina Anselmi [the first woman Minister in any Italian government, a Christian Democrat] – don't worry – in the mines equality is respected!*
11. *We don't delegate our liberation! Organise insubordination!*
12. *Malfatti reform – Communist Party reform – the precarious are organising!*
13. *35 hours – social wage – who pays? Capital!*
14. *Class struggle – organisation – here is our requalification!*
15. *Black work – marginal work – the social pact!*
16. *After Lama – try Benvenuto – in Tibet there is room for another idiot ["one with horns"]!*
17. *Cossiga and Berlinguer want power – and we're going to blow up the headquarters!*
18. *They'll be nothing left of the courts – we are all morally responsible!*
19. *Against capital: wildcat strike – blockade – absenteeism – sabotage!*
20. *Communist Party, unions: provocateurs, arse-lickers of the state!*
21. *DC-PCI = repression – organise insubordination!*
22. *Wages – breaks – no to black work – The best way to struggle!*
23. *Against overtime – against decentralisation – wage increases – no layoffs!*
24. *No one must be controlled – down with the sickness insurance cops!*

Cited in Nino Recupero, 1977 *"autonomia/organizzazione,"* Pellicano libri, Catania, 1978, p. 68

On Friday 22 April in Verbania, three worker militants from Magneti Marelli, including one sacked for political reasons, and four from Falck were stopped at a roadblock by the *Carabinieri*. Some guns were found in their cars, so they were suspected of returning from shooting practice in Valgrande. The seven workers were Enrico Baglioni, Riccardo Paris, Teodoro Rodia, Francesco Meregalli, Antonio Guerrero, Elio Brambilla and Emilio Cominelli.

On 25 April, during the Milan demonstration celebrating Liberation, which should have been concluded with a speech from Bruno Trentin, the Workers Committees of Marelli and Falck distributed hundreds of copies of a leaflet in Piazza Castello. In it they argued that since the sections of the petty and middle bourgeoisie arm themselves, "that the bosses have their private armed corps," so also the workers are entitled to do so.[280] The two Committees expressed their thoughts on the arrest of the seven workers in Valgrande. They had no problem with workers being armed, "except in the fact that these comrades have unfortunately fallen into the hands of the police." They stressed that the crime which was growing was perpetrated by the bourgeoisie with its private armies, with the restructuring and layoffs in factories, with the increase in charges and taxes, with deaths at work. Against this attack, "in recent months a new degree of recomposition of the proletariat has been achieved, which has seen enter into struggle, on the side of revolutionary workers, the unemployed, casual workers, the super-exploited in the black economy, women and young workers who, in schools and universities, are more unruly because they are simultaneously exploited and doomed to unemployment." The confrontation was strongly radicalised, so "vanguard workers and proletarians began to consider the appropriate means of struggle adequate to their strategic interests (abolition of the wage system, communism), they are thus armed and trained… These workers who were caught with weapons are comrades who fell into enemy hands and this is bad, but it is also a sign that new militants, new vanguards, in almost every department, in every factory, in every district and school, are posing the question of how to get sufficient power to organise themselves to leave behind wage slavery. It is a sign that thousands of comrades are taking what has been denied them."[281]

---

280 *L'orda d'oro*, op. cit., p. 326, testimony of Lucia Martini and Oreste Scalzone.

281 Leaflet by the Workers Committees of Marelli and Falk, also signed by: the Autonomous Factory Organisations of Alfa, Siemens, Face, Eni, Breda, Telettra, Carlo Erba, Snia; the Worker and Proletarian Patrols of Romana Vigentina, Lambrate, Bovisa, and San Siro district; the Communist Committees for Workers Power; the Workers Political Collectives; the Proletarian Communist Committees for Organised Autonomy for Workers Power; the Communist Committee (m-l) for Unity and Struggle, PC (m-l)I, Milan, April 1977.

On 26 April, the three sacked workers still at liberty presented themselves at the guardhouse. "The Red Guard waited for them, more menacing than usual. In the factory work stopped from 6 a.m. The PCI had stuck up provocative posters in the shops, but it did not show itself. On the contrary, in the workshops, marches led by the comrades of the Committee follow one after another."[282]

The arrest of the seven workers in Verbania happened while a discussion was going on in Magneti Marelli about "the process of construction of workers' organisation after the experience of the March Days, and the preparation for the exit from the factory of fired comrades and a debate about linking all workers situations…"[283]

On 29 April, at Verbania, the trial of the 7 arrested workers caught red handed took place. Around 500 comrades, including 120 from Magneti Marelli, attended. The trial was postponed to the next day. On 30 April, the workers' mobilisation increased to show solidarity with their arrested workmates. During the trial the defendants claimed the right of the working class to

---

282 *La Guardia rossa*, op. Cit. For the Executive of the Factory Council, the Verbania episode confirmed "on the basis of an explicit assessment of conduct contrary to the interests of workers and the masses," the correctness of the decision taken by the Factory Council the previous year when it expelled certain people from the union after the wounding of Palmieri. The Executive Council "calls upon all workers for the utmost vigilance and unity to isolate factory provocateurs, and to defend the Republican institutions now more than ever attacked by the forces of conservatism and reaction." The Lenin Section of the PCI inside the factory was even more explicit. In a leaflet it stated that "Baglioni, Rodia and Cominelli have declared in the factory that they belong to the area of autonomy, but they have never hidden their sympathies for the BR and NAP." The PCI also emphasised the responsibility of the company: "the actions of these figures [the workers arrested] in the factory were openly anti-union and above all anti-Communist, their actions took place throughout the most difficult time for the company and clearly played its game. We must condemn certain elements in the management who, supported by the work of these provocateurs, defended by all means (recruitment of shady characters, giving space to provocations) the discourse of ungovernability of the factory with the aim of drastically reducing staffing levels, particularly in Crescenzago, and blaming workers and the labour movement."

The leaflet distributed by the *Lotta continua* section in Sesto denounced "the frame-up of the seven comrades that workers know have always been at the forefront of the struggle. By making them out to be provocateurs they want to make an example of all the workers who have opposed sacrifices in the factories of Sesto San Giovanni," quoted in *Terrorismo in fabbrica*, op. cit.

283 *Operai e stato*, op. cit.

be "equipped with the tools" to support their demands. They were sentenced to two years without parole. This sentence encouraged the *Carabinieri* to again ask for the prosecution of some workers for participation in an armed gang. On 11 May, the prosecutor in Verbania transmitted, to the Milan jurisdiction, facts relating to participation in an armed gang, and the Public Prosecutor in Milan called for the issuance of arrest warrants against the already-arrested workers.[284]

In the meantime, the three fired workers continued to enter the factory until 15 May 1977, when they announced, on placards, the end of the fight against redundancies.

> The comrades decided to leave the factory, to demand from management a sum of 60 million lire [around €180,000 in 2017] that the boss would pay without any agreement being signed. Everything is at stake and everything depends on the use of force. The decision to leave the factory was a tactically correct decision to make, since the fight against redundancies represented a moment of confrontation with the boss and the growth of political organisation for workers, a growth that happened independently of their definitive return – or not – to the factory. The cash paid by the owner will be shared between the sacked comrades, the comrades in prison and a struggle fund for the Workers Committee and worker organisation in

---

284 "Chronicle of a Trial," *Cronistoria*, February 1980. Enrico Baglioni wrote a letter from prison to his comrade workers in which he only recognised the accusations which were of a political nature: "It is right that it is so, everything is political and nothing is legal, it represents well the crisis that hits the power of the bosses and underlines the strength of the workers and revolutionary communists." The real accusation against us is: "to be workers and to want to establish communism through the overthrow of this society, and they are right because this is the only way to do it." The arrests aimed at getting rid of those opposed to the restructuring plan for Magneti Marelli. In the letter, Baglioni distinguished himself from the Red Brigades, "not because they are not communist comrades," but because it is not yet time for the "storming of the Winter Palace," even if it is true that communism is approaching, "because the workers are from now on aware of the possibility of achieving liberation from work, thanks to advances in science and technology," because "the social character of production links us proletarians more and more to each other." Baglioni asserted his intent to participate in a legal battle which would highlight "all their contradictions." Letter: "We are accused of being workers" by Enrico Baglioni, July 1977, quoted in the *Lotta Continua* readers' letters section.

the factory.[285]

On 23 June 1977 the investigating judge Forno signed the arrest warrants requested by the Prosecutor and added a charge of aggravated robbery against Rodia and Baglioni.[286]

On 18 June 1977, simultaneously and acting in a coordinated way, two armed squads raided, around 3 p.m., the buildings of Magneti Marelli at 43 via Stephenson in Milan and Sit Siemens in Settimo Milanese (a suburb of Milan). The attacks were justified politically by the suspensions of workers in the two factories. After the actions the suspensions were revoked, a decision undoubtedly motivated by the cost of repairing the damaged plants.

The action at Magneti Marelli took place at 2.50 p.m. when two people dressed as *Carabinieri* arrived by car. The guard opened the gate and was immediately handcuffed. Another car arrived, a green Fiat 125, from which emerged four men and a woman, their faces not covered. They entered the warehouse and exploded seven drums of petrol.

About ten minutes later, the action was repeated at Sit Siemens. Three people, including one in a *Carbinieri* uniform, presented themselves at the gate under the pretext of having to defuse explosive devices inside the warehouse. The guard was handcuffed and left in a car in a meadow in Quinto Romano. The fuel drums were placed in three warehouses, each of 6,500 square meters, and connected to a timer. Two bombs exploded, the third was later defused by police. The raiders departed in a yellow Fiat 128 with the guard who was then released 5 km away. Fires ravaged the buildings resulting in damage worth 21 billion lire (more than €6 million at today's prices).

Prima linea claimed the attacks with phone calls to ANSA (National Press Association Agency) and *Corriere della Sera* ("we warn the Press against any attempt to link Prima linea with the Red Brigades") and a leaflet found in phone booths in Piazza Tricolore and corso Lodi in Milan: "Capital develops violence at every level of social productive relations, creates and centralises new institutions for political control over the proletariat. These are conditions necessary for its survival. The new international division of labour is the fundamental condition for the restoration of this command, to smash the unity and the political strength of the working class. This new form of command and

---

285 *Lotta Continua*, "New arrest warrants against the 7 Magneti comrades already imprisoned," 26/27 June 1977, and *Operai e stato*, op. cit. According to the testimony of Oreste Scalzone for the book *L'orda d'oro*, the money that the company gave laid-off workers was donated by them for the construction of a kindergarten for the children of Marelli workers. *L'orda d'oro*, op. cit.

286 "Chronicle of a Trial," op. cit. and *4 anni di lotte*, op. cit.

this new division of labour are inextricably linked. Disrupting the command, disrupting production and sabotaging the overall functioning of the capitalist machine are mandatory tasks for combative communist organisations... The working class therefore faces an alternative: either to blow to pieces the new power of command, the new operation of the machine of production, oppose the acceleration of its rhythm and the stratification of the workforce, or to make live in their own struggles in their own political initiative the ability to break the command, attack the opposed social bloc, sabotage production... In the revolutionary process we can see a dialectic between destruction of social relations and the re-appropriation of social wealth in order to build a fighting organisation of the class. It is in this organisation, in a process of prolonged civil war, that it expresses its political subjectivity and its capacity for a new social cooperation... The attacks against the multinationals Stet-Sit-Siemens and Fiat hit two crucial moments of the revival of the big Italian company as a multinational, a condition for the restoration of the unity and strength of command in Italy."

The leaflet cited as an example of an "attack aiming at the centres of training and organisation of [capitalist] hierarchies" the recent armed actions against the Iseo comapny and Federquadri,[287] while it underlined the importance of the "new form of command" in which participate "political cadres of social democracy, touched so far only in a marginal fashion" but whose "criminal function" in the future will be "highlighted and attacked by the fighters."[288]

---

[287] Federquadri was (and still is) an association of managers/professionals. The Italian word "quadri" more or less corresponds to the French word "cadres" and at Fiat, "the so-called *quadri* were managers below the rank of *dirigente* [executive], but with first-line supervisory duties or those of qualified technicians" (Garuzzo, *Fiat – the secrets of an epoch*). Garuzzo (a senior manager at Fiat from the late 1970s) also described the *quadri* as "the allies who did most for the success of the March of the Forty Thousand [see below]," pg 280.

[288] *Lotta Continua*, "Milan: a series of attacks," 21 June 1977; *La Prensa*, "They shot a foreman at Siemens, 5 thousand out of work because of fires," 21 June 1977; *Corriere della Sera*, "Other messages from the terrorists of Prima linea," 22 June 1977; *Lotta Continua*, "Prima linea: the view from behind," 22 June 1977; proceedings of the Assize Courts of Milan n. 921/80 folder 15 volume 3, and the interrogation of Massimo Libardi in front of the Assize Court of Milan 15 Dec 1983, quoted in the proceedings of the trial of Prima linea in Milan no. 921/80; Office of the Prosecutor of the Republic in Milan, "Closing speech of the representative of Public Minister Armando Spataro on 11 July 1981 concerning the proceedings no. 221/80 F G. and no. 228/81 F G.," pp. 875-876; Court of Milan, "Sentencing by Examining Magistrate Elena Paciotti concerning the criminal trial no. 921/80F on 3 June 1982 against Antonio Achilli and others"; *Il Giorno* article on the

Today, on 19 June [said the leaflet] armed groups of the communist organisation Prima linea have attacked: the spare parts distribution centre of Magneti Marelli in via Stephenson in Milan, the Sit Siemens warehouse in Settimo Milanese, the Fiat car park in Prato (Florence); they destroyed by fire stocks of finished products stored in these warehouses." The message continued: "Comrades, the cycle of workers' revolutionary struggles in all countries has shown that the consciousness that the workers have of their own needs, the antagonism between those needs and the capitalist system, the level of power that the class has practiced are such that they can break the rules of democratic compatibility, of the capitalist machine, foreshadowing a phase of confrontation with the bosses and the state. In fact, in this moment of crisis, capital doesn't programme the production of goods, but the general conditions of its rule over the workers.[289]

In a motion signed by 470 workers on 28 November 1977 and delivered to the court on 6 December the same year by a delegation of 20 workers, the workers of Magneti Marelli supported the political work lead in the factory by Baglioni and Rodia and stressed that "Baglioni, Rodia, Cominelli are workmates who personally very much committed themselves to protecting workers' rights and to all the struggles that have seen the working class of Magneti refuse to accept concessions and compromises in the face of exploitation and despotism in the factory"; "They also rejected the concept of delegation because they are convinced that all workers are invested personally in the management of trade union demands, in struggles and in any form of defence of their rights." As for the march inside the factory to the offices of Palmieri, chief of the guards, considered as one of the elements of the charges against those arrested, the signatories of the motion "not only support the legitimacy of this action but claim its collective responsibility. They consider that they have the right to take a decision collectively and to collectively oppose yet another abuse by the boss."[290]

---

trial of the Revolutionary Communist Committees-Prima Linea in Milan, 23 February 1984, p. 22.

289   *Corriere della sera*, "Attack on the FIAT warehouse at Prato. Thirteen cars and two trucks in flames," 20 June 1977, and Office of the Examining Court of Florence, "Arrest warrant no. *309/79A* r.m:c. no. 69/80, 9 June 1980."

290   Leaflet: "free our imprisoned comrades," Magneti Workers Committee, Falk Workers Committee, Alfa Romeo Workers Autonomous Collective, Snam Communist Collective,

Shortly before the trial, Enrico Baglioni and Emilio Cominelli, both held in the Fossombrone super-prison, wrote an "Open letter to the Magneti workers" in which they accused the PCI of being the "social police" needed by Italian capitalism to keep the workers on a leash. But workers were now aware of the fact that, thanks to new technologies, there is the real possibility of liberation from wage labour. This perspective clashes with the capitalist will to accumulate profits and those that reorganise themselves through the use of illegal and precarious labour. Enemies are also active within the working class, "some unconsciously, others dishonestly, become the spokesmen for the boss, saying they are against violence and for the right to life." For Baglioni and Cominelli "violence is the thing that we communists hate the most, because we want to build a world of peace, but we are forced to use it to achieve our liberation and that of all humanity."[291]

In Turin, on 9 January 1978, in front of hundreds of workers, the appeal trial against the seven took place. Their sentences were reduced and transformed into probation. Only two of them, accused of theft, were kept in prison. On 30 March, Rodia and Baglioni were also released. However, they were forbidden from living in Milan and its province ("and they are obliged to report each day between 8 a.m. and 8 p.m. to the *Carabinieri* barracks to confirm the place they choose to live following release"), but the small towns where they were confined became a destination for workers to go to discuss their return to the factory. Regarding the searches made by the guards inside the factory, on 3 April 1978 the judge in Milan condemned the Magneti company for illegal behaviour and cancelled the layoffs. The decision was later upheld on appeal. In September 1978 the labour court ordered the return to work of four of those arrested, two from Marelli and two from Falck, fired while they were in jail. These four workers could thus leave prison and go straight back in to the factory. For one of the four the decision was confirmed on appeal, while for the others the company did not challenge the initial judgment.[292]

Niguarda Struggle Committee, Polyclinic of Milan Collective, 5 Jan 1978.

291 Ibid

292 "Chronicle of a Trial," op. cit. and *4 anni di lotte*, op. cit.; Annex no. 3, Feb 1980. The examining magistrate justified the decision to expel Rodia and Baglioni from Milan in these terms: "the personality of BAGLIONI and RODIA and the seriousness of the facts alleged against them require the adoption, at the time of their release, of necessary precautions to prevent them persisting in illegal conduct in the factory where they worked until now. There is no doubt that a climate of fear has been established among the staff of Magneti Marelli because of the 'escalation' of terrorism and collective methods of intimidation practiced by the defendants. It is therefore considered necessary to impose a ban on the defendants from residing in any town in the province of Milan, notably in the area

On 10 January 1978, Francesco Meregalli, who had been arrested on 22 April 1977 with six other workers at Valgrande, was released from prison. On the same day a trial took place against 22 workers of the Policlinico hospital and on 12 January the Sit Siemens worker Antonio Muscovich was also put on trial. During the trial of the seven workers in Turin, a manifesto was published called *Fuori I compagni dalle galere* ("Comrades out of jail") written by the Magneti Workers Committee, the Falck Workers Committee, the Alfa Romeo Workers Autonomous Collective, the Snam Communist Collective, the Niguarda Struggle Committee and the Policlinico Collective.

Criminal trials and labour court actions against the workers "are two aspects of a single project that has its basis in the unity of the social base of the police and the capitalist state. In its structure and articulation, the state begins from the factory and concentrations of workers, where there are a court and police who can now count on the valuable contribution of the revisionists." In essence, the Worker Committees claimed that there was a sort of boss's law in the factories, with executive power exercised by guards and foremen, and a judiciary power run by managers. There were three procedures against workers:

- a standard procedure (warning letters leading to judgement and sentencing: a reprimand, a fine, suspension, up to dismissal with notice),
- a special procedure (based on reports written by the hierarchy, without the worker hearing about it) that triggers a sentence without notice, accompanied by an interim suspension while waiting for a criminal prosecution and a firing without notice,
- a penal procedure (workers are sent to a criminal court).

If order in the factories can't be maintained in this way, then recourse is made to the state.[293]

The revisionists of the Communist Party and the unions actively participated in "the elimination of communists from the concentrations of workers." They sent reports "to the judges and to the police of the state and the factory, in which they denounce, in every situation, the workers rebelling against the capitalist order, and they demand their dismissal." In this regard, the examples cited in the leaflet are countless: the Policlinics of Rome and Milan, Magneti Marelli, Falck, Breda in Sesto San Giovanni, Siemens, Innocenti Lambrate. "Magistrates and unions today are necessary tools in order to give legitimacy to the state, in an uncertain phase of transition to a new form of control." The real criminals, for the authors of the leaflet, are to be found in the bourgeoisie

---

where productive activity is carried out for the plaintiffs in this action."
293   Ibid

who, through restructuring and redundancies, organise the exploitation of home working, and increase prices and taxes.

"The bourgeoisie has not only reinforced – and continues to reinforce – its traditional police (first of all the *Carabinieri* and the counter-terrorism units) but also continues to arm dozens of private police forces (the gunmen of the bosses private police now number a hundred thousand). Factory managers, belonging to organisations like the *Federquadri* and *Comunione e liberazione* [a Catholic organisation, alread mentioned] also have a political role that precedes the directly armed organisation of the cadres of bourgeois order. Merchants, members of the liberal professions, etc., are armed, and these 'armies' equip themselves and train themselves against the working class, preparing to stop it with lead."

The proletariat must be convinced of the necessity of revolutionary struggle as the only means for its emancipation. Militants must not fall into the trap of a clash between the state apparatus and isolated individuals. The response during the trials must not limit itself to a technical defence accepting "the logic of the individual citizen before constituted society." In the same way it should not "politically reject the trial."

The behaviour of the communist militants during the trial "should be seen only from the perspective of how the comrades who are free can make use of it: against the bosses' and state courts, our defence relies on strikes and demonstrations that are going to visit these gentlemen, on the consolidation of the strength and organisation of the proletariat, on the expansion of the communist perspective."[294]

In the text a letter was published, among many, written by 70 Magneti Marelli workers from Crescenzago, addressed to their comrades Baglioni and Rodia detained in Perugia prison. In the letter, the workers reaffirm the political goal of autonomous organisation in the factory, they point out that the seven workers have been arrested to prevent the growth of the fight in the factory: "we will continue the fight that the bosses and the bourgeois state, with the help of bourgeois justice, have prevented you from leading. As always, we think that 'the only justice is proletarian justice'." Enrico Baglioni responds to the letter from prison on 28 May that prisoners are proletarians who generally do not recognise their own class, so it is necessary to "explain to them that there will be a better and fairer life only with the communist revolution that erases all forms of bourgeois power by the dictatorship of the workers."[295]

The news magazine *La Repubblica* published an interview with Luciano Lama, secretary of the CGIL, in which he advocated the limitation of wages,

---

294 Ibid
295 Ibid

increased productivity and mobility of workers in exchange for a reduction in unemployment and for investment in the South of Italy. He accused both bosses and workers of supporting the view that profits and wages were independent variables within the economic system, while, according to him, in a period of crisis, the two sides must respect their mutual interests. This thesis, according to which wage claims must take into account their "compatibility" with economic performance, was presented at the 24 February 1978 meeting of the General Councils and delegates of the CGIL in the EUR district of Rome. The motion was adopted by a large majority and would go down in history as "the EUR turning point" for its immediate impact on Italian society. It was the first time since 1947 that employers, government and unions had agreed to save the Italian economy from final collapse. The results of this collaboration were an immediate improvement in the national economic situation, lower inflation, a vigorous recovery in exports and renewed confidence for entrepreneurs. The union confederations' accepted with great understanding the partial annulment of the *Scale mobile*, containment of the number of strike hours and the signing of company agreements on mobility and productivity.[296]

In October 1979, Mario Grieco, a leading activist of the Workers Committee, was fired for poor performance. He had worked at Magneti Marelli since 1969 when many young people, especially from Sardinia, Puglia and Naples were hired. Some of his workmates described the situation in the factory like this, "for piece work there are two weights and two measures: 40 percent of workers who work with Mario perform individual piece work, while the other workers of the department perform team piece work. The first ones include all the comrades, the dissenters, the ball-breakers, the others are often linked to the PCI. The first are checked on each piece they produce, and are assigned slower tasks, which makes it harder for them to get by on piecework, the others have all the privileges. Basically, those who can't do team piece work, can't materially keep up with the required amount of production." Since the time of the first political sackings in 1975, conditions had changed in the factory, the company had transferred the entire Third section to a factory in the South and the foremen had taken some control over the workers. The boss's intention was to regain company competitiveness, by eliminating products that do not measure up, closing the foundry and the screw-making departments, using decentralisation of production and unofficial work and encouraging "voluntary" resignations.[297]

---

[296] *Storia d'Italia…*, op. cit., p. 523

[297] *Lotta Continua*, "Mario Grieco, Marelli worker, a Sardinian, sacked, one of those that the union will not defend," 26 Oct 1979.

The end of the movement

Immediately after the dismissal, a worker demonstration brought Grieco back into the factory, even though the union had "admitted the correctness of the dismissal." The Collective went to court to support the illegality of the dismissal, although the company offered a "substantial amount of money" to Grieco to give up his case. The Collective publically condemned this attempt at "corruption" by Magneti, and in the first round the court found in favour of the worker and after a year the company was forced to reinstate Grieco in the factory. Until the judgment was pronounced, Magneti continued to pay Grieco's wages with the intention of keeping him away from the factory and the organisation of the struggle. The court ordered an appraisal to verify the performance capabilities of the Frontor machine which Grieco worked on. For that, it used workers "selected by management." The result was as expected, and promised a defeat of the workers in the second round. The dispute ended in late 1981 when Grieco, in agreement with the Workers Collective (which the Workers Committee had started calling itself), decided to leave the factory in exchange for 20 million lire (around €60,000 today). For the Collective "this does not mean an abandonment of struggle or lack of confidence in the workers, but a simple fact: when the participation of workers in the struggle is not sufficient, no court finds in their favour, courts have always been in the service of bosses. Only when the workers go in to struggle with all their organisational strength can they make gains. So, given the weakness of the working class at this stage, the final judgment of the court could only be negative."[298]

Between 18 and 25 February 1980 the third Assize Court of Milan sentenced eight workers from Falck and Magneti Marelli for armed and subversive association. In fact this condemnation was aimed at the four years of struggles conducted in the factory but, for the Workers' Committee of Magneti Marelli, "the class struggle cannot be judged by the justice system."[299]

At the end of 1980, Enrico Baglioni was arrested again, this time accused of being one of the leaders of the fighting organisation Prima linea. In a letter from Brescia prison, Baglioni addressed himself to the workers of Magneti Marelli, "comrades of these twelve years," with these words: "1977 was an important year, a turning point for the trade unions in our country. The year of the EUR, the year in which unions officially recognized that we are a dependent variable of capital. We are no longer an autonomous and independent subject on the way to our liberation from the chains of wage labour. Three years have passed and they were three years of the restoration of deep bosses' and state

---

298 "'Normalisation,' the Magneti Marelli way," Magneti Marelli Workers Collective, in *Il Bollettino*, no. 4, February 1982.
299 "Chronicle of a Trial," op. cit.

power against us." We can consider that the workers' defeat was consummated after the "march of the 40,000" in Turin, a defeat paid for by revolutionaries in terms of repression and years in jail. Notably, Baglioni was accused of the attack on the headquarters of Marelli in via della Guastalla in Milan during Autonomia operaia's demonstration on 18 March 1977: "Comrades, I politically claim responsibility for this autonomous demonstration, I consider that it was a correct form of struggle to build a really autonomous alternative of workers against the rotten mechanisms of the union and the historic parties of the left, autonomous also from the economic mechanisms of capital and from the parliamentary cretins."[300]

Establishing a precise date for the end of the experience of the Magneti Marelli Workers Committee is impossible. As with any grassroots organisation, it is difficult to find any declarations of formal dissolution, and we only have the oral memory of the protagonists to go on, but this is beyond the scope of this research which is based on the written sources of the time. A grassroots structure such as the Committee is created and developed thanks to the maturity of the people who compose it, but it is subject to the demands of general confrontation. At the end of the seventies, the judicial and employer repression combined with the internal restructuring of the factory went along with a real general change of the situation in the factories and in Italian social reality. First of all, the restructuring changed the physical characteristics of the factories. Then the defeat of the worker resistance changed the political composition of the working class, the recognised vanguard of all demands for radical change in the political and social movements of that period.

At the end of 1979, the compromise between the DC and PCI had not paid off in the way that the reformists expected. The PCI rank and file grumbled, even though Luciano Lama, general secretary of the CGIL, annoyed Enrico Berlinguer, secretary of the PCI, because he continued to support the union's EUR line. In the June 1979 elections, the PCI lost a lot of votes and was therefore forced to change course, imagining an alliance with the Socialist Party in order to remove the Christian Democrats from power.

At the same time the bosses launched a general attack on the working class starting with FIAT Mirafiori. At the end of 1979, the management laid off 61 workers accused of committing acts of violence or making threats inside the factory. The attitude of the unions was extremely ambiguous, allowing the layoffs to be easily accepted. One year later, on 8 September 1980, FIAT announced that over 15 months they would let go of 24,000 workers, half of whom would be made redundant. Amongst them we can find the names

---

300 Letter from Enrico Baglioni: 'To the Magneti Marelli workers, to the comrades of these last twelve years," Brescia, 1980.

of those who played a leading role in the struggles which started in 1969. Three days later, FIAT announced that 14,000 workers would immediately be made redundant. The unions called for a total strike and blockaded all the FIAT factories. Enrico Berlinguer came to the factory gates and promised the workers total support from the PCI for their demands. FIAT announced that it would not proceed with the immediate redundancies. This decision divided the working class of Turin, between those who wanted to continue the struggle against the *Cassa Integrazione* and the redundancies and those who wanted to end the conflict, to the point that on 14 October 1980, on the thirty fourth day of the strike, an unusual demonstration took place in Turin: between 30 and 40,000 managers, team leaders, employees and workers from FIAT demanded the right to return to work. This demonstration, which was to go down in Italian history as the "march of the Forty Thousand,"[301] was the signal that the workers' movement was profoundly divided. The unions immediately came to an agreement with the FIAT management. This victory for Agnelli marked, for the whole of Italy, the end of the cycle of workers' struggles which had begun at the end of the sixties.

---

301 It hardly needs to be said that there was considerable Fiat management involvement in the organisation of the march. In Garuzzo's book he states: "It was not an easy operation to set up, also from a logistical point of view, because the heads, the *quadri*, and the loyal workers had not been in the factory for over a month and to make contact with them it was necessary to activate a delicate, widespread word-of-mouth campaign. … Fiat never admitted having organized the march…," *Fiat – the secrets of an epoch*, pg 81.

Lightning Source UK Ltd.
Milton Keynes UK
UKHW010411091220
374847UK00001B/15